AF361462

SICKLE AND VEIL

Sickle and Veil

Communist Gender Policies towards Muslim Minorities in Eastern Europe

IVAN SIMIC

UNIVERSITY OF TORONTO PRESS
Toronto Buffalo London

ISBN 978-1-4875-4692-2 (cloth)   ISBN 978-1-4875-4693-9 (EPUB)
                                 ISBN 978-1-4875-4694-6 (PDF)

Library and Archives Canada Cataloguing in Publication

Title: Sickle and veil : communist gender policies towards Muslim minorities
   in Eastern Europe / Ivan Simic
Names: Simic, Ivan, author
Description: Includes bibliographical references and index.
Identifiers: Canadiana (print) 20250311119 | Canadiana (ebook) 20250311127 |
   ISBN 9781487546922 (cloth) | ISBN 9781487546939 (EPUB) |
   ISBN 9781487546946 (PDF)
Subjects: LCSH: Muslim women – Yugoslavia – Social conditions. |
   LCSH: Muslim women – Bulgaria – Social conditions. |
   LCSH: Socialism – Yugoslavia. | LCSH: Socialism – Bulgaria. |
   LCSH: Soviet Union – Social policy.
Classification: LCC HQ1715.5 .S56 2026 | DDC 305.48/69709497 — dc23

Cover design: Alexa Love
Cover image: Archives of Yugoslavia/AJ 112f-1235-008.

The manufacturer's authorized representative in the European Union for
product safety is Mare Nostrum Group B.V., Mauritskade 21D, 1091 GC
Amsterdam, The Netherlands. Email: gpsr@mare-nostrum.co.uk

We wish to acknowledge the land on which the University of Toronto Press
operates. This land is the traditional territory of the Wendat, the Anishnaabeg,
the Haudenosaunee, the Métis, and the Mississaugas of the Credit First Nation.

This book has been published with the help of a grant from the Federation
for the Humanities and Social Sciences, through the Awards to Scholarly
Publications Program, using funds provided by the Social Sciences and
Humanities Research Council of Canada.

University of Toronto Press acknowledges the financial support of the
Government of Canada, the Canada Council for the Arts, and the Ontario Arts
Council, an agency of the Government of Ontario, for its publishing activities.

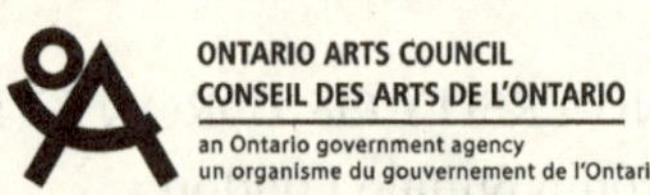

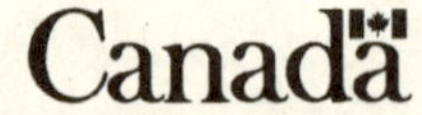

Contents

Illustrations

Acknowledgments

I would like to express my sincere gratitude to those who have supported me throughout this project.

This work would not have been possible without the invaluable guidance and insight provided during the initial stages of the project by Heather Coleman, Max Bergholz, and Catherine Baker, whose ideas helped shape its conception. I am particularly grateful to my former PhD supervisor, Bojan Aleksov, for his unwavering support and mentorship, which have continued to guide me academically so many years after finishing my PhD.

My time in Prague was made possible by the support of Stanislav Tumis, who generously encouraged the development of my research interests and teaching skills.

The research process was made considerably smoother by the assistance of Dajana Vasiljevičová[3], Radomyr Mokryk[4], Valeria Korablyova[5], Slavka Karakusheva, Andreja Mesarič[6], Jelena Gajic, and Elizaveta Bojko, who provided vital help with archival work and analysis. Without them, this massive project would not have been possible.

I owe a debt of gratitude to Andrew Hodges, whose meticulous proofreading and insightful suggestions significantly improved this work.

Special thanks to Branka Bogdan for reading various parts of this manuscript and providing valuable comments. I am also grateful to Plamena Stoyanova, Zhivka Valiavicharska, and Roumen Avramov for going out of their way to help me access necessary books during the challenging COVID-19 period. I sincerely thank the archivists at the Archives of Yugoslavia in Belgrade for their invaluable help in locating images, including the one featured on this book's cover.

Lastly, to my family, I extend my deepest thanks for their endless love and support throughout this journey.

Abbreviations

Abbreviation	Definition (country)	Translation
AFŽ	Antifašistički front žena (YU)	Women's Anti-fascist Front
ASSR	Avtonomnaja sovetskaja socialisticheskaja Respublika (SU)	Autonomous Soviet Socialist Republic
BKP	Balgarska Komunisticheska Partiya (BG)	Bulgarian Communist Party
BNZhS	Balgarski naroden zhenski sayuz (BG)	Bulgarian National Women's Alliance
CEC	Centralni izvršni komitet (YU); TSentralen izpalnitelen komitet (BG); Central'nyj Ispolnitel'nyj Komitet (SU)	Central Executive Committee
CK	Centralni komitet (YU); TSentralen komitet (BG); Centralen komitet (SU)	Central Committee (of the party)
ILS	Mezhdunarodnaja leninskaja shkola (SU)	International Lenin School
IVZ	Islamska verska zajednica (YU)	Islamic Community of Yugoslavia
JMO	Jugoslovenska muslimanska organizacija (YU)	Yugoslav Muslim Organization
KDBZ	Komitet na demokratichnite balgarski zheni (BG)	Committee of Democratic Bulgarian Women
KPJ	Komunistička partija Jugoslavije (YU)	Communist Party of Yugoslavia
SADUM	Duhovnoe upravlenie musul'man Srednej Azii i Kazahstana (SU)	Spiritual Administration of the Muslims of Central Asia and Kazakhstan

(Continued)

(Continued)

Abbreviation	Definition (country)	Translation
SKOJ	Savez komunističke omladine Jugoslavije (YU)	League of Communist Youth of Yugoslavia
SSR	Sovetskaja Socialisticheskaja Respublika (SU)	Soviet Socialist Republic
TKZS	Trudovo-kooperativni zemedelski stopanstva (BG)	Labour-Cooperative Agricultural Enterprises
VMRO	Vatreshna Makedonska Revolyutsionna Organizatsiya (BG)	Internal Macedonian Revolutionary Organization
TsDUM	Central'noe Duhovnoe Upravlenie Musul'man (SU)	Central Spiritual Administration of Muslims
WIDF	Međunarodna demokratska federacija žena (YU); Mezhdunaroden demokratichen sayuz na zhenite (BG); Mezhdunarodnaya demokraticheskaya federatsiya zhenshchin (SU)	Women's International Democratic Federation

Legend:
BG: Bulgaria
SU: Soviet Union
YU: Yugoslavia

Note on Transliteration

All titles, names, and inscriptions originally in Cyrillic have been transliterated in this book. Serbian Cyrillic has been transposed directly into the Latin script, with relevant diacritics employed. Bulgarian Cyrillic has been transliterated in accordance with the Bulgarian Transliteration Law, which was sanctioned in March 2009. Russian Cyrillic has been transliterated according to the GOST 7.79 System B standard.

In addition, I have provided translations of the titles of all primary sources in the bibliography alongside the transliterated originals, in order to offer additional context to English-speaking readers.

SICKLE AND VEIL

Introduction

Turdbibi Islamova lived in Soviet Uzbekistan. She was immersed in hard work from her earliest years, labouring in her rural household. Her relentless, yet unrecognized, work persisted after a marriage at the age of fifteen, which she did not consent to. Her parents did not bother to inquire into whether she held any affection for her intended groom. After her wedding, she was confined to her home, hidden behind a *paranja*, a full head-and-body covering in Central Asia. Her life revolved around hard labour, with no perceived benefits that she recalled. In 1930, however, a dramatic shift occurred when her entire community became a part of a kolkhoz named Stalin.[1] Her hard work was finally acknowledged and she was elevated to shock-worker status.[2] Later, she joined the party, and the paranja was no longer part of her narrative. Her brigade was recognized as one of the finest in Central Asia, and her fellow collective farmers chose her to represent them at the All-Soviet Meeting of Kolkhoz Shock Workers. On this occasion, she first glimpsed Stalin. She delivered a speech that credited him as an emancipator who "ushered women out of the dark life," and she was captivated by his proclamation that "women in the kolkhoz are a formidable force." Islamova's political ascendancy was meteoric. She was elected as a representative to the Supreme Soviet, the highest legislative body, and was appointed to head a regional executive committee. Under her leadership, an electric station, maternity ward, and cultural theatre club were established. She endeavoured to learn and master the Russian language, as she was determined to fulfil her party duties to the best of her abilities. Islamova was living the socialist dream, ever ready to serve both the party and her fellow citizens on the path to a better future.[3]

Behija Krkbešić was born into a traditional Muslim family in Sarajevo, Yugoslavia, and was confined within her home's lofty walls. She married young to an old-fashioned family who imposed stringent traditions upon its women. In her own words, she was "a house slave, whose voice must never be heard." She never ventured out of her house without her feredža – her face and body covering.[4] During the Second World War, her life changed unexpectedly when the Partisans took refuge in her house. She was introduced to a world beyond her imagination. Even her conservative husband joined the Partisan movement but unfortunately died, leaving her a single mother to four young children. Despite her circumstances, a bright new chapter in her life was just around the corner. Behija became involved in the communist-led People's Front and the local women's section of the party, the Women's Anti-fascist Front (Antifašistički front žena, AFŽ).[5] She poured her energy into the tasks she was assigned, and her shyness gradually dissipated. She avidly sought out knowledge, reading and learning more and becoming an active participant in meetings. Her efforts were acknowledged, and she became a party member in 1946, which she referred to as the brightest day of her life. Though she still wore a veil, she began to experience it as restrictive and felt it was incongruous with her newfound freedom and joyous life. One day, she declared her intention to discard the veil to her comrades. Her political career continued to flourish. Behija became a member of the AFŽ's regional council and vice-president of the local AFŽ. In time, she was elected to the city government. In addition, she assumed the role of secretary in her party cell.[6]

Muzafer Ismailova was a Muslim Turkish woman, from Kolarovgrad in socialist Bulgaria, born into poverty.[7] She was orphaned at the age of seven, and was therefore accustomed to hunger, wearing tattered clothes, and enduring the cold. After her parents' demise, she was taken in by an uncle who burdened her with all the household chores. Muzafer was barred from attending school and from playing with other children. At thirteen, she married a local boy and fled. They lived a life of deprivation, pinning their hopes "on the arrival of the Russians to liberate them" and usher in a new phase in their lives. One decade after the war, Muzafer was indeed living that dream. Her two children now attended school, her husband remained loving, and she had been elected as a councillor in the city's government. The leading party's women's magazine featured an article about Muzafer. It began with her sleepless nights, fraught with worry about fulfilling the expectations of those who trusted her. Her husband, too, was apprehensive, because of her limited proficiency in Bulgarian and fear of public embarrassment. Muzafer, however, drew courage from the support of her comrades, who fuelled her zeal to work even harder. She listened intently to the grievances and desires of the local community and dedicated herself to paving streets, installing street lights, and establishing a kindergarten. She encouraged other Muslim women to join the Fatherland Front,[8] undeterred by their husbands' resistance. She coordinated a reading group for them and assisted other women in securing employment. She never missed a meeting and even worked as a maid in the newly opened kindergarten. As the article emphasized, despite all her commitments, her home was well kept, and her children were clean, well nourished, and well behaved. She recounted tales of her poverty-stricken childhood and motivated her children to pursue education relentlessly. As she was determined to gain an education herself, she enrolled in an evening school. Despite her relentless efforts, however, Muzafer often pondered whether she was living up to the trust placed in her by the people and the party.[9]

A compelling thread connects the stories of Turdbibi Islamova, Behija Krkbešić, and Muzafer Ismailova. Despite the fact that they lived in different countries and thousands of miles apart, the narratives of their lives, as portrayed by the communist press, bear striking similarities. All three women emerged from impoverished families, accustomed to gruelling labour and mistreatment. They each encountered fraught relations with their traditional families, were married off at a young age, and supposedly started truly living their lives only with the socialist state's intervention. They embraced the socialist project from the outset and leveraged it for unprecedented social mobility. Their hard work was acknowledged by the party, and they reciprocated by dedicating everything they had to the future of socialism. Through these transformative experiences, they evolved into "new women," unshackled from the "chains" of traditions, veils, and gender bias. Their physical appearances altered too, as illustrated by the images of Behija and Muzafer featured in the magazine articles published about both women (figure 0.1). Both were pictured in modern attire; Muzafer was shown sitting in the front row at her evening school and Behija hard at work, a white shirt adorning her figure and a shovel slung over her shoulders.

This metamorphosis saw them become proactive advocates of socialism. Thanks to the opportunities they seized, they transitioned from passive victims to agents of change within their communities. They embodied socialist modernity, introducing electricity, kindergartens, maternity wards, and "culture." They were the living embodiments of the socialist dream.

In these narratives about transformations, gender roles and identities were crucial. The women's lives were the results of their personal endeavours, aided by party interventions. All three stories commence with the depiction of the difficult circumstances these women had endured since childhood, circumstances imposed by men and their traditional communities, which justified the party's intervention. A common theme across all three narratives was that communist parties dismantled structures that oppressed women, thus compelling men

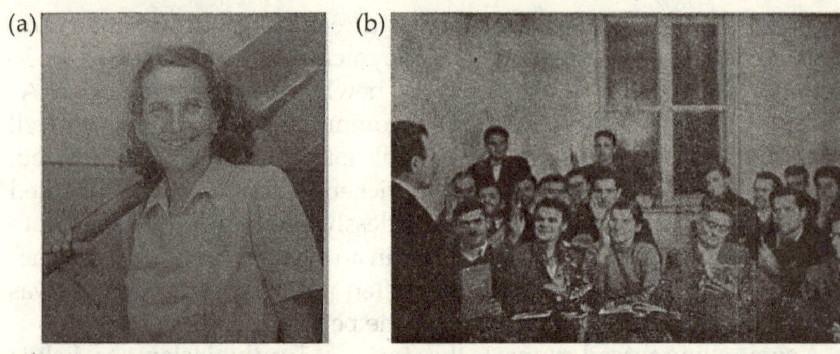

Figure 0.1. (a) Behija Krkbešić in the magazine *Nova žena*, and (b) Muzafer Ismailova in the magazine *ZHenata dnes* (front row, third seat from the left)

Source: (a) Courtesy of National Library of Serbia, Belgrade, and (b) courtesy of St. Cyril and Methodius National Library of Bulgaria, Sofia.

and entire communities to alter their attitudes. The women, in turn, capitalized on the opportunity to revolutionize their lives and endorse socialist projects, unburdened by limiting traditions or veils. In each case, veils were perceived as relics of a bleak past and as real hindrances to social mobility and an improved quality of life. In each story, men's role was challenged, as were gender roles and identities.

The concepts underpinning this book were driven by my personal struggle to navigate a myriad of questions linked to communism, gender, and Muslim communities. The book was born out of a curiosity to illuminate the reasons behind diverse communist regimes viewing veils as a threat. It goes further, however, by probing the peculiar fascination of communist states, colonial rulers, and modern politicians with gender and Muslim communities. What prevented the communists from envisaging an alternative approach to forcing women to unveil? How did the perspectives of the Yugoslav and Bulgarian communists evolve to assume a negative stance towards Muslim communities, considering them "backward"? How did the idea of backwardness occupy the minds of communist politicians, and were there any discernible disparities between the attitudes of male and female communist leaders? What provoked the apprehension among female communists towards veiled women? Was the discord merely an extension of an atheistic crusade against religion, or was there more to it in terms of class and race? How can we make sense of the Bulgarian case, which presents itself as the most extreme? Does the Bulgarian example explain all other instances, given that Bulgarian communists aspired to erase Muslim identities from the socialist nation?

As these questions suggest, this book's geographical focus is on socialist Yugoslavia and socialist Bulgaria. Nevertheless, a comprehensive analysis of these instances requires repeated reference to the Soviet Union, a crucible for the education, inspiration, and legitimacy of Yugoslav and Bulgarian communists. The book commences by establishing these ties, with Moscow positioned as the hub of interwar transnational undertakings. I explore the implications of this centrality for the "periphery," and examine how peripheral voices were at times re-contextualized but also frequently overlooked or muted. Nevertheless, throughout the manuscript, my analysis continually revisits the lessons that Yugoslav and Bulgarian communists learned from the Soviet model; I scrutinize how they adapted and used a variant of it to cater to their specific needs. Consequently, in each chapter, the analysis shuttles between diverse geographical areas, individuals, and communities of Central Asia and the Balkans.

It is important to recognize that other Muslim communities within Eastern Europe were targeted by communists with policies either similar to or marginally divergent from those considered here. For instance, socialist Albania has its own complex history of interacting with Muslim communities, among others, through a variety of gender policies. After the Second World War, the influence of the Soviet Union and Yugoslavia was evident among Albanian communists, but they ultimately charted a unique trajectory. This study does not, however, focus on Albania, and this decision is underpinned by an interest in scrutinizing instances in which Muslim populations did not form the majority. Despite Albania being a multi-confessional country, Muslims accounted for approximately 70 per cent of the populace by the late 1920s.[10] The veil, along with articles of men's clothing such as the fez,[11] while key political preoccupations, were transformed in this unique context, with consequences different from those in Yugoslavia and Bulgaria. In contrast with Albania, the environment in which the Yugoslav and Bulgarian communist parties operated bore remarkable political, economic, and social parallels, as depicted in chapter 2.

Because of the breadth of topics covered here, a wealth of primary sources from several countries underpin the findings described in this book. I have drawn on a broad array of materials, including archival documents, minutes from internal meetings and formal sessions, internal reports, correspondences, laws, curricula, newspapers, magazines, pamphlets, posters, films, and any other media that could illuminate this subject. These sources are written in many languages, such as Serbo-Croatian, Macedonian, Slovenian, Bulgarian, Russian, Turkish, and Albanian. They are located in the archives and libraries of former Yugoslavia, the former Soviet Union, and Bulgaria, and in an assortment of digital collections. The gathering of these documents would have been unfeasible without the invaluable assistance of postdoctoral fellows, graduate students, and research assistants who have collaborated with me on this project. They have also contributed their linguistic expertise in languages that I cannot read, such as Albanian and Turkish.

Thus, this analysis rests on the examination of thousands of documents, albeit the bulk of them originating from government and Communist Party institutions, officials, activists, and other related entities. Uncensored, first-hand accounts of individuals who opposed the party are indeed scarce. Nonetheless, these voices are not utterly inaudible. For instance, a detailed reading of the endless minutes from various party organizations or from the women's section of the party often uncovers genuine disputes, misunderstandings, differing interests, concerns, challenges, and opposition. This is particularly true in instances where these meetings were held behind closed doors. Secret service documents sometimes talked about these challenges more openly. Even documents and publications intended for public consumption frequently reveal more than their authors may have intended. Published resolutions from the women's sections of the parties, for example, indicate the issues at hand and the party's responses, and thus reveal the struggles, resistance, and challenges that initially compelled the party to react. If calls were made to activist women to redouble efforts at engaging Muslim women in reading groups in certain regions, it can be inferred that prior attempts fell short of success. Concurrently, publications such as *Žena danas* and *ZHenata dnes* (which translates literally as "Woman today" in both Serbo-Croatian and Bulgarian), *Rabotnitsa*, and *Kommunistka* fostered a unique array of images and narratives through their real or fictionalized stories. I, along with others who have analysed the communist press,[12] contend that even these texts were instrumental in shaping new possible identities for those willing to engage in the new regimes' projects. Therefore, despite the official nature of these sources, I have not discarded any, and I draw on them where appropriate.

This book moves back and forth between the Soviet Union, Bulgaria, and Yugoslavia. Although the analysis spans an extensive geographical area, it does not sacrifice depth of analysis for broad geographical scope. Occasionally, I bring up locations so minor that even inhabitants of those countries may struggle to locate them; this book thereby combines a micro- and macro-analysis. I show interconnections and elucidate communist policies, with a global character, aimed at Muslim communities. Also, I illuminate the unique peculiarities of each local case, placing gender policies within their distinct social, cultural, political, and economic contexts. Furthermore, I underscore similarities without proposing equivalences. For instance, while arguing that shared foundations influenced Bulgarian and Yugoslav approaches towards Muslim populations,

I also illustrate that the experiences of the individuals targeted differed because of a multitude of factors. By adopting a transnational historical approach, I seek to explain such global and local dynamics, and the interplay between communist centres and peripheries, while also paying close attention to the agency of local actors.

Transnational history allows for the examination of individuals and groups across diverse contexts, recognizing the influences of both national and transnational factors. It shines a light on transnational connections, an array of actors, and various forms of influence.[13] It spotlights many links formed through travel, border crossings, migrations, information flow and transfers, mutual perceptions, and interactions.[14] Transnational history also underscores and historicizes the agency of local actors. In this particular case, it allows for a perspective that moves beyond simply viewing local populations as passive victims of global processes and top-level political decisions.[15] While geographical and national borders somewhat distract from understanding connections and the formation of policies, I do not wish to trivialize the importance of borders and the structure of states, as I detail in all three cases. The transnationalism of dominant figures within the communist world also underwent a transformation, wherein non-state actors and covert revolutionaries became powerful state leaders who actively implemented policies and harnessed state resources.

The notion of *transfer* has been occasionally addressed in the field of transnational history. Augusta Dimou uses this concept in her analysis of socialism and its origins in the Balkans. She articulates that "the transport of cultural and intellectual 'goods' is an activity that resembles more a 'translation' (both literal and metaphorical), involving multiple strategies (rhetorical, cultural, social, political engineering) of adaptation, in contrast to an assumed mechanical, static, or simply mimetic activity of transfer from one context to another."[16] I concur with this kind of approach that underscores agency, adaptation, negotiation, and ultimately the creativity of the socialist periphery. In this book, I consider numerous levels of adaptations, from the structural and highest-level state and party echelons, to the individual agency of the populations. Scholars such as Diana Mishkova have also explored the concept of transfer, emphasizing the importance of studying the transformations that occur in the transfer process, with a focus on how ideas adapt to their new surroundings.[17] Mishkova's aim to highlight agency even when the power balance is asymmetrical has also heavily influenced the writing of this book.

Gender history has, for some time, benefited from the transnational history approach. Francisca de Haan posited that feminist historians have profited significantly from scrutinizing the transnational dimensions of feminism's history and the transnational processes that have shaped feminist and women's struggles.[18] Historians have begun to acknowledge Eastern European groups and actors, their internal connections, and their ties to the West, although a risk of attempting to fit Eastern European socialist and communist activists into the Western feminist canon persists, as if the Western feminist canon possesses some inherent value and is superior to the original Eastern European approach. This approach frequently attempts to understand figures such as Vida Tomšič, Spasenija Babović, Tsola Dragoycheva, Rada Todorova, Alexandra Kollontai, Inessa Armand, and numerous others from a Western-centric viewpoint. It suggests that labelling them as feminists would enhance the value of their work, yet this contrasts with these figures' own desires and actions, which actually caused real feminists to endure hardships, and imprisonment on occasion. As Zhivka Valiavicharska explains, socialist women from Eastern Europe and the Soviet Union consistently refrained from labelling themselves as "feminists." They also steered clear of the term *feminism* for their activities and did not conform to the North American and Western European timelines of feminism.[19] This book examines the connections among all these (and many other) people of various genders, observing their transnational influences while situating them within their own writings, speeches, and actions, and within their own social, political, and economic contexts. Their work was important, even when it went unrecognized outside the socialist bloc and did not align with the Western feminist canon.

When fused with transnational history, gender history provides compelling fresh perspectives that dig into the heart of the societies under scrutiny.[20] It shows how gender policies were constructed, who the pivotal actors were, how they functioned, how they adapted to constantly shifting circumstances, how they endeavoured to implement gender policies in practice, and how these policies impacted local populations. Further, gender history illuminates the strategies employed to negotiate gender policies at the local level. It covers how the populace resisted, or simply carried on with their daily lives, and how their communities were later transformed. Finally, this integrated approach helps to dissect the intricacies of the interplay between local and global dynamics, highlighting how gender norms and policies were shaped and reshaped within this context.

Despite these plentiful primary sources, an exploration of transnational history would be impossible without drawing heavily on the extensive body of scholarly work on Soviet Central Asia, socialist Yugoslavia, and socialist Bulgaria. This book would certainly not be possible without the many great authors who inspired me, and with whose analysis I will engage in every chapter. The Soviet case has been most thoroughly investigated, with crucial articles and books written by eminent scholars such as Adeeb Khalid, Marianne Kamp, Douglas

Taylor Northrop, Yulia Gradskova, Adrienne Lynn Edgar, Shoshana Keller, Eren Tasar, and others I cite frequently throughout this study. This manuscript additionally addresses some gaps left by these works, particularly regarding the influence of the Soviet case abroad.

Interest in socialist Bulgaria is on the rise, with flourishing debates among academics, from Bulgaria and beyond, concerning the character of Bulgarian assaults against Muslim populations. Scholars such as Ali Aminov, Mary Neuburger, Kristen Ghodsee, Fatme Myuhtar-May, and Zhivka Valiavicharska have made pivotal contributions to this field in the anglophone world. This book is further indebted to numerous Bulgarian-language studies by authors including Rumen Avramov, Stefan Dechev, Nurie Muratova, and Shaban Darakchi. This research enhances the field by introducing a more comprehensive gender analysis and linking up the Bulgarian case with the broader socialist world.

The Yugoslav situation is the least explored, except for key studies by Xavier Bougarel and Fabio Giomi on earlier eras. Much of the academic work on socialist Yugoslavia has focused on the "national question" in Bosnia and the ensuing post-socialist conflicts. I consult these works as well throughout the book, but I hope that more studies on social and cultural histories of Muslim communities will follow, particularly from a gender perspective. Furthermore, as this book illuminates, the Yugoslav approach was not formulated in national seclusion. Indeed, it exhibited stronger Stalinist tendencies than its Bulgarian counterpart.

Regrettably, some studies on socialist Yugoslavia and socialist Bulgaria are hampered by a narrow, isolationist, and nationalist perspective. It is not uncommon for them to succumb to nationalist leanings, bypass uncomfortable episodes in recent history, or provide unsophisticated explanations for such events.[21] On the flip side, a rising number of Bulgarian academics have written incisive and illuminating critiques of these approaches. Over the past two decades, Bulgarian academia has seen a greater emergence of critical voices than has research exploring the former Yugoslavia. A cohort of Bulgarian academics have actively countered the nationalist framework within their historiography; they have introduced nuanced perspectives and often daring interpretations.[22] For example, scholars such as Lilyana Aleksandrieva and Deyan Kyranov convincingly discussed the criminality of the Bulgarian state(s) and their actions against Muslim populations.[23] Tomasz Kamusella took the argument one step further, likening the situation to genocide,[24] though this sparked a debate over whether the 1989 expulsion should be examined as a standalone incident. My own inclination aligns with Rumen Avramov's view that policies towards Muslim populations should be analysed as a singular process that culminated in the events of 1989.[25] In this work I also use numerous excellent individual studies on Bulgarian Muslim communities,[26] gender policies,[27] the Bulgarian Communist Party and communism overall,[28] notable individuals who influenced policies,[29] and investigations into the relationship between Bulgarian communism and nationalism.[30] Scholars such as Avramov have also crafted remarkable studies on the catastrophic economic consequences of the "revival movement."[31]

As for socialist Yugoslavia, there is a tendency to overstate Yugoslav significance and uniqueness, while downplaying the influence of transnational factors and policies within the country that were directed at Muslim populations. Mainstream historiographies in the region frequently overlook Muslims in Yugoslavia, although a handful of recent individual studies have scrutinized the modernism of Yugoslav Muslim clerics,[32] immigration,[33] Islam in Bosnia,[34] and the process of unveiling.[35] The issue of gender, however, remains inadequately examined, particularly from a transnational viewpoint. Another complication arises from the lack of recognition and analysis of the relationship between the central power and the peripheries. The situation regarding the historiography of socialist Yugoslavia has been further muddled by Yugoslavia's disintegration, which gave rise to new research centres, of varying credibility, and studies with an insular focus on individual parts of Yugoslavia, thereby making their investigations even more isolationist.

Comparative studies on Yugoslavia and Bulgaria are exceedingly scarce. The most wonderful exception is an article by Pamela Ballinger and Kristen Ghodsee, which brings together the key issues of Yugoslav and Bulgarian gender policies on Muslim women. Ballinger and Ghodsee recognize numerous similarities in how Yugoslav and Bulgarian communists grappled with religion, secularism, and, consequently, their modernizing viewpoints on Muslim women. They reveal how socialist secularism was inextricably interwoven with ideas about gender equality, with the latter being a primary justification for control and suppression within religious communities. They spotlight the concept of "backwardness," a tool for justification, and discuss its relation to the construction of new socialist identities. The authors also observe different levels of coerciveness in the Yugoslav and Bulgarian approaches, but they find parallels in conceptualization, rhetoric, and the drive towards secularization.[36] The authors, likely constrained by the word count of a single research article, do not analyse the intricacies of the interplay between the Yugoslav and Bulgarian cases, or the particular features of the models of Bulgarian and Yugoslav policies. Many subtle aspects of Yugoslav and Bulgarian gender policies are also absent because of the large period examined. Nonetheless, to this day, this article provides the most comprehensive insight into matters of gender, communism, and religion in these two socialist states. It offers, if not a transnational history, then a comparative approach. It certainly provided much inspiration for this book. I will employ Ballinger and Ghodsee's concept of socialist secularism as an explanation for intrusive interventions into people's lives, thereby illustrating why the public/private dichotomy is not applicable and how it differs from the secularisms observed elsewhere.

As this book engages with a variety of population groups, I have used the most widely accepted names for each. In the Yugoslav context, the terminology for Albanians and Turks was relatively clear-cut, whereas for Bosnia I have employed terms such as *Bosniaks* and *Bosnian Muslims*. In chapter 2, I examine the significance of official terminology in the Yugoslav census for the establishment of Bosnia as one of the Yugoslav republics. The situation in Bulgaria is more complex, as the Bulgarian communist regime sought to forge a singular socialist nation, a topic I explore in the same chapter. Personal names and the label for the collective group became significant issues for the regime, which instituted assimilationist policies to eradicate personal and collective differences and identities. Given the significance of these policies, numerous Bulgarian scholars have addressed the topic. I adopt the terminology used by Fatme Myuhtar-May, differentiating between groups identified as Turks, Pomaks,[37] Roma, Tatars, and others.[38] None of these terms carry any negative connotations in this study.[39] When discussing communist policies that did not necessarily differentiate between these groups, I use terms such as *from Muslim backgrounds*. This also applies to communists who were atheists but who still had cultural ties to Islam, particularly in Yugoslavia. I also employ such terms when, for example, I examine the failures of the Bulgarian Communist Party to enlist Muslim women and men, as this pertains to people from all communities.

After this introduction, I situate Yugoslav and Bulgarian communist parties in a global communist world. The first chapter argues that pre–Second World War experiences and education in Moscow were crucial for both Yugoslav and Bulgarian communists in the development of their views on how to change society. The situation in their respective countries was remarkably similar. After violent events, both parties were banned and forced into underground activities, and both depended on the Comintern.[40] Furthermore, the leadership of both parties spent a significant amount of time in Moscow learning how to be proper Stalinists. It was then that Yugoslav and Bulgarian communists learned how to frame their gender policies towards Muslim populations in terms of Marxist discourse. They also learned how the Soviets approached the issue. The idea of "backwardness" was essential in considering policies towards Muslim minorities, and this chapter argues that Yugoslav and Bulgarian communists found a "solution" for their countries' backwardness in Moscow. Finally, Muslim women were at the bottom of the imagined social hierarchy, allowing communist parties to pursue aggressive social interventions vigorously.

The next chapter looks at the importance of nationality policies. Gender policies towards Muslim minorities in the Soviet Union, and then in socialist Yugoslavia and Bulgaria, were intertwined with broader approaches towards what was referred to as the "national question" and nation building. This part explores how communists approached and imagined nation building. I argue that Soviet approaches from Central Asia had profound effects on Yugoslavia and Bulgaria. Stalinist policies towards minorities were transferred abroad, but differences in how they were applied in federal Yugoslavia and unitarist Bulgaria determined the level of protection for Muslim minorities. Yugoslav communists followed the Stalinist nation-building model more closely, by creating new federal units that protected recognized nations. Bulgarian communists initially followed the Stalinist model, which protected Muslims, but without federal structures that could offer protection once Bulgaria commenced its de-Stalinization process. This chapter shows that policies towards Muslims became more hostile, while Bulgarian communists packed old nationalist approaches into a Marxist discourse. Muslim women's dress, particularly veils, was seen as an obstacle for new nation building in all cases.

The third chapter looks at how Bulgarian and Yugoslav communists used the Soviet Union as a model for legal transformation. They believed that Soviet laws were the most progressive globally and the only correct path for building a just society. They quickly passed and implemented new constitutions designed to transform the previous political and social orders. This section examines what these legal transformations meant for women's enfranchisement. I argue that they laid the foundations for tremendous changes in people's lives. Muslim women were afforded legal equality with men and with women from all other communities. They gained political, social, and economic rights for the first time. This part also focuses on what these forms of legal empowerment meant for women's political activities, and it shows that top-level politics was entirely dominated by men, with only a few non-Muslim women present. The inquiry demonstrates that because of this exclusion, gender policies towards Muslim communities were often insensitive to Muslim women's needs and desires. Finally, this chapter looks at the women's sections' activities in the two communist parties, in which the Muslim women of Bulgaria and Yugoslavia could find a space for political and social activities. These activities, however, often limited Muslim women to engaging with other Muslim women alone. Nevertheless, as this analysis demonstrates, some Muslim women seized new opportunities to make careers, opportunities that were closed to them before the war.

The next chapter turns attention to unveiling campaigns in Soviet Central Asia, Yugoslavia, and Bulgaria. It shows that the methods employed by the Soviets were readily used by communists in the Balkans decades later. The unveiling campaigns were imagined as collective efforts in which an individual was transformed, bringing the community to an imagined level of socialist modernity. The unveiling campaigns were violent and never considered the positions of targeted women. Yugoslav communists were the most successful in their unveiling program, banning the veils and eradicating them even in the countryside. Bulgarian communists were slower, dragging unveiling campaigns through many years, often due to poor party support in remote areas. Nevertheless, Bulgarian communists' approach was no less violent. This chapter shows that targeted women suffered from both communists and from their own communities. In the Soviet Union, many were murdered, raped, and bullied. In Yugoslavia and Bulgaria, they were equally under pressure, although violence was directed more outside the community. Targeted women eventually adapted to the situation by altering their clothes and bodily practices in all these cases.

The sixth chapter focuses on Muslim men. While aiming to change gender orders in Muslim communities, communists often considered Muslim men the main culprits behind any failure. This part shows how the discourse on Muslim men was framed from the early days of Soviet rule in Central Asia, portraying such men as deliberately keeping women in subjugated positions. The same discourse was used by Yugoslav and Bulgarian communists to justify campaigns and to explain failures. In all these cases, traditional masculinity was challenged by communist rule, with family relations and traditions changing. In Yugoslavia and Bulgaria, many decided to emigrate; others adapted to the new situation by paying lip service to the regime, and some resisted in the domestic sphere. The chapter also considers how men were targeted for their clothing and bodily practices. This resulted in traditional clothing and hats (the fez) being discarded and banned in Bulgaria, where even circumcision was banned and those practising it were persecuted. Finally, this segment reflects on how forced name changing in Bulgaria challenged Muslim men's dominant masculinity.

In conclusion, this book brings together gender policies towards Muslim minorities in the Soviet Union, Yugoslavia, and Bulgaria. It points to each case's similarities, continuities, differences, and peculiarities. It shows how ideas moved from one place to another, and it returns to individual stories of targeted people to point out how they resisted, adapted, or negotiated gender policies in line with their needs. It shows the final interconnectedness and the book's central argument regarding the consequences of paternalizing social interventions – these consequences being particularly dire when imposed without adequately taking into account the perspectives and desires of the targeted peoples.

Chapter One

Learning Together: The Moscow Years

In 1931, Maxim Gorky sent a letter to the workers of a factory in Uzbekistan, which had been renamed after him. He addressed women working in the factory, reminding them of their lives before the Soviet era: they were an unpaid workforce for their relatives, deprived of life's joys, ill with exhaustion, illiterate, and they faced the very grim prospects of perpetual backwardness and living conditions unfit for human beings. Gorky then exalted the Soviet successes of liberating women from their drudgery, from their chains, and from their male relatives. Women's lives became "lighter, brighter, and more reasonable." The Soviet state provided them with social infrastructure, and access to knowledge of the entire world. Finally, Gorky urged all women to fight for emancipation and serve as an example for other women around the world.[1] As Gorky was one of the main writers and ideologists of the Stalinist regime, his letter was reprinted in many publications. He addressed these local women in Uzbekistan, but also all other women in the Soviet Union, and international revolutionaries living, studying, and working in the country. According to Gorky, work in industry or on collective farms, combined with literacy, formed the backbone of women's emancipation and new gender relations. It was a solution that international revolutionaries could understand and reproduce in their own publications and works.

This chapter explores the influence of perspectives like Gorky's on the formation of world views among Yugoslav and Bulgarian communists. It argues that pre–Second World War experiences and education in Moscow were crucial for both Yugoslav and Bulgarian communists in developing their views on how to change society. The situation in their respective countries was remarkably similar. After violent events in the early 1920s, both parties were banned and forced into the political underground, and both depended on the Comintern. Furthermore, the leadership of both parties spent a significant amount of time in Moscow, where they learned how to be proper Stalinists. Through this experience, Yugoslav and Bulgarian communists grasped how to frame their gender policies directed at Muslim populations within a Marxist discourse. They also studied how the Bolsheviks approached the issue. The idea of "backwardness" was essential when considering policies towards Muslim minorities, and this chapter argues that Yugoslav and Bulgarian communists found a "solution" for their countries' backwardness in Moscow. Finally, placing Muslim women at the bottom of the imagined social hierarchy allowed communist parties to vigorously pursue aggressive social interventions.

Common Trajectories

The activities of the Communist Party of Yugoslavia (Komunistička partija Jugoslavije, KPJ) and the Bulgarian Communist Party (Balgarska Komunisticheska Partiya, BKP) in the interwar period had many similarities. Their interwar position was shaped by the political, economic, and social situation in their countries and by these parties' relationship with the Soviet Union and the Comintern. Understanding these interwar activities is essential in order to unpack how these communist parties formulated their views on Stalinism, gender and gender norms, ethnic minorities, and religious minorities during the later decades. The interwar period explains the similarities in gender policies directed at Muslim minorities, which were present once these communist parties had gained power after the Second World War. Additionally, examining the interwar period allows us to observe the continuities and differences in the regimes' policies.

Both Yugoslavia[2] and Bulgaria were economically underdeveloped and politically unstable agrarian countries on the periphery of Europe, with regimes that considered communism a grave threat. Both regimes, regardless of the ruling parties and coalitions, often enforced harsh measures against communists. After the First World War, Bulgaria reverted to its pre-conquest borders, while Serbia formed a new enlarged state.[3] Nevertheless, over 75 per cent of the population still lived in the countryside in both states, with indebted peasants, under-mechanized agriculture, and agrarian overpopulation.[4] Both countries had a small working class but a rising communist movement, and both countries had a significant Muslim population consisting of various ethnic groups with various languages and affiliations.[5]

Bulgaria faced similar social tensions to Yugoslavia, but it also had to confront a more complicated internal position due to the loss of yet another war. By losing the territories it had occupied, Bulgaria encountered more internal instability after a peace treaty was enforced that many in Bulgaria considered unfair. Nevertheless, the initial post–First World War government led by Prime Minister Aleksandar Stamboliyski attempted to normalize Bulgarian foreign politics by improving the country's relationship with Yugoslavia, and enact social reforms including the agrarian reform. This also enhanced Bulgaria's standing abroad, allowing Bulgaria to join the League of Nations. However, his peaceful politics cost him his life when he was ousted in a military coup and killed by the terrorist group VMRO (Internal Macedonian Revolutionary Organization).[6]

The Yugoslav state did not experience much stability either. Its internal politics were marked by constant struggles over social reforms, which were heightened with clashes over the country's desired political structure – namely, whether it would apply a federal or a centralized model. Beneath these clashes, there was also a struggle along ethnic lines between Serbs and Croats. These struggles culminated in 1928, when a prominent Croatian politician, Stjepan Radić, was murdered in the parliament, leading to a royal dictatorship in 1929 and the collapse of parliamentarism.[7]

The Bulgarian interwar trajectory was also like that of Yugoslavia in terms of the disastrous effects of the 1929 economic crisis and the suspension of the limited parliamentarism. In the Bulgarian case, the limited democracy was destroyed by the military, who suspended the constitution and all political parties. The country turned into an authoritarian state ruled by the monarch, Boris III, and it slowly turned towards Germany both economically and politically. The Bulgarian regime's ultimate goal was to reconquer the Yugoslav and Greek territories, and the state fulfilled these desires after forming an alliance with Germany in 1941, when the Bulgarian state occupied Macedonia and Northern Greece.[8]

In both Bulgaria and Yugoslavia, the communist parties' political life began with significant successes in gaining new members and supporters, and in challenging the ruling elite in the elections. Both parties formed at approximately the same time after the First World War, drawing on earlier socialist and communist traditions. The Bulgarian Communist Party was established in 1919, and its birth was rooted in a schism between two factions of the Bulgarian socialist movement – the Broads and the Narrows.[9] The Narrows faction, led by Dimitar Blagoev, founded the BKP and moved the organization closer to Bolshevik positions. However, the historian Emilia Mineva has argued that Blagoev kept some distance from the Soviet Union regarding the revolutionary process, opting for a more gradual approach instead of an instant revolution.[10] This approach included regular participation in the parliamentary and local elections, in which they made significant gains. For example, the BKP was second in the parliamentary elections in 1920 and 1923, just behind the Bulgarian Agrarian National Union, which formed the government.[11]

However, when Stamboliyski was overthrown and killed by the VMRO in June 1923, the Comintern criticized the BKP for their passivity in the coup event, and ordered the BKP to start an armed uprising. They abandoned their gradual approach and attempted a coup in September 1923, mainly in the country's western regions. However, communists failed to gather enough support and the coup failed. Georgi Dimitrov, Vasil Kolarov, and many other communists escaped to Yugoslavia and then further west.[12] The government's reprisal was brutal, and the BKP were banned. Communists then turned to sporadic terrorist attacks that often left many dead. The deadliest was their attack on St. Nedelya Church, in which around 150 people were killed, many of them belonging to the country's top-level political and military elite. As retaliation, the Military Union, which assumed power after Stamboliyski, killed about 450 communists without trial.[13] After these events, many more Bulgarian communists escaped to Yugoslavia and the Soviet Union, joining the Comintern apparatus or institutions such as the Communist University for the National Minorities of the West and the International Lenin School (ILS). Despite this exodus, the BKP still won a significant number of votes. For example, under the disguise of the Workers' Party, the BKP won the municipal elections in Sofia in 1932, after which the regime suspended the election results and the communist mandates.[14]

The Yugoslav Communist Party (KPJ) also emerged through the unification of several smaller parties in 1919, and it received its name at the Second Congress a year later. At that congress, the KPJ shifted towards more radical positions. They expelled moderate members and set the stage to join the Comintern, which would direct their development for more than two decades.[15] Just as in Bulgaria, the KPJ achieved significant electoral successes as early as in 1920, winning many major cities and districts. The regime reacted by suspending these local administrations, demonstrating that even Yugoslavia's purportedly democratic system would exclude the KPJ. Elected communist men were not allowed to take up their positions, although they were elected in major cities such as Belgrade, Zagreb, and Niš.[16]

The new Yugoslav state considered communism a grave threat. The regime was afraid of their political activities but also of the spreading of Bolshevik ideas. Once the First World War was over, the government organized special camps for returning soldiers and refugees, and especially for communists trying to return from various fronts.[17] The regime forced the KPJ out of the political system, and by 1920 they had proclaimed a decree to ban communist propaganda and all their activities. The decree was signed by Milorad Drašković, who was assassinated a year later by a young communist, which caused the government to ban the KPJ, revoke their parliamentary mandates, confiscate property, and conduct mass arrests.[18]

Over the following two decades, the KPJ worked underground. Their work consisted mainly of going on strikes, recruiting new members, translating Marxist classics and Soviet texts, organizing volunteers and aid for the Spanish Civil War, and of simply trying to survive the Yugoslav regime's brutal reprisals. Many communists were imprisoned or killed during this period. As the historian Jelena Kovačević notes in her discussion of Petar Miletić, a famous communist educated in Moscow, many communists were heavily beaten and tortured for days before any official imprisonment.[19] As the number of women in the party grew in the 1930s, they also shared their male counterparts' fate and were often heavily beaten. For example, Anka Butorac was arrested by the Zagreb police in 1930. She was beaten for days, and after her release, the party managed to smuggle her to the Soviet Union for protection, where she remained for the next five years.[20] Finding a route for these women to escape to the Soviet Union was often crucial for their survival, as they risked being arrested again. The KPJ developed a robust underground network to hide each member's identity. For example, when the twenty-three-year-old Vukica Mitrović was arrested, the police were not able to extract a confession or the names of other communists, despite beatings and tortures. Although these women were then released, they were often rearrested. Vukica Mitrović, together with many other women, did not survive one of those later arrests and was killed in 1941.[21]

Bulgarian women shared a similar fate during the interwar period. Heavily persecuted, Bulgarian communists were always in danger of their lives. For example, Tsola Dragoycheva was arrested several times during the 1920s. She was twenty-five years old when she was arrested in 1923 for participating in a failed communist uprising but was amnestied the following year. However, she was arrested again in 1925 in the wake of the attack on St. Nedelya Church. She was sentenced to death, but her sentence was postponed because of her pregnancy. She gave birth in prison, and her death sentence was commuted to a life sentence. Dragoycheva was amnestied after serving seven years in prison, after which the party sent her to Moscow.[22] Notable communist women such as Ana Maymunkova, Vela Piskova, Elena Gicheva, Rahila Nikolova, and many others did not survive the Sofia prisons. Dragoycheva, however, survived and became one of the most important Bulgarian politicians.

Both the Yugoslav and Bulgarian communist parties fought to survive during the 1920s, and they struggled to attract more women to their ranks. They were even less successful among Muslim women. In Bulgaria, Tsola Dragoycheva was a dominant figure, but in Yugoslavia it was only in the late 1930s that such an important communist woman ascended the ranks. Spasenija Babović was a Yugoslav counterpart to Dragoycheva, as was Vida Tomšič somewhat later. Another reason why the parties struggled to engage women was their hostility to various feminist societies. In the 1920s and 1930s, these societies became more prominent in Bulgaria and Yugoslavia, usually fighting for suffrage and economic and social empowerment. Following divisions between feminists and communists elsewhere in Europe, Balkan communists also believed that feminism separated women from the working class's broader struggles and thus served only bourgeois interests. However, in both countries, the number of women working in industry increased in the interwar period, and it became hard for the communist parties to ignore them. The KPJ placed questions regarding women on the agenda of their 1928 Congress in Dresden. They condemned the "bourgeois exploitation of the female workforce," and demanded an end to women's "political disempowerment, legal inequality, national suppression, and remnants of feudalism."[23] The party decided to form a committee that would focus on working with women and winning them over from the feminist and clerical societies. Indeed, in Yugoslavia, Catholic and Orthodox women's religious groups represented about a third of all organized women's associations during the interwar period. They were supposedly apolitical, focused on educating women in domestic skills and homemaking. The high levels of participation suggest that these societies likely had tremendous value for many women, but such a version of modernity was unacceptable to communists.[24]

The situation for women in communist parties improved following the Seventh World Congress of the Comintern, held in Moscow in 1935. Georgi Dimitrov, who held the highest position of the Comintern's general secretary, delivered the main speech on fascism and highlighted a new policy known as the united front. This was also important for the communists' attitude towards separate women's organizations, because Dimitrov criticized the underestimation of work for recruiting more women and addressing their concerns. He called on communists to work with independent women's organizations, or to even establish such organizations if needed. Dimitrov said that attempts to destroy feminist societies were harmful, and he called on communists to find the most flexible ways of approaching non-communist women.[25]

The Balkan communists dutifully followed the Comintern directives – they changed their approach and tried to be more welcoming to women. In Yugoslavia, many young women joined the KPJ, often young students. This was a double victory for them as these young women could infiltrate other societies and organizations to avoid the shadow of the KPJ's illegal status. Young communists were particularly active in the Youth Section of the Women's Movement (Ženski pokret), and they frequently clashed with older feminists during the discussions and readings of Marxist classics, which the older feminists tried to prevent. The conflicts grew to the extent that the Zagreb section of the Women's Movement abolished the Youth Section in 1938.[26] Nevertheless, through these and other young communist women's activities, the KPJ also managed to publish the magazine *Žena danas*, which became the official magazine of the KPJ's women's section a few years later. Many of these young women played significant roles during the Second World War and in ruling the country afterwards, in a true generational shift as many older interwar communists did not survive the purges. Mitra Mitrović, Vida Tomšič, Vera Aceva, Lidija Šentjurc, Vanda Novosel, and Ljubinka Milosavljević were all in their twenties. The KPJ also attempted to organize young women in Bosnia through the Youth Sections of the Women's Movement, but they were not so successful. The police in Sarajevo arrested the local communist leaders, Djina Vrbica and Bjanka Levi, as early as in 1936, and placed the Women's Movement under surveillance for communist activities. In Macedonia, the party established the Youth Section in Skopje and in other cities, but it seems that they did not engage with Muslim populations.[27]

The need to address "the woman question" prompted the KPJ to discuss and announce the first coherent gender program at the party conference in Zagreb in 1940. Vida Tomšič and Spasenija Babović became the first women admitted to the Central Committee, rendering Babović's experience in the Soviet Union even more important.[28] No women were elected in the KPJ's politburo, while Dragoycheva occupied that position in Bulgaria.[29] Vida Tomšič, who was more educated than Babović, presented a program based solely on the Soviet model and experiences. She promised gender equality as it existed in the Soviet Union: women would be legally, politically, economically, and socially enfranchised; the state would help with childcare; women would get equal pay; and the state would also protect female workers. Tomšič declared the Soviet Union the sole model for solving the woman question, shunning feminism once again. Furthermore, the conference's resolution emphasized the need to suppress feminism, as it creates divisions between male and female workers and blunts the class struggle. The core of this program remained for many decades. Tomšič did not mention national or religious minorities, as she assumed that all women would gain equal rights on the same path to socialism.[30]

The BKP also recruited more women in the 1930s, although not from Muslim communities. Bulgarian communists were also deeply suspicious of feminist organizations, often trying to disband them. Just as in Yugoslavia, many women from the universities joined the BKP, and in the Bulgarian case, they usually joined the Workers' Party, which the BKP controlled. Some of the newly recruited women advanced rapidly and were elected to the Central Committee of the Workers' Party, such as Lilyana Dimitrova. Other women, such as Yordanka Chankova, progressed through the BKP structures. She joined them in 1930 and then spent some time in Moscow at the ILS before returning to the country. She became a member of the Central Committee, but like Dimitrova she did not survive the war. Other ILS graduates, such as Dona Bogatinova, were luckier and survived the war, forging distinguished careers afterwards. Other women, such as Rada Todorova, Ekaterina Avramova, and Dora Belcheva, also held high-ranking positions within the BKP and the state apparatus because of their pre-war BKP experiences. However, all of them belonged to the Bulgarian majority population.[31]

Muslim men similarly struggled to climb the Communist Party hierarchies. It is doubtful that the leaders of the Balkan communist parties considered this a significant problem. For example, the Bulgarian communists Blagoev and Dimitrov were more concerned with creating a proletarian state based on the Bulgarian people's class identity rather than with attracting more religious minorities.[32] The KPJ was somewhat more open and more successful in mobilizing members from the Bosnian Muslim communities before the war. For example, Vahida Maglajlić from Bosnia became a KPJ member. After losing her life in the war, she became the only Muslim woman to receive the People's Hero medal. There is also scattered evidence that local KPJ sections were active in urban centres across Bosnia. In Mostar, a local party cell organized a secret meeting with women where they read excerpts from the work of August Bebel (a German socialist writer and politician) and the magazine *Žena danas*. Still, most communist people were recruited from Christian backgrounds.[33]

Both parties intentionally conveyed a very masculine image in their media. The KPJ's publication *Proleter* always used an image of a strong man to represent the working class. Pictures were generally rare in order to protect communists' identities, so the press relied on drawings and illustrations, but illustrations of working women were also a rarity. For example, for 1 May (May Day) in 1933, *Proleter* illustrated its first page with two workers who were secretly painting a star with a sickle and hammer, while the article explained capitalism's devastating influence on the working class. In contrast, according to the article workers and peasants were supposedly free with a secure future in the Soviet Union. Although women participated and organized numerous strikes in 1930s Yugoslavia, the illustrations in *Proleter* never featured them. Images of women and men who could be linked to Islam were non-existent as well.[34] This was also the case in the BKP's publication *Rabotnichesko delo*, in which pictures and illustrations almost exclusively featured men.

In addition to these many similarities between interwar Yugoslavia and Bulgaria and these two communist parties, Yugoslav and Bulgarian communists also shared direct mutual contacts and exchanges over the decades. These connections were also deeply personal, as Dimitrov's wife, Ljubica, was born in Serbia and represented the Bulgarian Communist Party at the congress at which the Yugoslav Communist Party was established.[35] After the First World War, both communist parties agreed to create the Balkan Communist Federation, an umbrella organization established in Sofia in 1920, which aimed to create a Balkan Soviet Federal Republic. As Maria Todorova has shown, the idea of a Balkan federation had been in existence for almost half a century at that point.[36] Such a state was supposed to solve nationalist territorial tensions and bring socialism to the Balkans. After the failed coup in Bulgaria, the organization was moved to Vienna and then to Moscow.[37] The idea of creating a Balkan superstate prevailed and ended only after the Tito–Stalin split in 1948. Furthermore, in the period before the Second World War, Yugoslav and Bulgarian communists also had mutual contacts in Moscow, and they were part of the same schools and institutions. Finally, within the Comintern led by Dimitrov, Yugoslav communists were always in contact with their Bulgarian counterparts.

The Moscow Influence

Time spent in Moscow was crucial for both Yugoslav and Bulgarian communists. Besides their own experiences from the Balkans, what they learned in Moscow shaped their approaches towards Muslim communities once the communists had gained power after the Second World War. In Moscow, their world views were moulded through collective activities in various organizations, including the Comintern, and through more formal education in various institutes and at the ILS. The

Comintern was crucial for shaping the lives of many international revolutionaries. As the historian Lisa Kirschenbaum shows, by the 1930s it had become an all-encompassing organization that coordinated revolutionaries in tens of countries.[38] Brigitte Studer, a historian of international Stalinism, has argued that the Comintern allowed the Soviet Union to be "the centre of a worldwide zone of circulation."[39] It directed numerous communist parties the world over, and published countless books and other publications in many European languages.[40] For Yugoslav and Bulgarian communists, Moscow was the transnational space in which they formed networks and developed durable ideas on what features a communist society should have.

For international revolutionaries in Moscow, the Comintern also organized direct education. The ILS was the most important of these educational institutions, operating between 1926 and 1938 with students mainly from the Americas and Europe. The school was an integral part of the Comintern, with the goal of Bolshevizing the international movement. Being active in the Comintern entailed developing revolutionary ideas and obeying rules that went beyond the national. The school was immersed in conspiratorial concerns, with students using pseudonyms and facing constant surveillance. It offered various courses ranging from short ones that lasted nine months to extensive ones lasting two to three years.[41]

The ILS's program was very Euro- and Russia-centric. It consisted mainly of numerous readings of the Marxist classics, and of Lenin's speeches, letters, and party directives; the history of the Russian Communist Party; and the history of the European labour movement.[42] Lessons were based on the Soviet experience, and students were taught about the Russian Communist Party's work and how to work with the masses. Soviet examples were used regardless of whether they were applicable in the students' native countries. The curriculum also changed with shifts in Soviet politics, for example, by adding lessons on industrialization and collectivization. Students had only a few lessons adapted to match up with their experience in their native countries. As the curriculum for Bulgarian revolutionaries shows, these lessons followed the same Soviet pattern, which defined what was worthy of attention, and how it should be approached. For example, the Bulgarian curriculum units very closely resembled topics from the book *History of the Communist Party of the Soviet Union (Bolsheviks): Short Course*, which was published a few years later and became a primary reference for international revolutionaries across the Balkans.[43]

Stalinist purges also affected the school. Texts written by purged authors were removed, and Nikolai Bukharin was removed from the principal position in 1929. In the 1930s, when the leading Bulgarian and Yugoslav officials attended the school, the conspiratorial atmosphere reached its peak. Self-criticism was commonly practised, while the curriculum was adjusted by Stalin's close associate Lazar Kaganovich.[44] The historian Barry McLoughlin writes that students were often purged as well.[45] These purges profoundly affected both communist parties, as, for example, Klavdiia Kirsanova was arrested and replaced by Valko Chervenkov, a future leader of the Bulgarian Communist Party.[46]

Communists educated in Moscow also had to accept core assumptions regarding the appropriate solution for nationalism, the "national question," and national minorities. The next chapter analyses details of that approach. At this stage it is important to note that in the curricula, international revolutionaries were taught that Tsarist Russia was a "prison of nations" that fostered racism and exploitation.[47] They also learned that Soviet solutions to the "national question" were the best and were universally applicable, with consequences for how the communist parties approached the issue back home. For example, the Yugoslav Communist Party changed its stance towards Yugoslavia as a state, and how Yugoslavia should be structured, in line with the Comintern's directions. The KPJ moved between various positions, from the idea that Yugoslavia should be dissolved to the solution that it should be a federal state. Eventually, with the Comintern's united front policy, Yugoslav communists decided that nations should have the right to self-determination, and they stopped advocating Yugoslavia's dissolution.[48] After the war, this would have profound effects once the communists had established new republics and defined new nations, as discussed in the next chapter.

The shift towards such national communism instead of international revolution was particularly noticeable after the Comintern's Seventh Congress. Georgi Dimitrov was the chief architect of the Comintern's "national line," which the historian Yannis Sygkelos has called a "Marxist nationalism." This meant that ideas about the world revolution were replaced with nationally oriented discourses and tactics, which would later have consequences for communists regarding how they approached various nationalities in their countries.[49] Regardless of the applicability of the term *Marxist nationalism*, communists staying in Moscow read and learned these core doctrines. For example, Bulgarian communists would first learn how the Soviet Union approached its "national question" before attending brief lessons on the "national question" for Macedonians, Turks, and Pomaks.[50]

Besides staying and studying in Moscow, communists were also expected to visit collective farms, factories, and new Soviet cities during the summer.[51] Furthermore, at the end of their studies, students went on a placement, usually to a factory or a collective farm, as part of their practical assignment.[52] Notable Yugoslav and Bulgarian communists also passed these assignments. For example, a future leader of the KPJ's women's section, Spasenija Babović, was sent to do fieldwork in the Caucasus after finishing a course at the ILS in 1934–5. She returned to Yugoslavia and was an influential part of the ruling elite for many decades.[53]

During its twelve years of existence, some 3,500 communists passed through the school. As Julia Köstenberger argues, Stalinization was a constant process.[54] Besides the theoretical curriculum, students learned to apply in practice and to themselves the principles of socialist competition, criticism, self-criticism, and conspiration.[55] Kirschenbaum writes that the idea was to make international communists seem reliable, unsentimental, and uncompromising. They were disciplined to become "proper" Bolsheviks.[56] Babović is an excellent example of this process, as during her entire career, she was a fierce Stalinist in her work methods. She placed the KPJ first, and she was uncompromising in following the party line and ready to crush any opposition. When she returned to Yugoslavia, she was arrested again, but the police could not gain any information from her. Once she became a member of the Central Committee, she had a chance to apply in practice what she had learned in Moscow, as did many other future leaders of Yugoslavia, Germany, Bulgaria, and Poland, who all passed through the school. They learned to view the world in a specific way and to justify any social interventions they deemed necessary in order to change their societies back home.

Another important example was the leading Bulgarian communist Tsola Dragoycheva. She attended the school and graduated in 1932, and she lived for some years in Moscow during the 1930s. During this time, Dragoycheva occupied a higher position in the Comintern hierarchy than any Yugoslav woman. She was a guest at the Seventh Comintern Congress in 1935, while in 1936 she worked in Paris on spreading the National Front politics to the Balkan communist parties. In 1937 she became a member of the Central Committee, and soon she entered the politburo and became the Central Committee's organizational secretary.[57] Like Spasenija Babović, Dragoycheva remained a fierce Stalinist for many decades. Kirschenbaum suggests that communists' belief in Soviet solutions went beyond simply suspending disbelief. Instead, it entailed internalizing a specific world view and maintaining their communist identities by making observations in a way mediated by these ideas.[58] For example, by examining the writings of Dolores Ibárruri, Kirschenbaum shows that Ibárruri's revolutionary truth structured her observational truth. Ibárruri and other international communists learned how to see the world. They learned how to behave and acquired an interpretative framework for analysing the world.[59] In Dragoycheva's biography, the gender historian Krassimira Daskalova writes that Dragoycheva was in touch with other leading communist women, including Ana Pauker and Ibárruri. This illustrates the existence of a network of influential communist women.[60]

John Bell estimates that between two and three thousand Bulgarians found a home in Moscow during the 1930s.[61] Men, however, dominated the Comintern and its educational institutions. Just like communist women, communist men learned what it meant to be *proper* communists. Besides Dimitrov, who led the Comintern and was at the top of the hierarchy, other Bulgarian and Yugoslav communists made careers in Moscow and later returned to their home countries. Valko Chervenkov fled from Bulgaria in the mid-1920s, becoming a Soviet party member. He was educated at the ILS and became its principal later in 1937. He was the school's last principal, and after its closure, he taught at various places in Moscow.[62] He also worked in the Comintern apparatus. Todor Pavlov became the dean of the Moscow Institute's Faculty of Philosophy, and he was later the BKP's leading theoretician. This education and the experience of being in the capital of the communist world were crucial not only for political control but for creating a sense of belonging. As Kirschenbaum argues, the ILS was a centre linking Moscow and the periphery.[63]

The experience of being in Moscow was undoubtedly enhanced by the fact that many revolutionaries escaped prisons and constant danger in their home countries. Dragoycheva and Babović were both arrested multiple times and barely survived torture. Amid economic and political crises in Europe, and the political, economic, and social disenfranchisement of women, the Soviet Union looked like paradise on earth. It was also common for international revolutionaries to leave their children in the Soviet Union, believing that this would offer them protection and the best possible childhood. Spasenija Babović left her child there and saw him again only after the Second World War had ended. As Kirschenbaum shows, personal life was inextricably linked with communist political duties. Communists' commitments shaped their personal lives, while "personal relationships influenced political understandings."[64] In Moscow, revolutionaries learned that there was no division between public and private life. Everything was at the party's disposal – their identities, sexualities, and relationships.[65] They also shared many direct connections – for example, Dimitrov's sister was married to Chervenkov, and they all lived in Moscow.[66] The behaviour of a revolutionary's spouse was just as important as their own behaviour. The same principles applied when these revolutionaries engaged in the practice of unveiling Muslim women in their own countries. As shown in chapter 5, good communists could not have veiled wives or daughters.

The Moscow experience, however, added further acceptance of violence to the mix. Yugoslav and Bulgarian communists escaped their countries to avoid oppression, but Stalinist purges brought another layer of violence, this time from within their ranks. Fear was familiar to all those educated in Moscow, and international revolutionaries were under constant surveillance. All their activities were recorded, which often resulted in extensive internal files.[67] I would argue that even the violence present in the Moscow years added to a sense of belonging to the communist world. To Yugoslav and Bulgarian communists, it added a global frame of reference. They learned that Soviet collectivization could be applied in the Balkans and that industrialization was something to yearn for. The same applies to Soviet policies in Central Asia towards Muslim populations. As Studer demonstrates, the Comintern had a long-lasting influence on international revolutionaries because it was an effective channel for the circulation of norms and representations.[68] Once these Muscovites had taken over both the Bulgarian and Yugoslav communist parties in the late 1930s, the importance of the learned norms and representations became even more valuable.[69]

Finally, during their stays in the Soviet Union, international revolutionaries were able to observe changes in gender relations and roles. The new social, economic, and political position of women was a domain in which the Soviet Union praised itself as having advanced further than all other countries. For example, the new opportunities that opened up for Soviet women were something that disenfranchised Yugoslav and Bulgarian women could observe in practice. While in Moscow, Balkan revolutionaries read Soviet magazines and pamphlets and learned how to "appropriately" interpret them. Regarding Muslim women and men, they read about Stalinist approaches towards the nationalities of Soviet Central Asia, and about new laws and "successes" in transforming the traditional societies.

Reading Soviet Newspapers and Magazines

International revolutionaries based in Moscow were expected to follow Soviet newspapers and magazines closely. Many revolutionaries who survived Moscow emphasized the importance of the Soviet press.

Additionally, besides direct reading, the Soviet press was translated and interpreted in the *Bulletin* (*Glasnik*) printed by the Yugoslav section after being granted the Comintern's approval. The *Bulletin* carefully followed the decisions of the Soviet government and the Central Committee, and explained its relevance for the Yugoslav communists.[70] *Pravda* was the leading publication to which party members subscribed, but revolutionaries read other magazines as well. These magazines provided revolutionaries with a framework through which to observe Soviet politics in order to follow the party line. Reading these publications was also a matter of prestige, as some of them were not widely available because of paper shortages, and the Comintern and international schools provided them. Furthermore, following and knowing the party line often meant being able to survive the Stalinist purges, although amid the unpredictability of the 1930s, there were no guarantees. Finally, like other international revolutionaries, Yugoslav and Bulgarian communists also contributed articles to *Pravda* and other magazines.[71]

The historian Matthew Lenoe observes that Soviet newspapers went through immense changes with Stalinism and its industrialization and collectivization projects. Newspapers became more militant, focusing on heroic sacrifices and class resentments. Except for periodicals aimed at women, editors of the prominent newspapers were all men. In 1929, only about 10 per cent of editors and writers were women. In *Pravda*, for example, international revolutionaries were able to read about the position of women mainly during the 8 March celebrations. During the rest of the year, the vast majority of articles addressed activists in general. They assigned tasks to the activists and offered examples of how these tasks should be fulfilled. The idea was to mobilize party activists in articles full of superlatives and epithets, and this model was applied in Eastern Europe after the war as well.[72]

Articles in *Pravda* on and around 8 March always discussed women's position in society and the changes brought about by the Soviet state. The main article would present the party leadership's stance and the new tasks for the activists, while the rest of the paper would contribute news and vignettes of how other activists had successfully completed similar tasks. The other leading articles also discussed the achievements of the Soviet Union regarding women's equality, and they established a framework on how gender relations were to be viewed elsewhere. For example, in these articles, *Pravda* attacked bourgeois politicians, legislators, priests, and others who claimed that a woman was "an inferior being whose fate was shame, slavery, and submission."[73] Instead, thanks to the Soviet state, Soviet women were supposedly active participants in the Soviet economy and builders of socialism with protected rights inscribed in Stalin's constitution. *Pravda* also regularly published the numbers of female students, politicians, hospitals, and day care units, and it called on the party organizations to recruit women into industry and politics.[74] Such articles provided foreign revolutionaries with an ideal that they should achieve.

After these featured articles, *Pravda* published pieces on Soviet women's new way of living, in both the cities and the countryside. These articles praised the new social mobility, including examples of successful career women who had been elected to top-level political posts.[75] They often published articles written in the first person, from both Russian women and various national minorities. Such articles talked about the repression of the "old regime" and the successes of the new Soviet state in industry, agriculture, and social institutions, which had made women's "joyful lives" possible.[76] These articles offered a solution, but for the foreign communists, they represented a possible different world that had already been achieved after the revolution in the Soviet Union. As analysed in chapter 4, the same approach was later taken by Bulgarian and Yugoslav communists in their own periodicals after the war.

Pravda also featured articles that supposedly showed perspectives of Muslim women. The story of Islamova which opened this book was probably the most typical of the ideal expected of women from Soviet Central Asia. The Soviet state and Stalinist policies provided the opportunity, and women had to accept the ideology and commit to the work. As a reward, the state would bring about social mobility and change to the entire community. Other stories from *Pravda*, such as the one about Tadzhihan Shadieva, followed the same pattern. Shadieva boldly chose to discard the paranja in 1926, and leave her abusive husband. She was sent to Moscow for further education, and there she encountered her future spouse. Upon completing their studies, both Shadieva and her husband were appointed leaders of the political sections at collective farms in two adjacent districts in Uzbekistan. Shadieva was the first Uzbek woman to hold such a position. This led to a socialist competition between the districts in cotton production, a competition in which Shadieva's district emerged victorious. As Shadieva climbed the political hierarchy, she featured in *Pravda* multiple times, talking about her work and bringing socialist modernity to her district,[77] only to disappear once she was arrested and sentence to ten years in prison in October 1938 during the Stalinist purges.[78]

These ideas – traditional practices and socialist modernity – were constructed through such articles, and they provided a framework for understanding the struggle for power in Central Asia. In many such articles, readers related to fascinating stories written in the first person by Soviet "East" women. They described the beautiful life the Soviet Union had given them and the fulfilment of their dreams, which they contrasted with the dark past manifest in the black veils. Yugoslav and Bulgarian communists could relate to this. They read straightforward solutions and recipes that they could apply in practice. For example, on 8 March 1939, *Pravda* featured an article and a picture of a young woman training to become a pilot. She described her military day and her training, learning maths, physics and mechanics, and flying the skies. Then she asked herself what kind of life she would have without the Soviet state. She imagined a "black veil, kitchen pots, doom … a life worse than death."[79] She then reflected on other women's lives, women who were not lucky enough to be within the Soviet borders, and she described the lives of these millions of women as oppressed, dependent, and enslaved.[80]

Pravda also published articles on Muslim men who were clinging to old gender norms. These articles included vignettes from life in Central Asia, and they were critical of "old" gender relations and traditions. For example, one piece described a situation in Tashkent in which a man did not allow his wife to visit the women's club and learn to read. However, after this woman's plea, the party activist Halim-Apa Kazakova intervened and convinced the man to allow his wife and daughter to attend the club and study. This activist was praised for successfully changing Tashkent with her immense energy and help from the Soviet state. She gave speeches to other women about new laws, lecturing them about their rights and the equality that the Stalinist constitution had brought them. She was active in the women's club, which had two schools, one regular and one for illiterate women, where she also worked on women's political education. Finally, on her initiative, hundreds of women were sent to study or work, while men in the old city had to accept the new reality and equality.[81] Such stories would be rewritten in a new local context – with new names but the same narrative – by Bulgarian and Yugoslav communists ten years later.

International revolutionaries not only read *Pravda* but also published articles. Consequently, the most important Soviet publication became a forum in which they could also seemingly participate. For example, Dolores Ibárruri wrote about International Women's Day and the Spanish Civil War for many years. She interpreted the Soviet Union as the ideal of freedom and women's liberation, for which Spanish women must fight. She observed poetically that in the Soviet Union, International Women's Day is a day of joy; in democratic countries, it is a day of struggle for basic rights, while in fascist countries, it is a day of covert protest or of the fight for liberation from fascism.[82]

Pravda's articles were of the utmost importance, but magazines designed explicitly for women included further nuances and explanations on how individual policies should be enacted. It is fair to assume that international revolutionaries, at least women, read those magazines, because after the war, the party's women's sections regularly subscribed to them.[83] Furthermore, their own magazines copied the look and structure of the best-known Soviet magazines, such as *Rabotnitsa*, *Krestjanka*, and *Sovetskaja zhenschina*.[84] *Rabotnitsa* at the height of Stalinism was not so different from the post–Second World War Yugoslav magazine *Žena danas* or the Bulgarian *ZHenata dnes*. *Rabotnitsa* usually opened with a feature article by or about Stalin. It then promoted notable shock workers, collective farmers, and other women who had distinguished themselves, including many from Muslim backgrounds.[85] Yugoslav and Bulgarian magazines did the same. All these magazines also featured news on successes regarding productivity, maternal protections, childcare, fiction short stories, and advice for homemakers on improving their *byt* – their way of life.[86]

Both in *Pravda* and in magazines designed for women, women were construed as needing special attention. The magazines created a patronizing relationship between women activists and women targeted for party interventions. Such publications addressed women activists, informing them of current policies and instructing them about immediate tasks, while creating narratives that the targeted groups were in dire need of such interventions. For example, they created a specific image of Muslim women in need of help, while the activists were portrayed as those responsible for bringing an imagined socialist modernity to these women in terms of family relations or dress.[87] It taught activists to think of Muslim women as policy objects, and also as real objects that should be unveiled, employed, and liberated from oppressive family structures. The veil was constructed as a hostile object; an obstacle on the road to socialism.[88]

These magazines also construed men as the main culprits, trying to preserve the oppression of women often through traditional family relations. For example, *Rabotnitsa* regularly wrote about Muslim women who were the "slaves" of their husbands in the past; however, socialism had liberated them, and they became shock workers. These women chose to unveil, becoming active builders of socialism. They were organized in brigades and broke productivity norms, creating "a new life" for themselves.[89] In that sense, these women became the bearers of modernity thanks to Stalinist policies. Choi Chatterjee notes that this transformation, while significant, still depended overly on the state and the party. Muslim women had to show public expressions of gratitude and personal and political subordination to the regime.[90]

Such writings are explored more in the following chapters of this book, which shows how the discourse established in Soviet magazines for women was imitated in socialist Yugoslavia and Bulgaria after the war.

Writings in the Soviet newspapers and magazines, therefore, served to inform readers about how to think in harmony with the party line. Articles such as these provided international revolutionaries with simple solutions for work among their own religious minorities. Minorities were supposed to become part of the socialist project, attaining the same level of imagined socialist modernity, while activists were placed in a powerful position as people who were supposed to enact and control. Communists who did not directly experience being in Moscow also formed their world views via Soviet magazines, newspapers, literature, brochures, pamphlets, and materials. These publications were smuggled abroad and read in secrecy, even in Yugoslav and Bulgarian prisons, and they were ascribed a tremendous value. These materials provided guidance and a legitimizing tool, telling local communists that they were on the right side of history. They offered a hope of a different world in which their goals were not unrealistic. Reports from many prisons and concentration camps, in which communists and anti-fascists were incarcerated, showed the value of any text coming from the Soviet Union, but also of the spoken word of those who had travelled to the Soviet Union already.[91]

Backwardness at Home

The idea of backwardness was an obsession of the Bolsheviks and of the Bulgarian and Yugoslav communists. They saw their countries as backward compared with Europe, and they also considered some groups of the population to be more backward than others. In this imagined social hierarchy, communists saw themselves as the working class's vanguard at the top of the pyramid. It was up to the communists, the "most advanced" group, to lead others and save them from "backwardness." This hierarchy also had a gender component – women were deemed "more backward" than men. Finally, there was a third component related to religion. Atheists were the most advanced group, while those who practised Islam were at the bottom of this hierarchy.

Of course, the idea of backwardness was not limited to the socialists. The local political and intellectual elites internalized the Balkan countries as "backward" and in need of catching up with industrial Western Europe. It was often an essential part of colonial projects, and it accompanied Othering and orientalizing.[92] The notion of backwardness in the socialist modernizing projects added different discourses via ideological explanations. For example, instead of fetishizing Euro-peanness and contrasting it with Turkish "backwardness," as Kumari Jayawardena writes in the case of the Kemalist revolution,[93] socialists fetishized their own imagined progressiveness as the vanguard of the working class. In practice, it was often socialist men, alongside a few women, who decided on this hierarchy, which was supposed to break what they considered to be a patriarchal society.

According to contemporary standards, both interwar Yugoslavia and Bulgaria were patriarchal societies in which women were disen-franchised politically, economically, and socially. Unlike other countries in Eastern Europe, Bulgaria, Yugoslavia, and Romania did not grant women voting rights after the First World War. In fact, for Yugosla-via and Bulgaria, the end of the First World War did not bring about any changes for women. Women were still not allowed to vote or be elected, while their social position was further hampered by a series of laws, of which the civil code was the most detrimental. In the newly formed Yugoslavia, six different civil laws were in force. For example, Serbian civil law passed in 1844 was still in power until the communists abolished it in 1945. This nineteenth-century civil code equated women with minors, stripping them of any political, economic, and social rights. Once married, women were deprived of any rights concerning economic activities, inheritance, divorce, or parenting, and they were legally obliged to "serve" their husband.[94] This code was based on even older Austrian civil law, which remained in effect in former Austrian parts of Yugoslavia, while for the Muslim populations, sharia law was in force. The new Yugoslav state aimed to unify the legal system and pass a new civil code, but this was not completed before the Second World War.[95]

In Bulgaria, similar provisions disempowered women. Daskalova shows that the Bulgarian constitution did not prohibit women from vot-ing but that women were not allowed to vote because the term *citizen* included men only.[96] The law professor Velina Todorova writes, on the topic of civil law, that women had a right to inherit only half of the share of their male counterparts, and even this was viewed with contempt. Meanwhile, the historian Ulf Brunnbauer claims that even after the First World War, women in the Rhodope region rarely inherited property in either Christian or Muslim communities.[97] Women had no rights to pursue the biological father of their children born out of wedlock, and – just as in Yugoslavia – women were barred from many professions and higher degrees.[98] Although the Bulgarian civil code was younger and based on different source documents, it included very similar stipu-lations to the Serbian code, particularly regarding the preservation of men's power and dominance. Furthermore, issues related to marriage and the family were regulated by religious canon rather than civil law, and the provisions were very similar in the canonical laws of the Serbian and Bulgarian Orthodox churches. Civil marriage did not exist, divorce was hard to obtain, interconfessional marriages were not possible, and spouses were supposed to observe gender norms within marriage as decided by the canon. Sharia law for Muslim populations was also the same in Bulgaria and in various parts of Yugoslavia, rendering Muslim women's experiences fairly similar.[99]

Yugoslav and Bulgarian communists were committed to changing their societies radically. These changes were supposed to be much deeper than simply political and economic reforms. They were intended to change the core of gender norms and relations. Indeed, they could draw on a long tradition of socialist and communist writers from their own countries who advocated such changes. For example, the Serbian socialist Dimitrije Tucović translated August Bebel's *Woman and Socialism* as early as 1909 and published his own article titled "The Struggle for Women's Liberation" the following year.[100] Yet it was the Soviet Union that provided the model of how that was to be achieved. While in Moscow, or through reading Soviet magazines, pamphlets, and documents, Yugoslav and Bulgarian communists learned how the Soviet Union approached "backwardness," seemingly solving the problem.

The Soviet idea that Muslim populations in Central Asia were "backward" was inherited from Imperial Russia and repeated countless times after the Soviet state was established. It was ultimately a European idea. Phrases such as the "backwardness of the Eastern peoples" were commonly used in the media and documents from the early postrevolutionary days.[101] As early as 1920, the Moscow centre directed all the relevant party committees and political units to intensify work on eradicating "backwardness." They insisted that it was activists' duty to fight religious prejudices, to spread literacy and schooling, and also to help the Muslim peoples "raise their national culture and create their own literature and their own schools," creating both class and national consciousness.[102]

Agitprop departments also received detailed instructions on how to approach the "backwardness" of Muslim women. Activists were instructed to fight signs of women's oppression, such as underage marriage, illiteracy, domestic violence, and veils. Backwardness was supposedly defeated by including these women in the workforce, organizing educational courses, and giving them a voice at rallies and assemblies.[103] However, as one activist from the party's women's section, the

Zhenotdel, explained, women's emancipation also depended on their rejection of religious prejudices. In her words, the sooner that happened, the sooner women would be on an equal footing with men.[104]

I argue that the discourse on Muslim women was cemented already in the first years of Bolshevik rule, and it was also spread by women themselves via many local congresses of the "women of the East." Many women delegates from Central Asia and the Caucasus spoke publicly for the first time. For example, Turkmen women met and talked about the need for education, equality with men, and the need to liberate other women. Their congress acknowledged that the people of the East were oppressed but that women were particularly oppressed for being women. The Bolsheviks promised to bring "culture and education" and to liberate women from "religious evils and bad family relationships." Women were supposedly forced "to live lives in the positions of prisoners and cattle." The congress then issued a resolution calling for the full abolition of the remnants of sharia law – dowries and kalym (bride money paid by the groom's family to the bride's family, dower). They also called for a struggle against traditions that exploited women and kept them "prisoners of men." The Zhenotdel was instructed to take all possible measures to promote this direction, to organize activists, courses, and schools, while courts would take special care to punish all those who still exploited women.[105]

The early 1920s also set the narrative regarding marriage practices, in which polygamy, dowries and kalym, and the abduction of women were mainly targeted. As one resolution of the executive committee of the Kirghiz Central Committee concluded, "By issuing a decree abolishing kalym in the Kirgiz Republic, the basis has been laid for the emancipation of Kirgiz women from the chains of everyday slavery that bind them."[106] Nevertheless, in the early 1920s, even Zhenotdel activists would be approached by peasant men to ask activists to decrease the price of certain women, so that they could marry them.[107] The Soviets also enforced the institution of civil marriage and divorce, bringing tremendous change to people's lives, as discussed in chapter 3. Here, however, it is important to note that this was the moment when the Bolsheviks established a model for other communists to follow.[108] The eradication of "backwardness" was supposed to be achieved through the liberation of women, attained through the Soviet laws, education, women's employment, and their economic independence.[109] Implementation of Soviet laws, particularly regarding women's property rights, kalym, and even polygamy, showed the limits of Soviet power. The orgburo of the party's Central Committee often had to call on local party organizations to take extraordinary measures and provide further assistance to implement the Soviet legislation.[110] It is unlikely that international revolutionaries were highly aware of these struggles.

These early post-revolutionary ideas about Muslim communities did not change much in the later period. The Bolshevik leadership established targets for activists and marked traditional practices as backward. By reading the Soviet literature, declarations, resolutions, and lectures, Yugoslav and Bulgarian communists learned how to approach their own Muslim minorities, which they did after the Second World War. Their approach was adapted slightly to the local surroundings, but as the following chapters show, Yugoslav and Bulgarian communists were ready to ignore their own experiences in order to fit Soviet models.

Of course, the "backwardness of women" was a myth that legal, economic, political, and social discrimination all facilitated. Even the communists' perspective that such backwardness depends on a lack of class consciousness was hard to sustain, as the Bulgarian case shows. The Bulgarian working class was small, as the country was predominantly rural. However, according to the historian Tatyana Nestorova, women held 44 per cent of industrial jobs in 1939. This was because women dominated the textile, tobacco, and food processing industries, which were a big part of Bulgarian industrial production.[111] Nevertheless, Bulgarian communists readily accepted that women required special attention. This was also the case in Yugoslavia, although Dimitrije Tucović insisted that because of the "material, moral, and intellectual poverty" forced upon women, their poverty was not much different from the poverty of the entire working class.[112]

Ultimately, once the idea that women lagged behind men (and that Muslim women lagged behind other women) had been established and accepted by the communists, it served as a justification for any kind of political action or intervention into the gender relations. The party leaders and its activists were supposed to liberate all the masses and bring about an imagined socialist modernity. How this modernity was imagined, and what it meant for gender policies, is analysed in the following chapters.

The Yugoslav and Bulgarian communist parties shared many similarities in the interwar period. Both were opposed to their respective state regimes and, after initial electoral successes, were pushed underground. Being a communist entailed a life of imminent dangers and often imprisonment. Many communists found refuge in the Soviet

Union, where they were educated in various Comintern institutions, institutes, schools, and most notably at the ILS. Yugoslav and Bulgarian communists' time in Moscow had a profound impact on them. They learned how to interpret Soviet policies and how to change society. At the same time, they were also at risk in the Stalinist purges, and indeed many lost their lives. Those who survived were even more Stalinized, ready to implement the party line at whatever cost. Many would later have a chance to apply the Moscow teaching in practice after the Second World War.

While based in Moscow, but also with copies reaching the prisons of Bulgaria and Yugoslavia, Soviet magazines and newspapers played a crucial role in establishing official world views. Revolutionaries read *Pravda* and other specialized magazines. Those in Balkan prisons smuggled and translated Soviet publications. They allowed revolutionaries to dream about Soviet paradise, and they offered solutions on how to bring about such changes to their countries. They read of tremendous successes with a solution to the "national question," the emancipation of Muslim women, new opportunities through collectivization and industrialization, new social, political, and economic rights, and new opportunities that Muslim people of all genders supposedly happily grabbed.

By considering their countries as particularly "backward" regarding gender norms and policies, the Soviet Union provided a model for Bulgarian and Yugoslav activists to follow. In both Bulgaria and Yugoslavia, women were politically, economically, and socially disenfranchised. The socialist revolution was supposed to bring equality and erase "backwardness." Indeed, this notion of backwardness created a specific class and gender hierarchy in which Muslim women were at the bottom. It provided a justification for any kind of planned social intervention directed at the Muslim communities once the communists were in power.

Chapter Two

Socialist (Gendered) Nation Building

By 1925, Faina Efimovna Nyurina was working as the head of the women's department of the Soviet Communist Party's Central Committee, and she was a member of the editorial board of the magazine *Kommunistka*. In that post, she wrote numerous articles on the position of women in the Soviet Union. She was one of those crucial people whose writing connected Sovietization efforts in Central Asia to the importance of working with women. In her view, the supposed backwardness and low cultural level of women were stalling the East's development, while if women unveiled, joined the party or Komsomol,[1] and completed paid labour, they held the potential of becoming a revolutionary influence in the new Central Asian states. Finally, the role of these "Soviet East Republics" was supposed to be of crucial importance for anti-imperial and anti-colonial work worldwide.[2] Nyurina was born in Ukraine, but by 1925 she was already working from Moscow, projecting to other regions what the new socialist nations should look like and what kind of transformation they needed to undergo to reach new socialist standards. Like many others, Nyurina was arrested and executed in 1938 during the Stalinist purges, and did not survive long enough to witness the unprecedented transformation in Soviet Central Asian republics.[3]

Gender policies towards Muslim minorities in the Soviet Union, and then in socialist Yugoslavia and Bulgaria, were intertwined with broader approaches towards nation building, the "national question," and the centre/periphery dichotomy. This chapter explores how communists approached and imagined nation building. It argues that Soviet approaches in Central Asia have had profound effects on Yugoslavia and Bulgaria. Stalinist policies towards minorities were transposed abroad, but the differences in how they were applied in federal Yugoslavia and unitarist Bulgaria determined the level of protection for Muslim minorities. Yugoslav communists followed the Stalinist nation-building model more closely, creating new federal units that protected recognized nations. Bulgarian communists initially followed the Stalinist model by protecting Muslims and offering "cultural" rights, but without federal structures that could provide protection once Bulgaria started the de-Stalinization process. This chapter shows that policies towards Muslims became more hostile when Bulgarian communists packed old nationalist approaches into a Marxist discourse. Muslim women's dress, particularly veils, was seen as an obstacle for new nation building in all cases. Gender imaginaries played an important role in nation building, continuing older processes in a new, socialist context.

The Bolsheviks and Central Asia

Policies towards the various nationalities and national minorities were set by the Bolshevik Party's top leadership in Moscow. These policies had direct consequences for how Bolsheviks and foreign communists approached gender in Muslim communities. In contrast to later Yugoslav and Bulgarian communists, the Bolsheviks did not have a blueprint for a socialist solution to the "national question" in practice.[4] They worked with the inherited pre-revolutionary situation, trying to Sovietize local populations and bring them to the imagined level of socialist modernity. The Bolsheviks opted for federalism early on, aiming to create new political units and "modernize" them. Stalin himself provided the rationale for federalism, pushing for it among the top leadership after the revolution. The idea was that the creation of new nations was an unavoidable part of the modernization process.[5]

In practice, Bolshevik modernization entailed reshaping indigenous societies in a European image. The historian Jeremy Smith points out that as early as in 1918, Stalin steered discussion on the "national question" towards the perceived "low cultural level" of the non-Russians. Stalin deemed them socially and economically backward – as lagging in their revolutionary development. For non-Russians in Central Asia and elsewhere to prosper, their regions needed their own schools, administration, and other institutions, in addition to a codified language and political autonomy, all of which would be supported by the revolutionary centre.[6] Indeed, over the following decades a lot of effort was put into education, institution building, and the general economic development of non-Russian communities.[7] The historians David Brandenberger and Mikhail V. Zelenov have asserted that nationality policy was a major component of Soviet self-representation, and it was regularly used to showcase Soviet modernization and a commitment to the liberation of various peoples.[8]

The Bolshevik nationality policies were far from straightforward
once applied. Many authors have highlighted the contradictory nature
of Soviet approaches in Central Asia: they were both imperial and anti-
colonial.[9] Immediately after the revolution, Stalin and Lenin promised
an end to imperial exploitation and called on Muslims to overthrow
their colonial masters.[10] Once the Bolsheviks had won the civil war,
Central Asia underwent extensive nation building. The tsarist territorial organization was rewritten, while Bolsheviks attempted to apply
the national-territorial principle to nomadic peoples with tribal affiliations, who generally did not define themselves in Soviet terms. The
idea was to divide Central Asia into separate states, each with their
own language, territory, and culture. Jeremy Smith has suggested that
economic differences made it impossible to settle new borders on an
imagined ethnographic basis. After much deliberation, the Central
Executive Committee created multiple republics that had never existed
before, establishing the Tajik ASSR, Turkmen SSR, Uzbek SSR, and
Kara-Kirghiz AR – which was renamed the Kyrgyz ASSR a year later.

Smith argues that these divisions were driven by the Bolshevik idea
that such political reorganization would help to improve the situation
of Central Asian Muslims, rather than by simple colonial attempts.[11]
The historian Adeeb Khalid contends that this was also a pan-Soviet
process of creating ethnically homogenous territorial entities driven
by the Bolshevik centre, but he also shows that local elites played an
important part in that process, taking opportunities to climb the newly
established state and party hierarchies.[12] Furthermore, the Bolshevik
ideas that emancipation and progress would come through education
and institution building were not so novel in the region. Khalid shows
that there was a strong local modernist tradition among intellectuals.
The Muslim modernist reformers called the Jadids advocated a modernist interpretation of Islam and criticized many cultural practices. The
Jadids also favoured cultural revolution, mass education, land reform,
and the emancipation of women, just as the Bolsheviks did.[13] The Bolsheviks implemented many of these ideas, but with an atheistic ideology and the state apparatus behind them.

As the historian Yulia Gradskova points out, when creating the new
republic, the idea of women's emancipation in the Soviet periphery was a
crucial element in – from the Bolsheviks' perspective – modernizing and
developing "backward" nationalities.[14] The Bolsheviks often divided
various nationalities into two broad categories – Eastern and Western –
and such a discourse had significant implications for politics: all Eastern nationalities were considered culturally backward and in dire need
of change.[15] Central magazines for women, such as *Kommunistka*, often

portrayed Central Asia as a single entity. They called it the Soviet East and highlighted problems linked to gender relations across the entire region. Throughout the 1920s, these areas were criticized for their "manifestations of barbarism concerning women"[16] and the Bolsheviks called on the regional leaders to fight slavery, veils, underage marriages, and kalym. To avoid being classified as "barbarian," activists in this region had to solve gender relations by bringing women into industry and agriculture and increasing literacy and women's political activities. Gender policies were, therefore, a tool for changing these communities but also a marker of women's imagined progress.

These core principles remained in later decades, and they guided activists and political leaders in evaluating the progress of newly created nations. The journal *Kommunistka* published many articles that defined Central Asian women as discriminated against, and they instructed their activists on how to approach the local party and the local populations. Adeeb Khalid also points out that the imagined liberation of Central Asian women was the personal mission of many European women in the Zhenotdel.[17] Polygamy, bride wealth, veils, and a lack of literacy were often mentioned as problems to be solved, while the state's progress was measured by the number of female workers, Komsomol activists, and communists.[18] The leading authors of *Kommunistka* also carefully counted and compared the number of women's clubs, meetings, conferences, and delegates. Women activists reading *Kommunistka* were told to place the position of Soviet Central Asia in the broader context of colonial countries that had not yet been liberated, as their own work must serve as an example of successful solutions. In that sense, they were reminded that local women's emancipation was the central problem of Sovietization in the East. At the same time, women's isolation in their households and from political life was designated as hindering the progress of Eastern republics across the board.[19]

The *Kommunistka* articles also targeted local party men, who had to be persuaded that women were an important force in the new states' economy, and that family relations and traditions hindered these new republics.[20] The new states intended to staff their administration with local women, while the entire party was supposed to be at work among them, winning over the non-party female *masses*. Male party members were supposed to be allies, which was often not the case in practice.[21] The party activists had to find a way of liberating women from the "feudal-patriarchal way of life and its economic, cultural, and legal relationships."[22] The sheer number of such wishful articles throughout the 1920s shows that resistance from the old social order was very much present.

As many authors have noted,[23] implementing emancipatory ideas was very challenging for Zhenotdel activists, even though the Bolsheviks made their ideas attractive to many local women and young people. Khalid argues that the Zhenotdel found willing recruits among the women fleeing abusive families and marriages, and who saw hope in the Soviet gender program.[24] However, resistance was fierce both among the party members and among the local population, particularly regarding unveiling, which will be discussed in chapter 5. Since the idea of success and progress for these nations was inseparably tied to gender relations from the very earliest days, and not only on the conceptual level, such resistance was particularly important.[25] After all, as one article in *Kommunistka* suggested, working with women was a national and state project, a part of the national politics of the parties in the new republics and raions.[26]

Nevertheless, women were struggling not only to climb the party hierarchy and the state apparatus but also, often, to achieve basic rights related to divorce, inheritance, employment, and general safety. The Zhenotdel and the party often blamed the entire society's "backwardness" for this, and that of Islam as religion. According to the historian Shoshana Keller, the Soviet government "used the women's liberation campaign as one of its primary weapons against Islam as a whole, never passing up a chance to declare that Islam must be eliminated because it oppressed women."[27] Meanwhile, the historian Cloé Drieu shows that Soviet popular artistic production, such as theatre and cinema, was also utilized in attempts to transform gender relations and delegitimize Islam's authority.[28] As is shown later in this chapter, the same approach was used in Bulgaria.

Incorporating new nations into an imagined socialist modernity also entailed control of religious activities. Church and state were separated throughout the entire country after the revolution, and all religious communities suffered a series of assaults. All religious organizations were disenfranchised in terms of family affairs, and all had many of their properties seized or destroyed. Yaacov Ro'i suggests that out of 20,000 mosques operating before the revolution, only about 4,000 still existed in 1929, with many more closed over the following decade.[29] This was part of the broader anti-religious campaign, in which all religious communities lost the vast majority of their land and religious objects, and many religious officials were killed.[30]

Besides destroying existing local institutions, the Bolsheviks aimed to control religious activities through (re-)establishing hierarchical institutions that were supposed to provide spiritual guidance and education. These institutions, in the form of spiritual boards, oversaw publishing activities, and were useful for controlling the actions of local religious officials.[31] A similar structure of spiritual boards had already existed in Russia before the revolution, with the Central Spiritual Board of Muslims (TsDUM) based in Ufa, led by the mufti.[32] It is unclear to what extent this organization existed in practice during the 1920s, and particularly during the destructive years of the 1930s. In any case, they were not able to protect and stop the gradual abolition of sharia courts, the confiscation of waqf property (an inalienable charitable endowment under Islamic law), and the closure of mosques.[33] Nevertheless, with changes in religious policies during the Second World War, Stalin's regime reorganized this institution in 1943. Alongside the establishment of the Orthodox Patriarchate, the regime established the Spiritual Administration of the Muslims of Central Asia and Kazakhstan (SADUM). It was led by a mufti as before, and it was supposed to be a bureaucratic umbrella organization for religious activities. The SADUM could open a madrasa and provide higher education there, while the regime also provided a budget for publishing activities.[34] The muftiate in Soviet Central Asia, and the Islamic scholars leading the organization, were dependent on the Soviet state, but often managed to find a space for protecting the interests of its believers.[35] It was dominated by a new male political and cultural elite in the Central Asian republics, successfully built by the Soviets[36] just as the Yugoslavs and Bulgarians did a few years later. Similar institutions existed in Yugoslavia and Bulgaria – namely, the Islamic Community of Yugoslavia and the Chief Mufti's Office in Bulgaria – both established after the 1878 Treaty of Berlin and reorganized after the communists came to power.[37]

One consequence of anti-religious campaigns and of the tight regulation of Islamic learning and religious observance was that religious practices became increasingly privatized and rooted in the domestic domain.[38] Furthermore, women were less visible to the authorities and under less official scrutiny. Fewer women than men were present in the state apparatus, the party structures, and public employment, and they were under less pressure to show loyalty to the regime. Prejudices about women's agency also served as a form of protection. Several authors have shown that family members often used such protections to perform religious rituals and practices, hiding behind women and blaming them if discovered.[39] Changing domestic religious practices proved to be difficult in all Soviet communities, particularly where the party organization was weaker in the countryside. As will be demonstrated in later chapters, this was also the case in Yugoslavia and Bulgaria a few decades later, where communists would be less able to control and eradicate religious practices from the domestic sphere. Finally, many officials were more concerned with measurable outcomes such as women's education and employment, leaving domestic religiosity intact for the time being.[40] Arguably, social life in Central Asia changed more during and after the Second World War because of the mass war mobilization. As the historian Douglas Northrop shows, migrations, wartime economics, mobilization, and ultimately a new generation born in the Soviet Union changed Central Asia more than the active efforts of Zhenotdel and party activists of the 1920s and 1930s. Long-term gendered nation building was apparently successful.[41]

As in other spheres, the Bolsheviks' approach to the national question, to nation building in Central Asia, and to their relationship with official Islamic institutions had significant consequences abroad. The previous chapter demonstrated that Soviet solutions were carefully studied by international revolutionaries through publications, while Soviet policies towards nationalities were also part of the curricula at the ILS. For example, the curriculum for Bulgarian revolutionaries emphasized that Lenin and Stalin had eradicated "backwardness" and promoted national freedoms on the basis of autonomy, which the Stalinist constitution guaranteed. Such an approach supposedly led to the creation of a multinational socialist state. In the 1930s, Bulgarian revolutionaries were taught that this was achieved thanks to industrialization and collectivization, the development of local national cadres, the promotion of local culture (supposedly "national in form and socialist in content"), the opening of clubs, theatres, and schools, the fight against illiteracy, and an overall increase in material welfare and well-being in these republics and areas.[42]

Finally, the creation of new republics and regions based on the establishing of new nations opened up the question of nationalism, which bothered both Yugoslavia and Bulgaria. As the previous chapter showed, the interwar Yugoslav state moved from one political crisis to another, with nationalism always at the fore. The Bulgarian interwar state was also drowning in nationalism, in which the Bulgarian political elites lamented territories they were unable to conquer in the First World War. Additionally, the issue of Turkish nationalism and its connection to Kemalism also often occupied the imagination of the Bulgarian politicians. And yet, the Bolsheviks were supposed to support national republics and regions. This support would guide them on their path to socialist progress, which would then suppress bourgeois nationalist discussions. The Bolsheviks discussed the dangers of nationalism for decades, while the historians Brandenberger and Zelenov revealed changes that Stalin made in the late 1930s, with his own editing of the *Short Course* in order to tone down much discussion of the threats of bourgeois nationalism. Furthermore, Stalin cut many instances in which the nationality policy was discussed in terms of modernization, including his own 1935 speech. In the *Short Course*, Stalin criticized "dominant-nation chauvinism," which was applicable to both Yugoslavia and Bulgaria. The Yugoslav communists interpreted this in a more literary manner by criticizing Greater Serbian chauvinism, while Bulgarians mostly avoided treating the dominant Bulgarian chauvinism the same way. Nevertheless, as Brandenberger and Zelenov show, throughout this period, the Soviet press continued to promote socialist nation building of various non-Russian peoples, thus demonstrating the complexity of the Stalinist approach.[43]

Yugoslav Communists and "Nationalities"

In reconfiguring the post-war Yugoslavia, communists drew on the Stalinist model and on their own Second World War experience. Regarding Muslim populations, crucial changes accompanied how communists structured the federal state, and incorporated local traditions and Muslim institutions, in a similar fashion as the Soviets did when encountering and adopting some of the Jadids' traditions. Yugoslav communists could rely on the modernist tradition, spearheaded by the existing institution of the Islamic Religious Community of Yugoslavia (Islamska verska zajednica – IVZ), led by the elected reis-ul-ulema. The reis was the supreme religious leader, in a semi-autonomous, indigenous official Islamic religious hierarchy.[44] The Islamic Religious Community was preserved in the interwar Yugoslavia; it was reformed in 1930 to include all other Muslim religious authorities in the state beyond Bosnia. This unification of religious leadership structures did not mean that various religious communities were brought closer together, as the reis-ul-ulema institution remained very much centred on Bosnia. Nevertheless, regardless of their real power in various parts of the country, the reis-ul-ulema had significant moral and theoretical authority.

The interwar reis-ul-ulema office's modernization was most evident with Mehmed Džemaludin Čaušević. He was elected before the First World War and remained the reis until he retired in 1930. During his tenure he strongly advocated for women's education and reforms in both male and female dress. He often praised Kemalist reforms, claiming that uncovering a woman's face was not against religious precepts. His writings and interviews provoked a fierce response from conservative ulema, which uncovered a deep split on the issue within the community. In the late 1920s, the unveiling of Muslim women polarized the community and led to heated debates in which the reis was even accused of turning his back on Islam. Only men participated in these discussions, and ultimately no changes were made. As the historian

Fabio Giomi argues, fierce local opposition postponed changes until the radical communist regime took power many years later.[45] Nevertheless, the modernist approach of the reis-ul-ulema and of many other influential Muslim men remained rooted in Bosnia, and it was welcomed and used by communists after the war.

Besides having the reis-ul-ulema as their religious leader, Muslims in interwar Yugoslavia were mostly politically organized by a party called the Yugoslav Muslim Organization (Jugoslovenska muslimanska organizacija, JMO). Like the IVZ, this was also dominated by politicians from Bosnia. The JMO often supported the government in order to protect the land privileges, and sometimes to protect religious and cultural rights. The historian Wolfgang Hopken rightly argues that the Bosnian Muslim political elite did little to tie the struggle for these protections with the creation of a cohesive Muslim nation in Bosnia.[46] Muslims in Bosnia were often exposed to various Serbian and Croatian societies that appropriated Muslims into their ethnic group, while the state did not recognize Bosnian Muslims as equal to Serbs, Croats, and Slovenes. Even less protection was available to non-Slavic Muslims in other regions of Yugoslavia. This was particularly the case in Macedonia and Kosovo, where the interwar Yugoslav state pursued Serbianizing policies. For example, the school curricula were designed in Belgrade, while most of the state officials and bureaucrats were Serbs. As the historian Stipica Grgić has argued, the relationship between the state and Albanians and Turks was strained at best, and often quite hostile. There was also a strong immigration drive to Turkey.[47] For communists, this was a good example of Greater Serbian chauvinism, equivalent to that of Russians, as elaborated in Stalin's *Short Course*.

The Yugoslav Communist Party always opposed Serbian hegemonic-nationality policies, but for a long time they had no consistent approach towards various nationalities. For example, in the case of Bosnia and Herzegovina, the historian Sevan Philippe Pearson has shown how Yugoslav communists changed their approach, most often as a reaction to Soviet politics.[48] In the 1920s the party's approach moved from supporting the Yugoslav centralist state to advocating each nation's right to a separate state. This stance changed again to support a federal Yugoslav solution in the 1930s. Pearson asserts that these changes were influenced by Moscow, and as he stated, Bosnia and Muslims played no central role in the nationalities policies. Instead, the party opted for Bosnia's autonomy at its 1940 party conference, as a solution to the Serbian and Croatian tensions. At the same time, the majority in the party leadership considered Bosnian Muslims to be either Serbs or Croats.[49] The political scientist Sabrina P. Ramet states that by 1938, the leading

Yugoslav communist politician Edvard Kardelj had agreed to the Muslims' "ethnic particularity," which was then vaguely confirmed at the party conference and in the wartime brochures.[50] The party accepted the special historical and territorial individuality of Bosnia and Macedonia, while also somewhat accepting the special ethnic status of Muslims in Bosnia. However, it would take decades for that ethnic status to be fully recognized.[51] There were no ideas to create a federal or autonomous unit for Turks, as they were considered an established national minority with their own state abroad.

Bulgarianness – the Bulgarian National Myth

As in Serbia, the targeting, abuse, and suffering inflicted on the Muslim population in Bulgaria was inseparably linked to the Bulgarian national myth of liberation created in the nineteenth century. It was then that the idea of *natural* Bulgarianness was fleshed out, based on language and religion. As elsewhere in the Balkans, this was the process of the new Bulgarian state trying to chart its nation and territories. Scholars such as Neuburger, Todorova, Merdjanova, and others have argued that the national ideology was built based on an opposition to Islam and "Turks" who were perceived as both oppressors and backward fanatics who slowed down the imagined progress.[52] The state targeting of Muslims for national homogenization, therefore, has a long history. For example, Theodora Dragostinova shows that the elite, including politicians, scholars, and demographers, defined who was part of the nation and who was not. They often used the census as a tool that would show them where "foreign elements" lived.[53] As this chapter demonstrates, the census continued to be important for such purposes in socialist times. Once Bulgaria had gained its independence from the Ottoman Empire, demographers often framed the narrative in terms of "pure" regions, spreading fears about population growth of those not considered Bulgarian. Dragostinova highlighted how ethnographers played a crucial role by insisting on a primordial Bulgarian nation defined by language, place names, folklore, traditions, and customs. This meant that "true Bulgarians" existed who simply did not know it yet.[54] The national myth also stated that certain Bulgarian populations lived outside Bulgaria, and therefore must be saved and brought back into the fold of Bulgarianness. Within Bulgaria, this discourse was often applied to the Pomaks. The Bulgarian national myth of Ottoman yoke was only strengthened by historians during Bulgarian state socialism, and twentieth-century Bulgarian communists in fact used the same myth.[55]

The trend in mass expulsions of Muslims was very similar in Bulgaria and Serbia before the Second World War. The first mass expulsions of Muslims from Bulgaria occurred after the 1877–8 Russian-Ottoman War, when Bulgaria gained limited independence. Several hundred thousand Muslims left Bulgaria, as in Serbia and Greece.[56] Unique to the Bulgarian government was an attempt to change the names of Bulgarian Muslims as early as 1912–13, in a campaign that would be repeated again several times during the twentieth century.[57] As Bulgaria managed to expand its territory following the victory over the Ottoman Empire, they gained a large Bulgarian-speaking Muslim population. Pomaks were particularly targeted during this early Christianization campaign. Myuhtar-May argues that the campaign was based on violence and nationalism. It was committed by insurgent bands, supported by the regular Bulgarian army, and enacted by the Bulgarian Orthodox Church. The campaign officially aimed to "return" the Pomaks to their old Christian religion. Myuhtar-May has convincingly shown that the actual objective was to consolidate newly acquired territories, regardless of the wishes of the resident populations there. Nevertheless, despite pressure and violence, the conversion campaign failed and most of the Pomaks retained their religion and names. After losing the Second Balkan War, Bulgaria was also forced to accept the peace treaty provisions that guaranteed freedom of religion for Muslim populations.[58]

Despite that, the idea that the state should *awaken* people's Bulgarianness was firmly established by the end of the First World War.[59] Contemporary scholars, such as Stoyu Shishkov, prophesized that the Pomaks were original Bulgarians just under the influence of Islam. This stance, as argued by Dragostinova, was accepted by the clergy, police authorities, state officials, and teachers.[60] Similar stances were present in interwar Yugoslavia, where notable scholars such as Jovan Cvijić claimed that Bosnian Muslims were ethnically Serbs.[61] Croatian intellectuals claimed that Bosnian Muslims were in fact Croats.[62] Still, the Bulgarian interwar governments applied different sorts of pressure in practice, likely due to the Turkey's proximity and fears of Kemalism.[63] This was particularly noticeable when the Zveno government applied its extremist policies in practice from the early 1930s onwards. It banned the vast majority of Turkish newspapers and societies, and enforced name replacements for almost 2,000 Turkish villages, giving them Bulgarian names. Turkish-language streams in schools were reduced, and less than a third of the Turkish schools remained open by the mid-1930s.[64] Anna M. Mirkova reveals a confidential police report from 1935 that argued that all legal measures should be taken to encourage the emigration of Turks and prevent Pomaks from leaving in order to gradually assimilate and convert them.[65] Finally, Zveno's pressures on the Turkish minorities forced some 100,000 people to leave the country between 1934 and 1939.[66]

Bulgarian communists, however, mostly ignored Muslim minorities in the interwar period, and scholars have not explored official BKP policy towards Muslim minorities in this period. The post-war socialist publications were also vague about party work among Muslims, with official histories being able to recall only a few Muslim names who participated in big events such as the September Uprising of 1923, and the Second World War guerrilla fighting. It also seems that a party approach towards Muslims was not separately defined, as can be seen, for example, in the brochure on the Popular Front in 1936, which was directed to all workers and peasants.[67] Many of the Bulgarian communist policies were a continuation of the interwar approaches, even those of the most extreme right-wing organizations. As explored in the previous chapter, learning in Moscow added another layer to the approach taken towards Muslim populations, allowing Bulgarian communists to frame old ideas within a new Marxist discourse.

War Experiences

In addition to the Yugoslav and Bulgarian communist parties' experiences in prisons and in Moscow, the Second World War shaped them profoundly. Both parties came to power at the end of the war, and both parties developed extensive mythologies regarding their war struggles.[68] Their armed resistance even began at the same time, when Germany invaded the Soviet Union in June 1941. The differences in their preparedness and the scale of the uprising were significant, and these differences ultimately decided how each would come to power in 1944–5. The Yugoslav communists mobilized people from all social strata, including many women,[69] while Bulgarian communists never managed to create a significant resistance movement. The BKP's most influential people, including Georgi Dimitrov, spent the war in Moscow. In fact, the Bulgarian fascist regime did not feel threatened by the communist Partisans until later in the conflict.[70] Bell writes that one of the reasons why the BKP failed to mobilize more people was because Bulgaria had been spared from the German atrocities, which were often the main motivation to join the communist guerrilla army in Yugoslavia.[71] Even in the summer of 1944, the BKP could count on approximately 4,000 fighters only. Contrary to the Yugoslav case, communism and liberation were brought to Bulgaria in September 1944 with the Soviet army. The BKP did not manage to recruit many women in their combat ranks, and their influence over minority women was non-existent.[72] In contrast, some of the crucial decisions for the future Yugoslav state were decided by Yugoslav communists during the war. They finally opted for the federal system, which proved to be one of the main differences from the Bulgarian case, where nations had no such protection.

Yugoslav communists first intervened in gender norms during the first days of their uprising. Women were accepted to the Partisan units, and already in August 1941, there were reports of Partisan women participating in military combat.[73] The historian Barbara Jancar-Webster estimated that over the following four years, the Yugoslav Partisans had around 100,000 women soldiers, of which about 25,000 were killed and some 40,000 were wounded. Furthermore, about 2,500 women gained officer ranks. As Jancar-Webster writes, most of these women were very young, often underage, and from rural areas.[74] The scale of the change in their lives cannot be overemphasized, and this transformation was also actively promoted by the Communist Party. Previously disenfranchised Yugoslav women were allowed to vote and be elected within the Partisan units and the liberated territories. The party formalized equal rights to political participation for men and women in February 1942, when they declared the Foča ordinances.[75] Yugoslav women achieved political emancipation through the war, and they became a part of the Partisan mythology in the post-war Yugoslav state. This mythology became an additional legitimizing tool for the regime and its activists to intervene in gender relations.

In both Yugoslavia and Bulgaria, pre-war communist women who survived the war held power positions afterwards. There were no Muslim women at the top of this hierarchy. However, in Yugoslavia, some Muslim women did join the Partisans, while others helped from in hiding. The most famous Muslim Partisan woman was Vahida Maglajlić, and she did not survive the war. Nevertheless, her case shows increased interconnectedness among Yugoslav Partisans of various backgrounds, particularly after 1942, when most Partisan units were located in Bosnia. Maglajlić was the daughter of a Muslim judge, and she became a communist before the war under the influence of her brothers. She also resisted her father's wishes to wear the veil. Instead, she finished high school, and according to her friends' memories, she often spoke to other women, describing having been discriminated against for not being allowed to study at university. She also spoke publicly against veiling. Even before the war, she gathered women from the town and talked about the need for education, social justice, and emancipation. She was also in touch with Dušanka Kovačević and other leading non-Muslim women from the party in Bosnia. Maglajlić was admitted to the party in 1941, and often used her veil to hide messages, ammunition, and other packages for communist fighters, becoming an important organizer. She also instructed non-Muslim women on how to wear the veil to stay undetected. Maglajlić was arrested and sentenced to death, but she escaped. Once in the woods with the Partisans, she continued her work among the Muslim women, delivered lectures, and organized Muslim women's work for the Partisans. She criticized Muslim women in liberated territories for wearing the veil and being "backward," but she also criticized men for their attitude towards women. She met women who lived in extreme poverty, where polygamy still existed, and where women's public participation was deemed unwelcome. These women heard their first political speeches from Maglajlić; they came to the meetings veiled and were sometimes followed by men. During these events, Maglajlić left a strong impression with her eloquence but also her appearance in trousers taken from a dead German soldier. She was also often sent to organize local governments – the people's committees – in the liberated territories, and for Muslim women, this was the first time they were voting and being elected. At the peak of her political career, Maglajlić participated in establishing the AFŽ and was elected to its Central Committee.[76] Maglajlić and her brothers were an integral part of the Yugoslav communist movement, believing in the revolution that was supposed to come with the communist victory. She climbed the party hierarchy, was trusted with the important tasks she fulfilled, and mobilized more women for the war effort.

Bosnia was the centre of guerrilla warfare during the Second World War from 1942 onwards, which brought Yugoslav communists into more contact with Muslim populations. Other women from the Muslim communities, such as Samija Bubić-Slipčević, joined the Partisans during the war and slowly progressed through the hierarchy.[77] Usually, Muslim women like Maglajlić had male relatives close to the party or who were already engaged in guerrilla warfare. The party members and the women close to the party were unveiled, but they were eager to use veils as a protection during the war. Maglajlić used veils to carry confidential messages, smuggle ammunition, and hide communists and Jews. There were also families helping communists hide in between missions or find escape routes in cities. Olga Marašović, a prominent AFŽ activist and a high-level politician in Bosnia and the federal parliament after the war, found refuge with many Muslim families in Mostar. She later recalled that this was the first time she lived with Muslims, and she fondly remembered their warmth, hospitality, and safety. She stayed at the home of a single mother with two daughters, and there Marašović learned how to wear the veil if needed. She then moved to another Muslim family, once again a solely female household, with male members either in the Partisans or already killed in combat. During a police raid, the three sisters living there kept the secret and their guest remained undetected. Marašović then moved to yet another Muslim family. In all these cases, she observed hospitality and bravery, but also a conforming to gender and religious norms. In all of them, she noticed the importance of the mother's role, while in the third family, she described how the mother prayed regularly while always asking Allah to help the Partisans win the war.[78] Other contacts existed as well. For example, the party activists claimed that they steered a group of about three hundred veiled women in Mostar, who held demonstrations against food shortages in December 1941. The veiled women attacked the city mayor, protested in front of his house, and ransacked the city's food storage facility.[79]

Despite all these examples of collaboration or the direct involvement of Muslim women in the Partisan movement, non-Muslim women heavily dominated the party's women's section, as the following chapters explore. There were no Muslim women in the AFŽ or party leadership once the Yugoslav communists had won the war. Instead, communists who had survived the pre-war Yugoslav prisons or Moscow dominated the party apparatus, while Muslim women's progression through the hierarchy was slow. Because of the AFŽ's and the party's hierarchical nature, the most critical decisions were made within the narrow top circle. Furthermore, the correctness of decisions was measured by a Stalinist interpretation of Marxism rather than their own experiences with Muslim communities. Bulgarian communists lacked this direct experience with Muslim women, but because of the Soviet influences, the post-war transformation was quite similar.

The difference from the Bulgarian case was that in Yugoslavia more men from areas with predominantly Muslim populations were closer to the top-level party leadership after the war. Their role is explored in more detail in the final chapter. The vast majority of these men did not identify with a religion. Many of them joined the party during the 1930s through the youth organizations – most notably the League of Communist Youth of Yugoslavia (Savez komunističke omladine Jugoslavije, SKOJ) – while the war and later the federal structure of Yugoslavia allowed them to obtain crucial political posts. They played an essential role in nation building and their influence culminated in the 1970s with Džemal Bijedić from Mostar becoming the federal prime minister of Yugoslavia.[80] This social and political mobility was remarkable considering that Muslims were still under-represented in the Partisans' ranks compared with other population groups, and the historian Wolfgang

Hopken offers data showing that by the end of the war, only 2.5 per cent of soldiers in Tito's army were Muslims.[81] One reason was that the old Muslim political and religious elite aligned with the Nazis.[82] The lack of support among Albanian and Turkish Muslims for Partisan efforts also informed distrust directed at the post-war party.

The Yugoslav Federal Model

The Second World War was a crucial point in the Yugoslav communists' frame of reference, and they formed policies based on various groups' loyalty towards them in guerrilla struggles. Pearson shows that during the Second World War, Yugoslav communists debated and decided on the future federative structure with the Soviet Union as the model, and this complicated the situation for Bosnia.[83] The historian Xavier Bougarel demonstrates that Edvard Kardelj's definition of *nation* strongly resembled Stalin's, and this definition viewed the nation as a community with a shared language and tight ethnic and cultural ties.[84] Muslims in Bosnia were still not considered a nation, and as Pearson shows, many communists did not favour defining religion as a national identity criterion. Finally, Bosnian Muslims lived in dispersed locations without the compact territory that was necessary according to Stalin's definition of *nation*. Some leaders argued that Bosnia should be an autonomous region because it lacked a titular nation. However, that would then create the dilemma of whether Bosnia would be attached to the Serbian or the Croatian nation. Nevertheless, Bosnian communists managed to convince Tito that Bosnia and Herzegovina should be the sixth Yugoslav republic. Bosnian Muslims did not gain a political status, and they would have to choose between Serbia and Croatia for their national belonging in a political sense.[85] Bosnia and Herzegovina was supposed to be a multi-ethnic republic – an equal home for Serbs, Croats, and Muslims. This federal structure was the first significant difference to the Bulgarian case. Yugoslav communists followed the Soviet approach towards nationalities, creating new nations, federal republics, and autonomous regions. There were no discussions to create a republic or a region for Pomaks or Turks in Bulgaria.

The way Yugoslavs approached Muslims in Bosnia can also be traced through changes in the state census. Scholars have observed these changes for a while, showing a progression from "muslim as a confessional group," to Muslim (with a capital *M*; in Serbo-Croatian the names of confessional groups are not capitalized) as a nation. For example, in the 1948 and 1953 censuses, Muslims were marked as a confessional group.[86] In the 1948 census, the Muslim populations were able to declare themselves only as Serbs or Croats in Bosnia, or as Turks or Albanians, which shows the new state's attempt to create a unified population in which religion would not be a marker of identity. In the 1953 census, people were allowed to declare themselves as Yugoslav, an option that many Muslims used. Therefore, in 1948 the vast majority of Bosnian Muslims declared themselves as "nationally undetermined," and in 1953 as "Yugoslav – nationally undetermined."[87] This shows that Bosnian Muslims successfully resisted declaring themselves as either Serbs or Croats, and they found a compromise solution to solidify their identity. The Turkish and Albanian populations were able to declare themselves as they wished. In Bulgaria, however, this right was contested in the early 1950s and more intensely following the de-Stalinization process.[88]

In the late 1950s, the first voices within the Yugoslav party criticized half-baked census solutions towards Bosnian Muslims. This also paralleled new trends in Yugoslav foreign politics following the Tito–Stalin split. The Soviet Union blockade forced the Yugoslav leadership to explore contacts with various other countries. By the late 1950s, Tito had invested much effort in developing the Non-Aligned Movement, with many Muslim-majority countries involved.[89] India and Egypt became crucial for the Yugoslav "third way" between the Cold War blocs. Yugoslavia's aim to position itself as the leader of the movement affected policies towards its own Muslims at home. At the first non-aligned conference in Belgrade in 1961, Muslim countries were strongly represented, and the Yugoslav government also tried hard to show that Muslims in Yugoslavia have full rights. Mosques were repaired, Muslim students sent abroad, and additional funds were provided for the IVZ.[90] In socialist Bulgaria, foreign policy trends were utterly different, with the Bulgarian socialist state considering Turkey a dangerous enemy.

In the 1960s the Yugoslav Communist Party progressed further in recognizing and protecting the rights of Muslim populations. In the 1961 census, there was a new option for people to declare themselves as "Muslim in an ethnic sense,"[91] which marked yet another change in the KPJ's policy towards nationalities. This recognized not only that all attempts to force the Muslim population to declare themselves as either Serbs or Croats had failed, but also that Yugoslavism was not compatible with the state's growing decentralization. Ramet explains that the party's line was to convince people that Muslim ethnicity and Islam were separate phenomena linked only by "culture."[92] At the same time, the party had to fight against identifying Islam with Muslim national identity, and they declared religious nationalism to be against its socialist ideology.[93] The "national question" was opened once again, even though the population was supposed to be unified within the Brotherhood and Unity paradigm and socialism, while national belonging was not supposed to be imposed.[94] All these changes were applicable primarily in Bosnia and Herzegovina. Censuses in Macedonia, for example, show that only 3,000 people declared themselves as Muslim in an ethnic sense.

Turks, Albanians, and Bosnians were divided by language, by different traditions of Islam, and by different emigration patterns. The historian Edvin Pezo indicates that in the 1950s, there was a large wave of emigration to Turkey, in which nearly 140,000 people left. He argues that the party leadership was surprised by this wave, and it was not a deliberate policy. Instead, Pezo uncovers a complex network of sociocultural, economic, and political motives. He asserts that the state's interventions into everyday life and restructuring of the Yugoslav economy along socialist lines were the leading factors. The confiscation of personal weapons just added to the reasons. At the same time, the Yugoslav and Turkish governments completed an agreement that allowed for such a migration. Pezo shows there was consequently a declining number of people who identified themselves as Turks. In fact, the number of Albanians in Kosovo even grew.[95] The final chapter of this book returns to the issue of Turkish migration (and that of others who passed as Turks to escape Yugoslavia) from Yugoslavia, relating these population movements to resistance to the communist policies, including new gender policies. In 1981, in the late Yugoslav socialist period, the census counted only 101,191 Turks, a decline from 259,535 in 1953, while both the Albanian and the Muslim population had doubled.[96]

Despite more protection because of the federal state structures, the Yugoslav communists continued the previous state's practice of trying to regulate and control Islam in a similar fashion to the Russian tsarists, Bolsheviks, and Bulgarians. The Islamic community's modernist tradition proved to be useful for their successful adaptation to a new socialist Yugoslav state. The first issue of the Islamic community's *Bulletin*, published in 1950, carefully declared such modernism. The IVZ was to be closely tied to the state in order to support its modernizing efforts, to support modern education and science, and to explain it all in religious terms. The *Bulletin* declared good relations with the party, and full support for the communist government: Tito's picture was on the first page, before an article by the reis-ul-ulema, Ibrahim Fejić. In his editorial, Fejić emphasized that for the first time Muslims in Yugoslavia were equal to other religious groups and ready to engage in large socialist projects full-heartedly, particularly in large projects such as the country's industrialization and modernization. He endorsed the separation of the state and religion, welcomed the state's modernizing efforts, and promised to support and help the progress of the Yugoslav peoples.[97] The next article in the *Bulletin* was about Tito's speech when he had received the Islamic community's delegation: he had promised them equal rights and the freedom of religious expression. At the same time, Tito clearly explained that the IVZ would be supported as long as they served the state's interests, without ties to foreign centres as was the case with other religious organizations, by which he meant the Catholic Church.[98] The IVZ was to be strictly Yugoslav; it would function within the state's legal framework, while in return it would be protected and aided financially. The deputy reis-ul-ulema went further and compared Tito with divine providence, appearing in the country's darkest hour to save it from fascists. In his words, under the "wise direction of genius leader Marshall Tito all Yugoslav peoples were united in brotherhood and unity, guaranteeing equal rights and progress for all communities."[99]

The IVZ's modernist line supported other issues of importance to the party as well, for example, those regarding secular education and the education of girls for which the *Bulletin* called on Yugoslav Muslims to endorse modern education and science. Husein Talić, the president of the Ulema-medžilis (Council of the Ulema) in Sarajevo, wrote about the tremendous achievements of science in the Islamic world in the past, and he called for its revival in Yugoslavia. He strongly criticized people, particularly in the countryside, and blamed their illiteracy for allowing various enemies to spread prejudices and harmful traditions. Talić called on everyone to continue the work of the previous reis-ul-ulema, Čaušević, on education, particularly regarding girls' education. He welcomed the literacy campaigns and expressed hope that soon everyone would be able to read and write. Finally, he explained that literacy was the first step towards the inclusion of everyone – and particularly women – into the state's economy and productive labour.[100]

This kind of writing, however, was not simple repetition of the official party narrative. The leaders of the IVZ were aware not only of their party dependence but also of the negative discourse of backwardness that was imposed on their communities. Their choice to embrace the communist narrative of modernization and frame it in Islamic terms was an important act not only for the IVZ's survival, but also for bringing what they considered to be positive changes to the community. It was a way of controlling the narrative. The official communist narrative was adopted and changed to fit their needs. Communist gender policies were negotiated, and the parts that the IVZ considered useful, such as women's education and labour, were supported.

The extent to which the calls by the reis-ul-ulema and his colleagues were effective among non-Bosnians is debatable. Nevertheless, the Yugoslav communists managed to establish a very good relationship with the IVZ and its leader, the reis-ul-ulema Fejić. The state provided hefty monetary donations and did not discriminate against Islam over other religions. Thanks to the communist powers, the modernist strand of the Islamic community was able to solve issues, such as women's education and unveiling, that had previously shaken it to the core. The IVZ's first resolution, published in 1947, stated that the organization had a particular responsibility to "liberate" Muslim women from a "backward custom" that impeded their development. The IVZ called for veils to be discarded, and they helped Muslim women to participate in developing the Yugoslav economy. The IVZ's leadership explained that there were no religious barriers to the unveiling, adding that every Muslim man would be a patriot who would help with the "awakening of the Muslim woman's consciousness."[101] In chapter 5, I will discuss the IVZ position regarding veils further. By working closely with the party, the IVZ was able to play a significant role in negotiating Yugoslav nationality policies. This combination of factors was crucial for the divergence present in the Yugoslav and Bulgarian case: the Yugoslav case entailed new republics and regions, a recognized distinctive identity for the Muslim populations, and a positive relationship with the IVZ.

Post-war Stalinism in Bulgaria

The situation in Bulgaria was different because of the unitarist state's structural organization, its proximity to Turkey, and the fact that Bulgarians were the only "big nation" in the country, unlike in Yugoslavia, where no nation predominated to that extent. The Bulgarian socialist state did not envision republics and autonomous regions. For example, a Pomak republic was never created; nor were there plans for the political autonomy of either Pomaks or Turks. Although there were differences in how the communist regime approached Turks, Pomaks, and Roma Muslims, I argue that the difference was mainly in the timing of various assimilationist policies rather than in the final intent. The racialization of the Pomaks was also very similar to the racialization of the Turks. During most of the twentieth century, the Pomaks were defined as Bulgarian Muslims who had been supposedly forcefully converted to Islam, while the Pomaks themselves were barely included in such debates. *Bulgarian Mohammedans* was also a popular phrase of that time.[102] The sociologist Shaban Darakchi claims that this linguistic and religious situation often meant that the Pomak population positioned themselves between Turks and Christian Bulgarians, allowing for fluidity of identifications.[103] The historian Fatme Myuhtar-May argues, however, that Pomak identity was not weaker, more fluid, or less relevant than any other identity.[104] Nevertheless, these ideas about Pomak identity meant that the Pomaks have been often aggressively pressured to assimilate since the Bulgarian state's early days. In the socialist period, the dominant public and scholarly discourse maintained that the Pomaks were forcefully converted to Islam in the past and that their assimilation reversed such a process. Similar ideas existed, and continue to exist, in Croat and Serb intellectual circles about the Bosnian Muslim populations. Nevertheless, such views were discouraged during the Yugoslav socialist period, although the party was unable to control them in the 1980s.[105]

After the Second World War, the Bulgarian communist regime changed the country's politics towards minorities in line with Stalinist principles. The Turkish population (re)gained certain rights, mostly in terms of schooling and publishing activities. Attempts to rename the Muslim populations and Christianize them ceased. The same applied to other ethnic minorities such as Roma, Jews, and Armenians.[106] Besides following the Stalinist principles of *liberating* national minorities, scholars suggested that one reason for a conciliatory approach was the new regime's need to gain allies, or at least not to antagonize a large group of people.[107] However, even Georgi Dimitrov did not fully adhere to protecting Turkish rights. The historian Stefan Dechev brought Dimitrov's words to Traycho Kostov, another leading communist politician, stating that the country should provide full rights to national minorities, but to be careful when it comes to the Turks.[108] Declassified documents show that the party was very hesitant in building trust with the Turks, and they organized the resettlement of Muslim populations as early as in the late 1940s. Those who lived close to the border with Turkey were moved to inner Bulgaria, and hundreds of families deemed as "dangerous elements" were forced to leave in 1948. The Bulgarian historian Mihail Gruev argues that by 1948, the regime felt stable enough not to seek support from Muslims, which resulted in these resettlement campaigns.[109]

Nevertheless, the BKP was officially committed to religious and ethnic equality. The party opened its doors to more minorities, and at least temporarily moved away from the discriminatory approaches of the previous Bulgarian regimes.[110] Fatme Myuhtar-May states that in the first decade after the war, the communist regime was more accommodating towards Muslims, while many Muslims supported the regime if only for not being as heavily discriminated as before.[111] The anthropologist Daniel G. Bates notes that this was the only period when the public curricula promoted the Turkish language. Turkish teachers were recruited or sent abroad for additional training, and Turkish newspapers published regularly.[112] In line with Stalinist values, the regime promoted Turkish folklore, costume, theatre groups, and libraries in which books by approved Turkish authors could be read. These arts were supposed to be "national in form, socialist in content,"[113] which perfectly reflected Stalinist policy towards nationalities.

A brief closer inspection of the permitted Turkish theatre groups shows how they served a specific agenda for the new regime. They were racialized, and gender played an important component. As one article that reported on Turkish theatres' visits to Sofia explained, young Turkish women performers were "brave pioneers in the struggle against century-old backwardness, religious fanaticism, and ignorance."[114] Participants in these art groups were supposed to be torchbearers for socialism, bringing it to their own communities in a manner reminiscent of the Bolshevik writings of the 1920s and 1930s. Women were the cornerstone in the new gender policies that sought to overcome the nation's supposed backwardness. For example, the same article then detailed the hard struggle of a young girl named Yulvie, who tried to persuade her conservative mother to let her join the art group. Yulvie's mother was afraid that Yulvie would embarrass herself in front of men, shaken by the fears instilled by "hodzhas."[115] She also recalled that in the Qur'an, "it was written that such a woman would be punished."[116] Eventually, Yulvie left without her mother's approval, and after performing in many Turkish villages in the Rhodopes, she married the theatre's conductor. Finally, when Yulvie's son was born, the mother softened and reconciled with her daughter and her choice of career. Socialist family and socialist progress transformed Yulvie's mother, too.[117]

Such articles in the leading magazine for women reveal the purpose the state ascribed to minority art groups. They were supposed to promote folklore, but at the same time be a tool used to attack their own communities' religious and cultural practices. Identification with folklore and with use of the local culture was neither new in nor unique to Bulgaria. In Romania, for instance, similar ideas about folklore and modernization were present in Ceaușescu's time and used for "modernizing" purposes.[118] Yulvie from the story was at the same time a modernizer, but also a guardian of old Turkish songs and dances. Yulvie's village and their practices were deemed backward, but then the village and practices transformed and became modern, once sanctioned by the state. Many of these Turkish folklore groups did not survive much longer, after the state embarked on aggressive assimilationist policies.

The new 1947 Bulgarian constitution guaranteed minority rights, and placed minority schools on an equal footing with public schools.[119] However, all religious schools were closed after 1949, and religious schools were traditionally attended by Muslim men.[120] The same approach towards religious education was taken in Yugoslavia, as the party wanted education to be fully secular. The new education policies in both socialist countries were secular, elementary schools were mandatory, and there was no gender segregation in the classrooms. The new Muslim authorities from both the mufti office in Sofia and the IVZ in Sarajevo agreed with such an approach, despite this making it harder for them to educate their own ulema. Nevertheless, the closure of Muslim schools and mosques in this early period was driven by atheism, which affected other religious communities as well as Muslims.[121]

The relatively tolerant approaches taken towards Muslims in Bulgaria were only temporary, and even then, as the historian Milena Savova-Mahon Borden argues, the party imposed a range of stereotypes on other Muslim communities. This was a process of defining what is "Bulgarian" and "ours,"[122] just as in the analysed case of the folklore groups. Furthermore, there were other inconsistencies in allowing for certain rights and putting pressure on populations at the same time. Turkish educational and cultural institutions experienced a period of relative prosperity, but about 150,000 Turks still left the country in 1950 and 1951. Bates argues that even more people would have left if Turkey had not closed its borders, which it partly did because some of those being sent to Turkey were Roma.[123] At the same time, the historian Tchavdar Marinov asserts that many Pomaks were prevented from leaving, with the party leaders insisting that "Bulgaro-Mohammedans" belonged to the Bulgarian people.[124] Apparently, the same logic did not apply to the Roma populations, particularly as approximately 45 per cent of them declared themselves as Muslims in 1946. Many of them asked to leave for Turkey, hoping for better treatment and less racism.[125]

The anthropologist Ayşe Parla notes that Turkey maintained privileged immigration policies for Balkan immigrants throughout much of the twentieth century, a privilege not available to others who wanted to move to Turkey. After the First World War and with the establishment of the republic, Turkey welcomed new immigrants, hoping they would be a constitutive element of the new republic. Some 825,000 Turks from the Balkans moved to Turkey, which accounted for about 10 per cent of the entire population. Many were recruited into the military and the administration; they held elite positions and were granted citizenship.

Only in the late 1950s and 1960s did Turkey become more closed to Balkan immigrants. Nevertheless, even then, Turks from Bulgaria were welcomed, particularly because of the Cold War tensions.[126]

It is debatable to what extent this first wave of post-war immigration was a deliberate act instigated by the Bulgarian government, and to what extent they simply saw a window of opportunity to decrease the number of people who seemed disloyal. As I have shown earlier in this chapter, the same immigration wave occurred in Yugoslavia at the same time. The Turkish population still remained higher in Bulgaria than in Yugoslavia, and Bulgarian communists enacted other measures to promote assimilation. For example, the pressures on Turks to not declare themselves as Turks started as early as in 1953, and the resistance towards these measures is discussed the last chapter. Women also resisted this process known as "passportization," which involved obtaining identity cards. This required them to appear without their veils and to be photographed, a practice that led to consequences explored in chapter 5.[127]

Towards One Socialist Nation

The real change in Bulgarian politics towards Muslim populations occurred in the late 1950s. Stalinist policies towards minorities entailed at least some protections, and with Stalin's death and later de-Stalinization, the breaks to Bulgarian nationalism loosened. Savova-Mahon Borden notes that de-Stalinization entailed a new wave of cultural nationalism. The communist regime aimed to strengthen its position through ethnic nationalism, presenting itself as a leadership of and for ethnic Bulgarians. Some scholars posited that the turn towards ethnic nationalism was driven by demographic concerns and the irrational behaviour of communist leaders, but Savova-Mahon Borden challenged these views, showing that the regime deliberately promoted cultural nationalism based on ethnicity, and that it saw ethnic diversity as a threat to its power.[128]

Ali Erken has recently argued that the failure to create a Balkan federation between Yugoslavia and Bulgaria in 1948 allowed the Bulgarian government to turn to nationalistic policies directed at Muslims. According to him, Bulgaria gave up on its internationalist ambitions and focused on re-emphasizing its Slavic identity. Equally, Turkey embraced a strong anti-communist stance and became one of Bulgaria's main enemies.[129] The problem with Erken's argument is that assimilationist policies towards Turks often came after attacks on the Pomak populations. It is more likely that together with ethnicity, religion played a major role. As Savova-Mahon Borden has argued, the Bulgarian communists considered ethnic differences a potentially subversive element, although their approach was inconsistent and escalated with de-Stalinization.[130]

Ali Eminov and Fatme Myuhtar-May have highlighted the importance of the 1956 session of the Communist Party's Central Committee, not only for Zhivkov's stabilization in power and the onset of de-Stalinization, but for instigating changes in the approach they took towards minorities in Bulgaria. The party announced a need for Muslims to "develop a sense of being inseparable from the Bulgarian nation."[131] The party resolution was a very specific mixture of bureaucratized communist language about raising "the political and cultural level of the Bulgarians with Mohammedan faith … to actively engage them in the building of communism"[132] with nationalistic goals. In practice, this entailed an active assault on Turkish minority rights, and the first attempts at forcefully changing the names of the Muslim populations.[133] The same session of the Central Committee had consequences for other minorities, and they became increasing hostile towards the Roma, Tatars, and Pomaks. The Bulgarian state also contested the recognition of Macedonians as a distinct entity. Eminov states that by 1956, Macedonians of the Pirin region had been issued new passports in which they were identified as Bulgarians, ending the previous strategy of fostering of a unique Macedonian cultural identity. Two years later, the BKP went further and aimed to assimilate the Turkish population by closing schools, educational establishments, and language instruction, starting the "cultural revolution" and unveiling process examined in the following chapters.[134]

Savova-Mahon Borden argues that the BKP provoked ethnic conflict in order to create homogenous ethnic units.[135] Bates notes that many Muslims were integrated into Bulgarian society to a considerable degree and showed strong support for the Communist Party, but attacks on names antagonized many and showed that they had no future in such a state.[136] Additionally, the late 1950s also saw attempts to rehabilitate the Rodina movement. Rodina, known for its interwar endeavours to foster Bulgarian state nationalism among the Pomaks, which included name changing, was dissolved in 1947.[137] Nevertheless, after the already-mentioned April Plenum of 1956, the party slowly refashioned Rodina's activities as patriotic rather than fascist. From the 1960s, even some former leaders who had been previously marked as fascists were praised for fighting against religious fanaticism.[138]

The transformation of Bulgarian society following de-Stalinization was profound in many areas, including state structure. The government introduced the 1959 reform of administrative units, which entailed increased centralization and more party oversight. The newly created district units of the BKP had more control over public life. Mihail Gruev claims that this reform strengthened the BKP's capacities, allowing them to try to interfere more harshly in people's private lives.[139] This may explain why certain interventions in Bulgaria came later than in Yugoslavia, as was the case with the unveiling examined in chapter 5. The reform certainly put in place the infrastructure for further assimilation campaigns, which intensified from the 1960s.

The next crucial intervention from the top levels of the party came in 1962, when the politburo announced a resolution that set the stage for aggressive assimilation policies directed at the Pomaks and Turks. The resolution was bluntly entitled "Measures against the Turkish Self-Identification of Gypsies, Bulgarian Muslims (Pomaks) and Tatars." It included drafts of policies and intentions for the following two decades. The resolution opened with the statement that the BKP "has always been guided by Marxist-Leninist theory on the national question" and then it explained that the party had undertaken a number of measures to eradicate "the great economic and cultural backwardness of the Turkish and Gypsy population."[140] The party then praised itself for the new educational opportunities, health care, and low unemployment it had achieved. However, the party aimed to counter "Turkish reactionary propaganda and religious fanaticism," embodied in these people's attempts to register themselves as Turks. It was supposedly helped by their education and religious services in the Turkish language. Therefore, the politburo ordered the party organizations, unions, the youth organization, and other social organizations to fight "the Turkish religious and chauvinistic propaganda and its pan-Turkish and pan-Islamic aims and aspirations."[141] The resolution also gave instructions for a simplified name-changing procedure through "a large and systematic popular persuasion."

Pomaks, and smaller communities such as Muslim Tatars and Roma, were targeted first, as if to test out an assault on the larger Turkish community. This resolution placed pressure on Pomak people of all genders to change their traditional attire, change their names, and abandon religious customs. People registered as Tatars, Roma, and as Bulgarian Muslims "should be registered with their real nationality."[142] Furthermore, these people were forbidden from moving to cities and areas with a more compact Turkish population. The Turkish language was removed from their schools, and other children were not allowed to live or study in groups with Turkish children. The Bulgarian Academy of Sciences was ordered to provide studies on the "historical truth about the results of the assimilation policies of the Turkish oppressors, about the mass and individual conversions to Islam."[143] During the politburo meeting when this resolution was announced, only Bulgarian men were present. As Myuhtar-May shows, this was the moment when the politburo decided to proceed with the "revival process," establishing the assimilation policies of the following decades.[144] Aleksandrieva and Kyuranov also argue that since at least the early 1960s, Todor Zhivkov had affirmed the idea that assimilation was generally a good thing, with only the means to be decided on.[145]

The first forced name-changing campaign began shortly after the 1962 resolution. It targeted the Roma and Pomaks, who mounted strong resistance that forced the regime to pause the campaign in 1964. Over these two years, the regime employed violence, which was blamed on the over-zealousness of local party officials.[146] This pause, however, did not mean the abandonment of the name-changing ambitions. A politburo session in November 1967 concluded that the process of renaming the "Bulgaro-Mohammedans" was slow and unsatisfactory. Two years later, in February 1969, the Central Committee decided to accelerate the "natural process of resolving ethnic differences." Scientific institutes were called upon to use their research to help this process.[147] In July 1970 the BKP's Central Committee decided to rename all "Bulgaro-Mohammedans." The government no longer tried to conceal the renaming, and instead sought to speed it up and spread it all over the country.[148] As Eminov shows, this directive was carried out over the following two years, in which all Pomaks were forced to adopt Bulgarian names.[149] The mounting pressure on Muslim populations was also reflected in the census data. For example, in 1975 the number of people who declared themselves as non-Bulgarian decreased considerably. That same year, the section recording a person's nationality was removed from identity cards.[150]

State institutions adopted a similar approach to attack the Roma population. From the late 1950s, the Roma were systematically discriminated, silenced, and expected converge with the majority of the Bulgarian population. Interest in the Roma past or contemporary culture was discouraged, and later even seen as a threat.[151] The anthropologist Carol Silverman demonstrates that the government denied the existence of the Roma, while simultaneously implementing assimilationist policies from the 1960s similar to those for the Pomaks, including the forced Bulgarianization of their names. In the 1970s the public performance of Romani music was banned, followed by the banning of the public use of the Romani language in the 1980s. Muslim Roma were also affected by general anti-Muslim measures such as the banning of circumcision and the wearing of shalvari trousers, which I discuss in more detail in the following chapters.[152]

Despite this divergence from the Soviet approach of protecting at least some rights for national minorities, Bulgaria retained close relations with the Soviet Union at all levels of government. Bulgaria nourished cultural relations and exchanges with the Central Asian republics, and Bulgarian cities had special relations with Soviet Asian cities. For example, Haskovo was a city twinned with Tashkent in northeast Uzbekistan, and there were many visits and exchanges. When Tashkent was hit by an earthquake in 1966, workers from Haskovo helped rebuild the city. The historian Christopher Scarboro conveys the uneasiness of Bulgarian correspondents in Tashkent, as the city conflicted with their image of a "modern socialist city" and "oriental backwardness," and even more so with the Soviet policy of ethnic particularism.[153] The correspondents' reports also conveyed a certain maturity and self-confidence present among Bulgarian communists, in which they no longer had to translate all Soviet policies into Bulgarian settings. Instead, the old tropes about backwardness and socialist modernity were packaged in a new language and adapted to new political aims to the detriment of the Bulgarian Muslim populations.

After the attack on Muslim communities had started in the 1960s, the party gradually destroyed all Muslim organizations and institutions. Daniel Bates argues that in practice, from the 1970s onwards the Muslim minorities had no public voice, organizational infrastructure, or visible symbols in public.[154] Turkish-language schools merged with Bulgarian schools, and soon all teaching of the Turkish language ceased.[155] These were all steps that led to the forced expulsion of Bulgarian Muslims in late May 1989, when Todor Zhivkov announced an imminent bout of ethnic cleansing, leading to mass protests and hunger strikes by Turks and other Muslims.[156] According to information from the Ministry of the Interior, the names of 822,588 people were changed, while 309,592 were expelled from Bulgaria in 1989. This means that the names of at least 10 per cent of the total Bulgarian population were changed.[157] Since no federal units were created based on these identities, as in Yugoslavia, there was no political structure to protect them from unitarist government. Mahon argues that all these assaults on Muslim populations had unintended consequences for the BKP, namely that they only strengthened the targeted people's identities.[158] Tomasz Kamusella argues that this event should be considered on its own in order to underline that it was a unique form of ethnic cleansing.[159] While I agree with his characterization of the events as deliberate ethnic cleansing, these events must be placed within a broader perspective and historical contextualization. As this chapter shows, and many other scholars have also demonstrated, these events were part of a long process of attacking the rights of Muslim populations, in addition to the abuses and humiliation inflicted upon them by the societal majority. Also, observing the long-term process of scapegoating, abusing, and excluding the Muslim population helps to explain how such massive crimes were possible in 1989. After all, in September 1989, the party's politburo was still referring to these people as "descendants of Islamized Bulgarians" and as having been deceived by Turkish nationalism.[160]

Numerous Bulgarian historians also participated in all parts of the process of eliminating Muslim communities, providing the party with justifications for forcible assimilations. Since the de-Stalinization process and the 1956 session of the Central Committee, there was a specific alliance of communist politicians and academics who assaulted the rights and identities of Muslim populations. For example, Stefan Dechev points to an edited collection compiled by many historians working at the Bulgarian Academy of Sciences, which explored the history of Bulgarian Muslims in the Rhodopes, opening the floodgates to pseudo-historical works aiming to demonize the Muslim populations.[161] Scholars were invited to participate in the agitprop meetings of the Central Committee, where they offered insights on the party's strategies for integrating the Pomaks into the "socialist nation" as early as 1959.[162] Dechev also shows that historians provided inflated numbers of deported and converted Christians, which led to rising panic about the "biological" shrinking of the nation and demographic catastrophe.[163] During this entire period, BKP leaders and scholars did not use the word *nationalism*, thus superficially avoiding the interwar rhetoric. As Eminov observes, they instead opted for a range of cliches, with the revival process and "the grand excursion" being the most cynical,[164] and the words *progress* and *modernization* were also commonly used. Therefore, it is crucial to observe interventions by critically examining the language around them, with full contextualization.

After the de-Stalinization process, Savova-Mahon Borden argues, BKP policies were guided by ethnic nationalism, in which the communist regime saw itself as the leadership of ethnic Bulgarians.[165] For that process to happen, I argue, the Bulgarian Communist Party's gender program was crucial, and visible from the first years of its detachment from Stalinism. The party targeted gender relations, family relations and customs, people's dress, and circumcision in order to deny people their identities. In the next chapter I will explore how communist enfranchisement brought tremendous changes during the first decade after the war, but also how it turned out to be a tool for penetrating previously closed communities. By removing gendered differences, the BKP aimed to eliminate Turkishness and Pomakness, aiming to create an imagined Bulgarian socialist nation.

The idea of a unitary Bulgarian socialist nation had been in the making since the early 1960s and was actively pushed into circulation in the 1970s. It entailed gradually assimilating Muslim groups into a larger "Bulgarian socialist nation,"[166] while in the 1980s it was publicly endorsed at the BKP's 13th Congress. The BKP still claimed to derive its politics from Marxist-Leninist ideology, although, as Savova-Mahon Borden indicates, the party never explained from which exact concepts they drew inspiration.[167] Tomasz Kamusella rightly suggests that this entire policy entailed a process of the denial and suppression of Muslims' ethnic and confessional identities. In theory, Bulgarian communists imagined that the Bulgarian nation would be more socialist than ethnically Bulgarian.[168] In practice, this meant that ethnic gendered differences had to be erased, be it by redressing people of all genders, or by putting a stop to the practice of Muslim boys' circumcision. All religions were viewed negatively; the difference was that Bulgarian communists picked up and developed more orientalizing views towards Islam than towards other religious communities. Islam was seen as the main obstacle in the modernization process for decades, and from the mid-1950s the Bulgarian press for women had been printing more articles that pictured Islam negatively. A typical article would contrast the lives of women in Muslim communities with women elsewhere in Bulgaria. For example, a certain Suad from Sudan found a new life in Bulgaria and praised women's achievements and equality, contrasting it with Sudan. As Suad explained, "Mohammedan religion puts women in shackles, in chains and limits them to domestic life."[169] Islam would have no place in a socialist society. Such articles were not present in the Yugoslav press, as the country was trying to build relations with non-aligned countries.

As for sexuality, the unified socialist Bulgarian nation was imagined as exclusively heterosexual, with only two genders imaginable. The same was the case in Yugoslavia. Non-heterosexual sexualities were considered as barely existing, and they were not discussed in relation to other identities. Male homosexuality was prohibited by the penal codes in both Yugoslavia and Bulgaria from 1951. The difference was that the Yugoslav penal code targeted only men, while the Bulgarian one targeted all people who had same-sex relations threatening with up to three years in prison.[170] Sources on same-sex desire in socialist times are hard to locate generally due to the continual erasure of non-heterosexual experiences. They also did not play a part in framing and implementing policies towards Muslim populations from the state and the party, as they considered sexuality to be inherently heterosexual.

Nevertheless, in both countries non-heterosexual peoples of all ethnicities and religion suffered from discrimination, abuse, and prosecution.[171] Unfortunately, the experiences of non-heterosexual Muslims are not uncovered in this work either. Socialist Bulgaria came to be envisioned as the country of one Bulgarian nation, engulfed in what Mary Neuburger defined as national and socialist sameness.[172]

———————◼❘◼———————

Soviet policies on national minorities had a profound impact on international revolutionaries, including on the future leaders of Yugoslavia and Bulgaria. The Bolsheviks aimed to create new nations, with their own republics and regions, led by loyal local political elites. These new nations were supposed to be modernized by the Bolsheviks, and created in their European image. Gender policies were particularly important in defining new nations, and often their success was measured by progress in achieving rights for women. The Bolsheviks carefully analysed the number of women in politics, the workforce, education and other fields, promoting women's involvement as a solution to indigenous "backwardness."

Yugoslav communists applied Stalinist principles in creating new nations, republics, and autonomous regions. After the Second World War they established political institutions filled with local populations, which opened a space for many Muslim men and some women to climb these hierarchies. Yugoslavia's new federal structure also provided more protection for Muslim populations, and during the decades of Yugoslav socialism the rights of Muslim populations increased with better access to politics, education, and religious practices.

Bulgarian communists initially embraced the Stalinist protections given to minorities. They allowed schools, institutes and publishing activities to flourish, and they promoted various forms of artistic production. Nevertheless, the regime was distrustful towards Muslim communities even in early socialism, and it reversed its policies once it felt it had a more secure grip on power. After the regime had embarked on the de-Stalinization process, Muslims' rights were gradually revoked, cultural and educational institutions were abolished, and the population was pressurized to discard their identities, change their names, and declare themselves as Bulgarians. Eventually, the policy of "one Bulgarian nation" did not leave any space for ethnic and gender differences. Once all these attempts to erase Muslims from the country had failed, the regime engaged in even more aggressive expulsions of Muslims to Turkey.

Chapter Three

Communist Enfranchisements

Communist politicians such as the Soviet Serafima Ljubimova, the Bulgarian Tsola Dragoycheva, and the Yugoslav Vida Tomšič loved to remind women of their legal, social, and political discrimination before communists had come to power. Dragoycheva often wrote in *ZHenata dnes* that women were treated as slaves: without political participation, equal salaries, and labour rights, they struggled in poverty and illness together with their children.[1] Yugoslav communists described the "old" Yugoslavia in the same terms, as the most awful place for women to live.[2] They also loved to write about Muslim women's position, describing it in even more dire terms: they considered these women the disempowered slaves of family relations and traditions.[3] Naturally, both communist parties looked to the Soviet Union for the solution to such disempowerment.[4] In Tomšič's words, they were taught by Lenin that the victory of the revolution and abolition of old laws was the first step towards the working people's new life.[5] Women's rights became the cornerstone of the new legal transformation enacted by Balkan communists, who translated and adapted Soviet legislation to their countries.[6]

Bulgarian and Yugoslav communists believed that the Soviet laws were the most progressive in the world and the only correct path for building a righteous society. After the war, both countries quickly declared a new constitution and laws to change the previous political and social orders. The legal transformation affected every religious community because the state declared a separation of the state and religion. Family affairs no longer fell under the scope of religious institutions, and limitations were imposed on the activities of religious institutions in education and political affairs. This chapter also examines what these legal transformations meant for women's enfranchisement. It argues that it set the foundations for tremendous changes in people's lives. Muslim women became men's equals under the law, and the equals of women from all other communities as they gained political, social, and economic rights for the first time. Finally, this chapter highlights troubles that emerged in implementing the legal transformation in all communities.

The Soviet Model

The Soviet legal transformation of Central Asian societies was much more complex and gradual than Yugoslav and Bulgarian communists were aware of. Yugoslav and Bulgarian communists picked up universal Soviet laws in their European form and used the 1936 constitution as their starting point. In Soviet Central Asia, however, the 1920s were marked by a more gradual transformation until at least the mid-1920s. For example, the Bolsheviks did not insist on abolishing sharia and adat (customary) courts immediately after the revolution, and they were tolerated as a parallel legal system. The Zhenotdel was one of the fiercest critics of this situation; they insisted that it disadvantaged women. For years, the Zhenotdel leadership advocated the traditional courts' abolition, but it was very aware that Soviet laws had still not been enacted in these early days of Soviet rule. The human rights lawyer and Marxist Anne McShane has shown that the Zhenotdel represented women in both the Soviet court system and the traditional courts.[7] The institutional tension remained for years, with local people turning to both the Soviet courts and the local courts according to their personal needs. The Zhenotdel celebrated any diminishing of the local courts' powers, but with the weak party structures the struggle for authority was far from straightforward. Local men with power often resisted any transfer of authority to Soviet courts, particularly related to family affairs.[8]

The change came during the mid-1920s, when the Soviet state felt more secure in its power in Central Asia. Issues that had bothered Zhenotdel activists for years, such as polygyny, kalym, underage marriages, and the abduction of women, were all abolished and banned in Uzbekistan in 1926. Such criminalization of local practices followed elsewhere in the region in the mid-1920s as well.[9] Magazines for women such as *Kommunistka* triumphally explained that sharia and adat were responsible not only for defining "women as property" but also for women's weak cultural and political awareness, the poor state of the nation's health, and obstacles to economic development.[10] Such writings were aimed at activists, and they hardly reflected strong feelings on the part of the local populations.

New laws also introduced divorce procedures and property divisions similar to other regions of the Soviet Union. Divorce became available to women and men equally, and some women did try to exercise this right. As Northrop shows, these laws were often lauded as much needed in Central Asian societies,[11] although the Soviet state did not build enough of a safety net to replace old patriarchal family structures. New social and economic institutions for women who needed protections to escape abusive and violent marriages were in their infancy or even non-existent. Even if women managed to get to safety, they often struggled to gain other rights such as the fair division of property upon divorce. The Zhenotdel activists were well aware that men often barred women from receiving property, buildings, and tools, and that local traditions always overruled Soviet laws.[12] Anne McShane argues that the Zhenotdel alone was not capable of supporting the mass female populations. McShane also shows that many women were further abused and even murdered for obtaining a divorce and for daring to transgress traditional cultural norms.[13] The right to divorce also led to a further backlash in the form of a moral panic, wherein divorce was perceived as "becoming endemic."[14] Indeed, this argument emerged in all other places where new divorce laws were implemented that challenged the patriarchal order.[15]

Despite the challenges in enforcing the new Soviet laws, Central Asian societies were changing. The legal transformation was gradual, but even so, many women paid with their lives for the attempt to exercise their rights. More were killed when the Bolsheviks decided to transform societies further with the Hujum (assault) campaign and unveiling, as explored in chapter 5, transformations that Yugoslavs and Bulgarians pursued as well. Nevertheless, as Soviet state power grew, so did the apparatus to implement laws and protections, bringing about a long-lasting transformation. With collectivization and industrialization from the late 1920s and 1930s, this transformation process accelerated, encompassing all of society.

The focus in Soviet magazines also moved from legal transformation, which by that time had allegedly stopped polygamy, dower, and other practices, to supporting women's work on the collective farms and in political organizations.[16] This change of tone was also important for international revolutionaries, who, as analysed in previous chapters, read Soviet magazines to find inspiration for their own societies. Instead of lamenting the situation in "backward societies," articles from the 1930s began showing the Soviet power of laws as applied in practice, bringing justice in cases of arranged marriages, the selling of women, and other supposed traditional practices.[17]

Legal Transformation in Socialist Yugoslavia and Bulgaria

The Soviet legal transformation that brought legal equality to women was a source of much pride, and it was promoted as a path for all other communists to follow. The Bulgarian and Yugoslav underground communist press wrote about progressive Soviet legislation for decades before they were able to enact such changes in their own countries. The 1936 Soviet constitution was lauded as the most progressive piece of legislation, bringing equal rights to all its citizens.[18] Communists educated in Moscow had lessons on Soviet legal transformation at Lenin's international school.[19] In these lessons, but also in the Soviet press, Yugoslav and Bulgarian communists could relate to the pre-revolutionary situation regarding women's rights in Russia and compare it with the situation in their respective countries. After all, women's political, economic, and social disempowerment was the same, and even the legal situation was similar since religious institutions held jurisdiction over family matters. Laws related to marriage and divorce were very similar for Orthodox churches in all three cases, as well as the sharia provisions within the Hanafi school of thought. New Soviet laws were universal; they replaced the authority of the sharia courts and customary laws, and just like the Bolsheviks, the Yugoslav and Bulgarian communists aimed to unify their legal systems. The difference was that Yugoslav and Bulgarian communists had a prepared recipe they could follow.

Communists aimed to set the stage for a radical transformation of their societies, and they viewed enacting the new constitution and the Family Code as the most important legal tasks. The legal transformation closely followed Soviet ideals, while Soviet interwar laws and the 1936 constitution served as models. Significant parts of the Soviet constitution were literally translated and only slightly adapted to Yugoslav and Bulgarian settings. The Yugoslav communists were slightly quicker at announcing new laws, but in Bulgaria, the core legal changes had also been completed by the late 1940s. In both countries, women gained legal equality, and Muslim women were encompassed in that process.[20]

The interwar Yugoslav legal system was replaced in the first year after the war. As early as in 1945, Yugoslav communists organized a referendum to abolish the monarchy and elect constitutional parliamentary members. For the first time, all men and women, including Muslims, had the right to vote and be elected. The enfranchisement started within the Partisan units with the Foča ordinances, enacted in the liberated territories in 1942. Despite this new political opportunity, there were no women from Muslim backgrounds among the candidates for the constitutional assembly. The women on the list were primarily pre-war communists, who then dominated Yugoslav politics for a decade. Some Muslim men from the party were elected, and they strongly advocated the upcoming changes.[21]

The newly drafted Yugoslav constitution was crucial in defining the position of religious communities within the new socialist state. The discussion in the constitutional assembly demonstrated how Soviet ideas were adapted to Yugoslav practice. Leading communists such as Milovan Djilas defined broader approaches towards religion. The party, then, made sure that assembly members from Muslim backgrounds discussed the position of sharia courts, laws, and the Islamic community more broadly, and that the assembly members from Muslim backgrounds offered their support and justification for the forthcoming changes.

Gender and family relations were central in discussions over the position of Islam in the new Yugoslav state. A lawyer from Bosnia, Zaim Šarac, explained that sharia law and sharia courts had no place in the new state, as this would entail a return to gender inequality. Šarac said that all citizens who wanted to get married would have to register the marriage with the civil authorities. Šarac argued that Muslims supported such a solution simply by voting for communists in the previous elections. He also said that Muslims in Yugoslavia never wanted to be a privileged religious community, but only to be on an equal footing with the Orthodox and Catholic communities, and that the constitution would bring such guarantees.[22]

Hasan Rebac, an old social reformer from Bosnia and an interwar politician,[23] explained that these new laws were actually good for sharia law. He argued that the changes would fix what religious communities were interpreting "wrongly." He said that Muslims in Bosnia had pressurized the old Austria to interpret sharia laws so that Muslim girls were exempt from education. Rebac blamed their misinterpretation of the Qu'ran for the fact that over 90 per cent of illiterate women in Yugoslavia lived in Bosnia. Rebac then argued that the new regime must not allow women to be subjugated within family law and that the new constitution must guarantee equality.[24] By arguing these positions, Rebac drew on his modernizing views from previous decades, in which he addressed women's inequality many times. This time, he had the full party power behind him, as they had found a common interest.[25] For the Yugoslav communists, it was important to gain support for such big changes from such notable people from the community, even if these people were not necessarily communists.

Milovan Djilas further explained that the state and religion were going to be separated. He rejected suggestions from the Orthodox Church that both religious and civil marriage should be equally valid. He also declined proposals that the sharia courts retain jurisdiction over certain fields, particularly those linked to family issues. Finally, Djilas said that the state may financially support those religious communities that support the new state, and he expected religious communities to play "a positive role."[26]

The new Yugoslav constitution was announced in January 1946. The historian Miroslav Jovanović demonstrates that it had many direct translations and minor adaptations from the Soviet 1936 constitution.[27] The constitution guaranteed certain rights regarding religious freedoms in theory. However, churches and religious communities had lost jurisdiction over marriage, family affairs, and education. The state and religion were separated, and the state now prescribed education and family law. The constitution allowed religious communities to educate clergy under "broad supervision by the state." Religious communities' political activities were forbidden, and the state reserved the right to help them financially.[28] The Yugoslav constitution also had a separate article proclaiming that women were equal to men in all spheres of society. This gave all Yugoslav women equal political, economic, and social rights for the first time. Just as the historian Carmen Scheide notes in the Soviet case, the male standard was set as the norm and women were put on an equal legal footing with men and defined separately.[29]

In Bulgaria, the legal transformation was very similar to Yugoslavia – it was just slower as the Bulgarian communists took longer to obliterate all the remaining opposition. Bulgarian communists also modelled their legal equality of women and men on Soviet laws and the Stalinist constitution. Ananieva and Razvigorova emphasize that one of the new Bulgarian government's first legal acts in late 1944 was to guarantee the political and legal rights "of both sexes" in the Gender Equality Ordinance.[30] The constitution that was declared in 1947 formalized the rights of men and women, with a text almost identical to the Soviet and Yugoslav constitutions.[31] Article 72 of the Bulgarian constitution was the same as article 24 of the Yugoslav constitution. Women were declared equal to men, with guaranteed equal salaries for equal work and special work protections. Both constitutions also declared their intention to protect the interests of mothers and children by establishing maternity wards, kindergartens, and maternity leave. The Bulgarian constitution also had the same provisions and wording for civil marriage, a separation of church and state, state education, and a ban on religious organizations' advocation of political positions.[32] Further statutes defined how the Chief Mufti was elected, which in practice meant control from the party.[33]

With the new constitution and Family Code, both Yugoslav and Bulgarian communists abolished sharia in family relations.[34] Yugoslav communists announced a new family law in 1946, and this meant that

Muslim communities were placed under the same universal law as all other groups for the first time. The state took the family under its "protection." As an article in the AFŽ's leading magazine explained, "This was a measure to combat church influences, which destroyed the family, and traditionally enslaved women."[35] This new code replaced all earlier laws and defined marriage as between a man and woman, giving them equal rights and responsibilities. Nevertheless, the law did not allow men to take a woman's last name, and children would take the father's last name by default. The law also defined joint property and introduced a valuation for domestic work in case of divorce. It also introduced alimony and defined the procedure for divorce. Both men and women could start the divorce process for a set of reasons previously unheard of in sharia law. The law did not recognize no-fault divorce; of the many reasons the law did accept, it allowed divorce if the partners were incompatible and their relationship was disturbed.[36]

The Bulgarian Family Code was announced in 1949, and it combined the Gender Equality Ordinance and the Marriage Ordinance. It was more detailed than the Yugoslav version, but the basic provisions regarding civil marriage and parents' obligations towards children, divorce, and alimony were the same. Civil marriage was confirmed as the only legal kind. Both parents had equal responsibility towards children, and divorce was possible for many reasons previously unheard of in Muslim communities, and alimony was also modelled on the Soviet laws. The minimum age for marriage was set to seventeen for women and eighteen for men. The code was also universal across the entire country, and so it established new norms for Muslim communities.[37]

Given women's legal situation before the war, the new constitution and accompanying laws brought immense changes. Disempowering state laws and practices of customary and sharia law were swiftly removed. The new legal framework set the foundation for the political and economic enfranchisement of Muslim women. It promised them equal political participation and employment rights, equal access to education, legal protection, divorce rights, property divisions, and an equal share of inheritance.

Socialist Pronatalism

Another area of communist intervention common to all Eastern European countries related to motherhood, which was placed under special protection by the state according to the Soviet model.[38] Communists considered motherhood as inseparable from womanhood, and they drafted special protections for employed women and placed such promises in the constitutions previously mentioned. These motherhood protections were also considered a form of women's empowerment. The new socialist states promised to build a universal welfare system that would protect everyone, including Muslim women. They promised free services for children, new provisions regarding pregnancy and maternity leave, and new job protections for pregnant women and mothers. These measures were supposed to help employed mothers rather than to restructure how domestic work and childcare were performed.[39]

Once again, by following communist publications, one could argue that Yugoslav and Bulgarian communists found inspiration in the Soviet Union. Although not a novel invention, crèches and kindergartens were rare before the war in both countries, and almost non-existent in Central Asia before the revolution. The Bolsheviks invested a lot of resources in building them and making them available, at least in cities and towns. As the historian Yulia Gradskova has highlighted, these new services for children were typical Soviet spaces – ideological and physical objects through which a new society was built.[40] In the decades following the Second World War, all socialist countries invested much effort in constructing childcare services and in making them widely and freely available.[41]

The Bolsheviks considered day care facilities, kindergartens, playgrounds, and schools as some of the most visible markers of the Central Asian transformation. Collectivization was supposed to bring all these institutions into farms, while some regions even organized socialist competitions over who could establish more nurseries. The quality of these nurseries is debatable, particularly as they were often opened quickly, with poorly trained staff and facilities.[42] Nevertheless, they are telling of broader efforts to ease motherhood, since fatherhood was not mentioned.

Legally, the Soviet Union pioneered paid pregnancy and maternity leave, which increased over the decades. Interwar Yugoslavia and Bulgaria did not have such benefits. Not many Muslim women worked in non-agricultural activities, but those who did had to work until the day of the baby's delivery. In the countryside this was the norm for everyone. With collectivization this was also supposed to change, as collective farmers were also entitled to such benefits. In industry, women were barred from certain jobs deemed harmful to motherhood. Some communists interpreted this as enfranchisement as well, although the consequences were that women were barred from certain well-paid industrial jobs regardless of whether they planned to have children. Similar legislation was passed in socialist Yugoslavia and Bulgaria decades later.[43]

After the Second World War, both Yugoslavia and Bulgaria included pro-natalist policies in their legislation and practice in a very similar way. Initially, both states copied Soviet laws regarding childcare services, child benefits, pregnancy and maternity leave, and monetary incentives. These benefits depended on women's employment status, and since they were provided by the state, monetary benefits and leave were more accessible and were used more often. Pregnancy and maternity leave was proudly provided by the socialist states, and it increased with each reform. Initially in Yugoslavia, women could use up to ninety days of paid maternity leave and extend it using regular paid vacation afterwards. In Bulgaria the provision was the same. It increased in 1973 to six months for the first child, with one more month for each subsequent child. The benefits peaked with the 1986 Labour Code, which offered two years of paid maternity leave.[44]

In these early stages of socialism, the only notable difference between the Yugoslav and Bulgarian approach concerned access to abortion. Bulgarian communists copied the Soviet law from 1936 in its entirety, while the Yugoslavs copied the same law but permitted abortion under certain social conditions. In both countries, abortion was often used as the only form of contraception; it was very widespread and was often conducted by fortune tellers in the countryside. The AFŽ's leaders were very concerned with the extremely high numbers of unsupervised abortions and with the many medical complications and deaths of women that followed. Thanks to strong advocacy by people like Vida Tomšič, the social conditions under which abortion was permitted were expanded in 1951, despite strong opposition from many Yugoslav doctors who wanted a stricter approach. Abortion was not made illegal; however, it was not considered a woman's right but a necessary evil until socialism had been built. The Yugoslav position changed a few decades later, and the party legalized abortion entirely as the woman's choice in the 1970s.[45] The fact that the first law permitted abortion for social reasons marked a significant difference with the Bulgarian case, as many women could claim poverty and obtain a free and safe abortion at clinics.[46] Such clinics, however, were more readily available in cities, while in the countryside, women used the unsafe services of village healers throughout much of socialism.[47] In Bulgaria abortion was decriminalized in 1956, although Bulgarian women still had to get permission from a special committee. What is more, access was further restricted in 1968 and 1973. The partial ban meant that abortion was not available to married women with fewer than two children. Nevertheless, abortions remained frequent and were often the only available form of family planning.[48]

The Bulgarian state engaged in more radical pro-natalist policies after de-Stalinization, but as Deyana Marcheva shows, by 1951 the state had announced the Decree for the Promotion of Fertility and Multiple Children, which increased child benefits while also taxing people without children.[49] The Bulgarian press also urged women to have many children. For years mothers were celebrated for having multiple children. Stories featured of their success and pride upon receiving "Mother-heroine" medals, which the state introduced for mothers with eight or more children.[50] Women were also praised for their professional achievements, but in such articles they also thanked the state for care and improvements in living standards. They explained that having children is not only important for the state but also a joyous moment in women's lives.[51] In the early 1950s, such articles could still feature photographs of Muslim families in which women wore headscarves, a representation that would later disappear.

Differences between Yugoslav and Bulgarian approaches became visible in the 1960s. The historian Ulf Brunnbauer argues that the Bulgarian state intensified its pro-natalist propaganda in the post-Stalinist period, and they were obsessed with attempts to increase fertility rate. At the same time, the state again supported dependence on the family units for childcare and older persons' care.[52] In the Bulgarian women's press it became impossible to see positive pictures of big Muslim families. The Bulgarian state still wanted to increase the fertility rate, but new measures were introduced only amid concerns regarding the low fertility rate of the dominant group. For example, the child allowance that the families received encouraged them to have up to three children. As the historian Bistra Anachkova shows, childcare benefits were paid to families monthly and the amount depended on the number of children in the family, while a lump sum was given for the birth of the first three children.[53] On the individual level, however, there is no doubt that many women were better off with more money, services, and protections, regardless of what the state demographers and policy planners intended. It seems that the Yugoslav party leaders were not concerned with increasing the birth rate as much as they were worried about decreasing the mortality rate of mothers and children, which was very high in the countryside. The reasoning was that with the improvements in living conditions due to socialist development, the birth rate would also increase.[54]

Pro-natalist policies were universally applied to all groups in Yugoslavia in terms of laws, monetary incentives, and pregnancy and maternity rights. As for the Muslim populations, in the later stages of Yugoslav socialism, there were concerns over ethnophobic and racist voices angered by the very high birth rate in Kosovo among the Albanian population. These voices grew stronger in the 1980s amid the collapse of Yugoslav socialism after Tito's death. Although the discourse shifted towards anti-natalist policies regarding Muslim populations, the state did not abolish pro-natalist incentives. Rada Drezgić has clearly traced the re-emergence of racist discourse among Serbian demographers, which was particularly prominent after the collapse of Yugoslavia.[55]

New post-war legislation also envisioned new access to health care, with special protections for mothers and children written in both the Yugoslav and Bulgarian constitutions. Many Muslim communities had to wait for decades for health care facilities specifically aimed at women to be built. After the war, hospitals and maternity wards were rare all over the region because of the previous absence of investment and the war destruction. In Yugoslavia, the number of doctors was low even in the major cities, while the rural areas would be visited by a doctor only during health campaigns. Areas like Kosovo, Montenegro, and Macedonia, where most Muslims lived, often had no doctors at all. Folk-healing practices were dominant in all communities, and the tremendous efforts that the Yugoslav state made to build more hospitals and train more doctors, nurses, and midwives would take decades to reach more remote communities.[56] The situation in Bulgaria for health care development was similar. In the early 1950s, the party instructed the Ministry of Health to staff Turkish areas with more doctors, particularly women doctors, and to construct new health centres and maternity wards.[57] The media reported on these efforts, and *ZHenata dnes* proudly announced that a poor Romani woman named Ayshe Mustafova Kezimova was the first to give birth in a new suburban maternity ward in Sofia. This demonstrated that their health care was "organized on the USSR's example ... without any racial discrimination."[58] Nevertheless, maternity wards and medical services outside urban areas barely had an effect on Muslim communities. The number of doctors from a Muslim background was also negligible. The gap between Muslim and non-Muslim regions was obvious in terms of access, infrastructure, and medical staff.

New Legislation in Practice

The effects of these legal changes are harder to trace, particularly in early socialism. Scattered reports show that the application of laws that empowered women was far from straightforward for Muslim communities, and for other communities where the state and party apparatus could not or did not want to enforce new laws. For example, the party's struggles to implement measures such as equal inheritance and alimony, were remarkably similar in both countries in rural areas. Customary practices that disempowered women proved very resistant and hard to break. The internal reports were full of claims that inheritance practices were intact in the countryside communities during the entire socialist period, and communists were certainly aware of the problem. In Yugoslavia, in the early 1950s, the AFŽ formed a committee to examine family relations in the countryside. They uncovered domestic violence, abuses, the state's inability to enforce laws in family matters, and many other discriminatory practices. Women regularly gave up properties to their brothers, while their community sometimes shunned those who dared seek their inheritance.[59] As further internal reports suggested, notions of shame and women's subjugation in the house were common to all religious communities in the countryside. Men usually initiated divorce, and women often did not ask for joint property to be shared. As these issues were so widespread, internal reports did not distinguish between Muslim and non-Muslim communities.[60] These reports, however, were not systematic. The statistical bulletin data did not capture these issues, and even for the number of divorces, it did not stratify the report in line with people's nationality or religion. Still, by observing regions and areas with predominantly Muslim populations, it seems that the divorce rate was lower than in the country as a whole.[61]

The press occasionally tackled the government's struggles to enforce legal equality and transformation in practice, lamenting that there are areas where Muslim women "still live in feudal relations." One article from 1955 in Yugoslavia is particularly telling of the failure to change the situation in the countryside ten years after winning power. The article depicted cases of violence in which women were heavily beaten, and yet they refused to report it because of fear and a lack of support. The author interviewed local judges in Bosnia, who claimed that women would come to them only if they were expelled from their houses, even if they had suffered abuse for years. The divorce process was often not initiated at all. The author also questioned the women he met at the court and the police station. Some expressed a fear of being homeless with their children, while others who had already been driven out asked only for minimal monetary support. Once the reporter had followed up with the local communists and party leaders, they confirmed that almost nothing had changed in the countryside. In their words, the husband was still the law. Even though the author tried to end on an optimistic note, calling for the local party and women's sections to do more work, he admitted the party's failure to change society.[62] Such articles aimed to mobilize and shake the local party into action, but they also show a lack of social support, and the absence of meaningful government programs that could effectively support victims. Such programs did not exist before socialism either, and since the socialist state was organized around "productive" labour, women who did not work outside the home had few options and feared homelessness and poverty.

During the early socialist period in Bulgaria, information about the extent of domestic violence would reach the public as a side note in articles discussing a large number of divorces. In passing, an article mentioned a young, hard-working woman who was heavily beaten for years and was often saved by the police and neighbours. However, it seems that except for a divorce, no actions were taken against the perpetrator.[63] In another story set in a Muslim household, which may be fictional, a man told a teacher that he would beat his wife for not wanting to attend the literacy course and for being too conservative. Although in a position of power, the female teacher just asked for the reasons, and she did not scold the man. She also did not report him. Instead, the teacher expressed understanding for the man when he narrated his story and described that he wanted to bring his wife to the store, discard the veil, and send her to school. The wife saw these as attacks on her personality and as an attempt to separate her from Allah. Despite the violence, the wife was offered no sympathy, as she would rather "listen to the hodzhas," than to her modern and handsome (repeated several times) husband. Domestic violence was simply ignored if not justified.[64]

Finally, in both Yugoslavia and Bulgaria, divorce, although legal and seen as a positive step towards equality by the party leadership, was most often depicted negatively by the press and experts. Divorce was justified only in cases of gross domestic violence, with visible physical injuries. In many other cases, people were criticized for asking for a divorce and blamed for not trying hard enough to make their marriage work. Children were often at the centre of such debates. For example, the Bulgarian *ZHenata dnes* depicted divorce as inflicting great misery on children; they argued that divorce in a socialist society should be rare. Many articles were devoted to people deemed "reckless," who did not understand that "marriage is not only a personal act but is of interest to all of society."[65] The same discourse existed in Yugoslavia.[66] The women's press published stories about trivial reasons for divorce, and they urged people to reconsider, particularly if they had children.[67] Throughout the entire socialist period, experts published articles, booklets, and brochures about the "negative" aspects of divorce and blamed "broken families" for almost all social problems.[68]

Despite these challenges and sometimes half-hearted approaches to socialist transformation, legal changes slowly changed Muslim communities, even in remote areas. The state apparatus constantly expanded in both countries, and its expansion brought changes alongside rapid urbanization and industrialization. In both countries, the number of people living in the countryside fell from about 75 per cent in 1946 to about 33 per cent at the end of socialist period, which allowed the state to impose new norms and control more easily.[69] For example, civil marriages were registered in most cases. Furthermore, Darakchi writes that in Bulgaria, "stealing girls" ended after it had been prohibited by the new regime. Parents still played a crucial role in choosing a spouse, but practices had to fit the new legal models such as the minimum age for marriage.[70] In the Yugoslav countryside, the practice of "stealing girls" persisted in the form of pre-arranged customs, albeit prescribed within the limits of the law. However, even there, most of the marriages were registered in the local government offices.[71]

Because of urbanization, new benefits related to motherhood, such as monetary incentives or access to free childcare, were also taking root. In the countryside, both countries tried to organize day care and kindergartens during the peaks in seasonal labour, but these services often had poor facilities and untrained teachers. In Yugoslavia, they were mostly abandoned after collectivization failed, with the government hoping that expanding the cities and towns would also improve the situation for the nearby population. Nevertheless, childcare arrangements often remained traditional, with working women relying on the help of grandparents or relatives. As in Bulgaria, the uptake of kindergartens was comparatively lower than in other Eastern European countries. For example, the economist Mieke Meurs demonstrates that even in the 1980s, only 8 per cent of Pomak households, 6 per cent of ethnic Turkish households, and 6 per cent of Roma households used nurseries for children aged between one and three years. That number can be explained by the maternity leave available at that time. However, Meurs also provided data showing that Christian households used preschool more for care of children aged three to seven, as compared with all other groups. This difference was particularly visible among the Roma and Pomak children. The lower number of Bulgarian Muslim women who used these services is not surprising, considering that it allowed the government more control and often violent abuses during the redressing and anti-circumcision campaigns, as examined in chapters 5 and 6.[72]

What did not change, in the Soviet Union, Yugoslavia, or Bulgaria, was how domestic chores were gendered and divided. Legal equality did not translate into sharing domestic chores, and the party did not promote such ideas confidently. For example, there were booklets on the education of small children in which *mothers* were told to divide up the domestic chores among their children equally regardless of gender. However, calls for men to participate were not so easy to find.[73] Ulf Brunnbauer states that the inner functioning of Bulgarian households barely changed, with men not participating in domestic chores.[74] Ultimately, all these regimes tried to offer a technological fix, either with services or with kindergartens. For example, the Bulgarian *ZHenata dnes* often wrote about the new kindergartens and day care facilities, workers' eateries, and laundry services, calling them "the true revolution in women's domestic life."[75] However, women outside the main urban centres had to wait many decades for such a fix, if it was ever accomplished.

One of the first things that the Bolsheviks, and later the Yugoslav and Bulgarian communists, did after coming to power was to enact a legal transformation that established what was then considered equality between women and men. Yugoslav and Bulgarian communists followed the Soviet model and they quickly implemented a new constitution and laws, which were often direct translations and minor adaptations of Soviet laws. Muslim communities were encompassed in that process. The state took away religious communities' authority in family affairs, guaranteeing new rights in the constitution and family law. Women and men were equalized in terms of rights and responsibilities towards children. Access to divorce, which was previously unknown in these communities, was governed by sharia laws and courts. Women also gained legal access and equality in relation to property, economic activities, education, and political and social activities.

Communists also saw new laws on motherhood as an inseparable part of this legal enfranchisement. They pioneered pregnancy and maternity leave, and enshrined special protections for mothers and children in the constitution and in law. The state also promised free and widely available nurseries and kindergartens, in addition to health care facilities. Although it would take decades for these to be built and widely available, many Muslim families did use them.

This chapter has also shown that legal transformation was sluggish in affecting Muslim communities in practice. The party often struggled to impose new laws in areas with weak party infrastructure, with women struggling to enjoy guaranteed rights. This was particularly evident with inheritance, and with rights regarding property division after divorce. The state's safety net was often inadequate, leaving many women in a hard position, often enduring gendered violence because of a lack of options for them and their children. Communists quickly learned that passing new laws was far from enough to bring about the imagined transformation of the targeted communities.

Chapter Four

Crafting Socialist Identities: Turning Muslims into Comrades

In the summer of 1935, the engineer Kemar Ragimova became the focus of the party's magazine *Rabotnitsa*, and of an internal correspondence with the Central Committee. The press explained that Ragimova was forcefully veiled when she was thirteen; a few months later she was married, and at the age of fifteen she was already a mother. She had no right to leave the yard. Her life changed, however, after Soviet power was established in Azerbaijan. Kemar began not only to go out into the street, but also to advocate among other women to break free of traditional bonds. In 1926, Kemar stopped wearing the veil and began to study. After her husband's death, she was left alone with four children, but thanks to the party's help, she continued her studies and became an engineer in the oil industry, while her oldest daughter enrolled in medical school. Ragimova exceeded production quotas and lived the socialist dream. At the height of Stalinism, Ragimova became a celebrated role model – as a previously downtrodden Muslim woman – and made a career for herself in the Stalinist system. In recognition, she was elected to the Baku Council, and the papers quoted her saying that "Soviet power creates true miracles."[1]

Ragimova was one of many such women that the regime promoted. This chapter turns its attention to new opportunities and challenges for Muslim women and men in creating new lives within socialist states. It examines how communists imagined social mobility for and the transformation of Muslim communities, and what it meant for many who found careers in industry and the newly collectivized agriculture. It shows that pathways for Muslims who wanted to use new opportunities were far from straightforward, with obstacles from both their communities and the regime's understanding of Muslims as a *special case*. Socialist regimes anticipated that individual participation in the socialist economy would eventually have a spillover effect on the entire community. This chapter also explores the space for political activities, showing that high politics was entirely dominated by men, with only a few non-Muslim women present. Due to this exclusion, gender policies towards Muslim communities were often insensitive to Muslim women's needs and desires. Finally, the chapter looks at the activities of the party's women's sections, where Muslim women from Bulgaria and Yugoslavia could find a space for political and social activities. These activities, however, often just limited Muslim women to engaging with other Muslim women. Nevertheless, as this chapter demonstrates, some Muslim women seized new opportunities to pursue careers that had been closed to them before the war.

New Social Mobility

Throughout the entire socialist period, many women from Muslim backgrounds achieved unprecedented social mobility through the new legal equality, as well as through education and employment policies. To a certain extent, post-war mobility in the Balkans was similar to that in Soviet Central Asia after the revolution. The Bolsheviks drew on classical Marxist theories and believed that social mobility and the emancipation of "backward groups" would come through employed labour. *Pravda* published many articles insisting that "the women of the East" should enter paid employment if new nations were going to progress towards socialism. Destroying harmful traditions and sharia laws was seen only as the first step.[2] In the 1920s and 1930s, a significant number of women in the Soviet Union entered schools and universities that had been previously closed to them, and a range of new employment opportunities opened up. With Stalinism's rise, labour became a focus. Ambitious industrialization and collectivization projects accelerated changes, and the Soviets needed female labour more than ever before, resulting in many Muslim women entering factories and collective farms, while others found work in the administration sector, the education sector, or in science.[3] Industrialization radically changed the landscape not only with new industries, but also with entire cities being built. Urbanization followed, and both changed the countryside too. The historian Wendy Goldman shows that the change was immense for women from all communities, as by 1935 women comprised 42 per cent of all workers. The unprecedented movement of people from the countryside to new industrial areas did not leave many communities unaffected.[4]

Collectivization and industrialization were not only tools for economic development but were also imagined as critical for further social and personal transformation. By joining collective farms alongside other peasant women, women from Muslim backgrounds were supposed to become educated and proactive builders of socialism. Muslim communities, then, were supposed to achieve "the same level" of socialist development, with cultural differences erased. *Pravda* exclaimed that collectivization "has awakened" the women of Central Asia, who were only recently "liberated" from veils, kalym, and slavery. The leading Soviet publication explained that by becoming factory or collective farm workers, these women were fully exercising their rights and becoming part of a "growing army" of qualified leaders in the socialist economy.[5] Collective farms were also supposed to offer all services available to workers in factories – particularly access to health care.[6] In practice, the construction of these services was slow, and they were often unreliable, but the political, social, and economic landscapes nevertheless radically transformed the lives of Muslim women and men. Finally, the Hujum and brutal oppression, as explained in the next chapter on unveiling, also contributed.

Women from Central Asia who achieved social mobility featured in many Soviet publications, which were later translated and distributed in both Yugoslavia and Bulgaria. Mamlakat Nahangova made the front page of *Rabotnitsa* in 1935 with a picture with Stalin, and she quickly became a celebrity (figure 4.1). Mamlakat was a young shock worker who broke a record in cotton collecting, for which Stalin personally congratulated her. In contrast to Ragimova, Mamlakat was born in the Soviet Union, and according to the press, she therefore never knew "the life of slavery," and so her voice was "loud and clear."[7] Ten years later, *Žena danas* in Yugoslavia published a three-page article about Mamlakat, praising her work achievements on a collective farm, and her desire to learn and *advance* herself even more. The Yugoslav version of the article followed Mamlakat's life after becoming famous upon returning to Tajikistan from Moscow. Her social mobility started with hard labour; she then progressed through school, Komsomol, and further studies and eventually gained party membership. Through all these achievements, Mamlakat expressed an even greater desire to learn, and to serve the party and Stalin. In 1945, Mamlakat was presented as an accomplished woman, and as an active agent of socialism who also enjoyed all its benefits.[8]

This story, typical of the Stalinist press, revealed a model for social mobility: it usually addressed women or workers from impoverished families, and it demonstrated that the new legal framework was supposed to open up unprecedented opportunities that could be fulfilled through hard work and learning. Groups deemed the most oppressed were supposed to benefit the most. Women in the Balkans were promised equal chances of embarking on a career trajectory like Mamlakat's.

Figure 4.1. Cover page of the December 1935 issue of *Rabotnitsa*, featuring Stalin and Mamlakat

Source: Author's personal collection.

Regardless of their background, women could advance their social position thanks to their hard labour, a willingness to learn, and loyalty to the party. The idea here was to craft new socialist identities, a new woman and man, which became a common trope throughout socialist Eastern Europe.[9]

Just like the Bolsheviks before them, the Yugoslav and Bulgarian communists believed in the power of laws, decrees, and resolutions for changing social reality. The media was supposed to foster those changes, and party activists were supposed to speed up their propagation. All these communist parties invested a lot of effort and media space in showing that this new world was not only possible but also actively created for those who had been disadvantaged by the previous regimes. Numerous Yugoslav and Bulgarian magazines for women featured articles about new rights, which detailed the changes to political, economic, and social rights. They explained women's rights to vote and be elected, and to choose a profession and education. At the same time, these individual rights were presented as collectively important. The transformation that legal changes instigated was supposed to be individual and collective. For example, the media called on women to use the new constitution, which allowed them to elevate themselves personally and become "socially useful" regardless of their background.[10] The Yugoslav and Bulgarian press used the exact same phrases. As *ZHenata dnes* stated, thanks to the 9 September and the changes that followed (referring to 9 September 1944 when a coup d'état led to the establishment of a communist-controlled government), Bulgarian women were free and equal citizens who became ministers, members of the parliament, university professors, scientists, workers, shock workers, and collective farmers.[11]

A comparison between the "old oppression" and the new socialist changes was often used as a tool to promote new opportunities for women. The most prominent communists, such as Tsola Dragoycheva, often reminded readers that Bulgarian women had no right to vote and be elected, were not allowed to pursue notable careers, were paid much less than men, and lived without state welfare. Dragoycheva repeated that men had been allowed to beat women, kick them out of their homes, drink away women's money, and spend women's wealth. The state did not protect families, and women could not own property, while pregnant women worked in factories, fields, and streets right up until the day they gave birth. As neither protections for women nor modern health care existed, the umbilical cord was cut with a rusty sickle, leading to a high infant mortality rate. After listing all the evils of old Bulgaria, Dragoycheva wrote that they had changed all this thanks to the Soviet army, the party, and the people's uprising. In Dragoycheva's words, thanks to "Dimitrov's constitution," Bulgarian women now had endless possibilities, and it was up to these women to use them.[12] Such articles certainly served to shamelessly promote the regime, but their importance in showing new possibilities to women should also not be neglected.

After these top-level legal and policy changes, Yugoslav and Bulgarian communists regularly posited that employed labour was a means of emancipating both an individual and the entire community. For example, when applauding women enrolled to become nurses, *ZHenata dnes* wrote that these newly educated Turkish women were supposed to return to their villages, work at the collective farms in health care, and "fight against prejudice, superstition, and bigotry."[13] The article did not miss the chance to state the following: "Gone are the days when the Turkish woman, hardened by religious fanaticism, languished in ignorance. Assisted by their Bulgarian sisters, she [the Turkish woman] has woken up to a new, free life. Now she is a teacher, a collective farmer, a people's councillor, a public figure."[14] The article also featured a collective image of forty-three women dressed in white, smiling and supposedly accepting this new role. Even their bodies were reshaped through education and labour. Labour was further connected with a variety of life situations. For example, the press praised the first women who arranged a civil marriage, explaining it in terms of their desire to work in factories and be emancipated.[15]

It is no coincidence that in these media representations, Muslim women were presented as in need of additional help. In the imagined gender, class, religious, and race hierarchy, Muslim women needed their "more advanced sisters" to lead them and validate their efforts. The principle in the print media was similar and rather simple. Work outside the home was emancipatory, but on that road towards emancipation, the male workers needed communists; female workers needed male workers; male peasants needed any workers; female peasants needed male peasants; and Muslims needed non-Muslims to lead and guide them.

Magazine and newspaper articles were followed by other media that disseminated imagery of new socialist identities. Exhibitions, posters, and films played an important role. In the early socialist period, these were very similar in Yugoslavia and Bulgaria. For example, Yugoslav and Bulgarian Stalinist films shared aesthetics, plots, and characters while differing only in language and location. The 1949 Yugoslav film *The Factory Story* (*Priča o fabrici*) and the 1952 Bulgarian film *Danka* had a very similar female textile worker as the heroine and the same kind of story about heroic women overcoming obstacles for the good of the new socialist country. In both cases, labour was the key component of emancipation and personal transformation, and it became one's purpose over all other possible identities.[16]

Most of the labour heroines presented in the press and films were from the dominant, non-Muslim populations of Yugoslavia and Bulgaria. In an early Yugoslav film called *The Lake* (*Jezero*), the only reference to the local Muslim community ridiculed the "backwardness" of a local *hodža* who did not believe that a hydro-dam could ever be built.[17] A few years later, the film *Zenica* portrayed more issues from

Muslim communities as a side story. There are scenes depicting a traditional Bosnian Muslim household, in which the father forces women to be veiled, hidden from the world. Eventually, a young Muslim girl named Emina, still veiled, decides to join in with the construction of the Zenica steel industry. She gets a job as a courier, and is defended by her new colleagues when her father storms the factory to bring her home. A male technician intervenes and insists to Emina's father that women are equal under the law, to which her father replies that for his household and his children, he is the law. It culminates in Emina refusing to go home, and her deciding to stay in the factory. Other male colleagues also approach Emina's father, explaining to him not to worry, and that these are new times. As a result, Emina keeps working and transforms into a new woman, with several respectable workers trying to woo her. Her father's patriarchal authority is permanently broken. Eventually, she requests that the main engineer send her off for additional education, as she is keen to progress her career, while the factory succeeds in changing the entire city and all its communities.[18]

At around the same time, the Bulgarian film *Adam's Rib* (*Rebro Adamovo*) placed the young Muslim woman Zyulker, who was eager for education and a career, at the centre of the plot. Once again, it was her father who was depicted as someone who tried to keep her in a state of *backwardness* by arranging a marriage for her and forcing her to leave school. The heroine was then abused by her husband, and eventually managed to escape violence. After many difficulties, and with the help of her first teacher (with whom she falls in love), she manages to become a teacher herself. After she is transformed, empowered, and full of self-confidence, she decides to return to her old village as a teacher, ready to transform the community as well.[19] In both these films the trope is the same: the new state opened up unprecedented opportunities to everyone, while the personal bravery of Muslim women, and help from non-Muslim men, allowed the old patriarchal structures to be broken and new life to commence. As argued by Nadège Ragaru, this, and later films such as *Time of Parting* (*Vreme razdelno*) were showing clear power relationship committing symbolic violence by shaping perceptions and identities, making the dominated accept their subjugation.[20]

The Education of Future Socialists

The focus on teachers and educators in these first films also reflected the regime's strategy. Socialist regimes invested a lot of hope that through socialist education, a new generation of loyal and proper socialists would emerge. The Soviet Stalinist press was full of stories of new opportunities, created through schooling that was free and open to people from all backgrounds. The creation of a secular, non-segregated educational system in Central Asia was also a source of much pride. After the revolution, the typical stories followed Muslim women who used the opportunity to obtain basic literacy unavailable to them beforehand. Illiteracy was presented as a colonial legacy that required not only additional funding for school infrastructure, but also support to break old prejudices.[21] However, in the 1930s, it became more common to read articles about women who had obtained the highest degrees and scientific posts. For example, *Rabotnitsa* often featured stories about women who passed through all levels of schooling, even finishing doctoral degrees despite their disadvantaged background.[22]

Yugoslav and Bulgarian communists also inherited countries that were severely illiterate, while in the areas with a predominantly Muslim population it was harder to find a literate person than not. According to the official statistics from 1931, just under 73 per cent of people in Bosnia were illiterate, with female illiteracy much higher – reaching almost 100 per cent in some villages. All interwar governments proclaimed the fight against illiteracy to be the main objective, but there were few improvements.[23] In Bulgaria in 1934, illiteracy rates were also remarkably high among the Turkish population, with 80.6 per cent of men and 96.6 per cent of women unable to read or write.[24] After the Second World War, both communist parties engaged in a tremendous effort to eradicate illiteracy, bringing perhaps the most visible long-term change to the Muslim and other communities. Both women and men were encompassed in large literacy campaigns and crash literacy courses, although it seems that both regimes targeted women the most. One reason was that more women were illiterate than men, while another reason was the ideological explanation that women have to be literate, as they are the first educators of future generations.[25]

Communists implied that women would spread their teaching to the children as well, and Yugoslav communists, for example, launched a program to train "mothers as the first educators." The AFŽ was supposed to teach mothers to properly educate their children from as early as possible, and then to work closely with a school on further socialist education.[26] They also published many small brochures to educate new mothers, and organized countless public lectures. These were supposedly based on socialist science; they shunned prejudices and dismissed traditional practices. This drive to *modernize* women was a global trend that viewed women as a resource in promoting an agenda through education – it was not unique to the communists. It was used in every modernizing project, from colonial ones to internal modernizing projects in capitalism.[27] What was unique about this case was the framing of modernization and education in Marxist discourse, and the imposition of newly imagined gender relations through education on religious minorities.

The Yugoslav AFŽ spearheaded crash-course campaigns to eradicate illiteracy. Thousands of activists held literacy courses, very often in areas where Muslims were the dominant population. Material for these courses came from the party's presses, often from simple newspapers and magazines. The students learned to read and write, but also to interpret the radically changing world around them. If they managed to find educators, the AFŽ encouraged courses in the Turkish and Albanian languages, although they constantly lacked qualified people and course materials. They were also encouraged to devote their first written words to Tito and the party.[28] Literacy courses were usually followed by further programs providing education on motherhood, hygiene, food preparation, and general household economics, and many Muslim women completed these courses as well.[29]

In the early post-war years, Georgi Dimitrov also announced that the struggle against illiteracy was one of the main priorities. He expected teachers to be the main government's force, and in their absence the same expectation was placed on all literate women activists. The Bulgarian National Women's Alliance (Balgarski naroden zhenski sayuz, BNZhS) was supposed to spearhead constant care for women's education, political upbringing, and the "advancement of their cultural level."[30] However, Bulgarian literacy campaigns were slower than the Yugoslav campaigns in the immediate post-war period, probably because Yugoslav communists were able to mobilize many more women to participate in them. It seems that the Bulgarian efforts were more concerned with non-Muslim peasant women, and that only from the early 1950s did Bulgarian communists put more effort into educating the Muslim minorities. This was part of a broader educational program, as the politburo allowed for new Turkish high schools to be opened, and it directed the party cells to find "suitable progressive" teachers who speak the Turkish language, so they could be sent to Turkish villages on a two-year tenure. The politburo also sent a plea to the Bolshevik Party for six teachers from Azerbaijan to work in the new high schools and to be advisers for the ministry. The Ministry of Education was also tasked with making a plan for new schools and reconstruction of the old ones. The plan included more funds for books and other educational aids. The number of stipends for Turkish boys and girls was to be increased at medical schools and at agricultural colleges and universities. Stipends were supposed to be given to students from working-class families or from poor and middle-income peasants who showed loyalty to the government. A new curriculum was developed, with the Qu'ran and religious studies removed. It was a comprehensive plan – the first of its kind that focused on children and young people in order to create a new Turkish elite loyal to the Bulgarian socialist state.[31]

As the Yugoslav and Bulgarian communist regimes felt more secure, they switched their focus from crash courses on literacy to ensuring that the entire population received mandatory elementary education. The change for Muslim communities was immense. The new education was secular, without gender segregation in classrooms. Girls could no longer be exempted from elementary education on religious grounds. Resistance to sending girls to schools was widespread in both Yugoslavia and Bulgaria. Usually, the women's section was tasked with ensuring that parents complied with the law; but often the party and the administrative apparatus had to be involved.[32] The regular practice in the countryside was to allow only boys to attend school, and it turned out that communists would need decades to break such practices. In all rural religious communities, the education gap was big, as even when girls were included in elementary education, more boys were allowed to go to high schools.[33] Nevertheless, routes to high schools and all universities were open to Muslim students, in a system without tuition fees and with available dorms, canteens, and stipends. By the end of the socialist period both Bulgaria and Yugoslavia had new generations of Muslim students who used these opportunities to enter careers and professions not available to them beforehand. The transformation was particularly stark for Muslim women as many, despite all these obstacles, managed to make high-level professional careers for themselves. Valiavicharska considers all women in Bulgaria as a whole, and shows that by the early 1970s, women in Bulgaria made up 68.5 per cent of those in post-secondary professional education, and 51.6 per cent of those in higher education, which set a remarkable standard globally at that time. Nevertheless, Valiavicharska also argues that women who challenged normative femininity, patriarchal roles, and the gendered division of labour faced various forms of backlash during the entire period, demonstrating the complexity of changes and the resilience of patriarchal norms in all communities.[34]

Education programs in Bulgaria and Yugoslavia were remarkably similar, with a strong emphasis on science and mathematics. Religious education was removed from schools, and the closure of certain Islamic educational institutions – the mektebs and madrasas – heavily affected communities. For example, scattered reports from Yugoslavia show that women were particularly unhappy when mektebs in Sarajevo and Novi Pazar were closed.[35] Bulgarian communists also closed all mektebs in 1952, leaving only one madrasa open, albeit without a female division.[36] Throughout the following four decades, secular schools dominated in a similar manner, although Yugoslav and Bulgarian approaches started to differ with de-Stalinization, as Yugoslavia became more open to various Islamic publications. For example, in the late 1960s the Yugoslav state permitted the publishing of brochures about the Islamic character of education in Yugoslavia. One such brochure, published by the IVZ, explicitly called on parents to pay particular attention so that children would gain a religious education adapted to Yugoslav socialism. It also insisted on equal attention to both boys and girls in terms of education, inheritances, and parental love. The brochure stated that the family was the key to the future generation, as it decided whether a child would be a believer and a good worker and citizen.[37]

Finally, despite breaking the old gender segregation in the education of boys and girls in Muslim communities, socialist education was still heavily gendered. Boys and girls learned the same curriculum, but girls were encouraged to enter certain professions, such as health and education, while technical high schools for skilled trades were heavily dominated by boys. This was particularly important, for as the next section will show, work in industry was particularly valued. Entering these trades, crafting new careers, and gleaning benefits from participating in the socialist project proved easier for Muslim boys than for girls.

From Muslims to Shock Workers

Women worked in industry before the Second World War, but their numbers grew significantly after the communist takeover. Women comprised about 27 per cent of industry workers in Yugoslavia,[38] and about 38 per cent in Bulgaria in 1960. While the overall number of workers rapidly increased in Bulgaria, the number of women in industry grew even faster. Women particularly dominated the textile industry and food processing, besides non-industrial jobs in education, arts, health, accounting, etc.[39] By the end of the socialist period, Bulgarian women made up about 50 per cent of the total workforce.[40] However, because of the policy of erasing the identity of the Muslim populations, it was impossible to deduce from official statistics to what extent women from Muslim backgrounds found jobs in these sectors. One could become a "heroine of socialist labour" in almost all occupations, and from the scattered evidence it is clear that some Muslim women found new careers in industrial labour, even receiving awards and prizes.[41]

Work in industry was imagined as the pinnacle of one's achievement. In following the Soviet model, Yugoslav and Bulgarian communists also heavily promoted the notion of shock work. A shock worker was supposed to tirelessly surpass daily work quotas, be innovative in their work methods, and lead a respectable socialist life. Becoming a shock worker brought prestige and pride, and it could also bring monetary and other benefits. Soviet periodicals aimed at women had promoted the idea of achievement through work since the advent of industrialization. Alison Rowley shows that from the early 1930s, the Stalinist press had insisted on improved living standards by working outside the home, with many women featuring as shock workers on the covers.[42]

Muslim women who managed to become shock workers were featured in countless articles in the top Soviet journals. Yet, taken together, these articles all had similar tropes. Shock work was an achievement that proved a point and undid existing bias and prejudices about Muslim women's labour.[43] The feature articles were usually stories of liberation and of a long road from literal slavery to the freedoms that Soviet power brought with it. At the end of that road lay meaningful work in the Soviet economy, and personal emancipation and healing through completing such labour.[44] As another Stalinist article explained, labour itself had shifted meaning, from being a joyless burden to a joyful privilege that resulted in a life of prosperity.[45]

At the height of Stalinism in the mid-1930s, shock work was an ever-present feature in Soviet politics. When Maxim Gorky addressed women shock workers who were building the Moscow–Volga Canal, he explained that their "honest, heroic work" showed how work transformed humans. In his words, the ultimate truth of Bolshevism lay in that transformation, and, finally, how beautifully Leninist and Stalinist principles organized women. As Gorky emphasized, shock work allowed these women to bury the past with their hands and build the new future. For him, it was a prime example of how socialism had uncovered the truth about gender equality, allowing women to become more self-aware regarding their rights and importance.[46]

Even though shock work lost some of its importance for the Soviet Union after the Second World War, Yugoslav and Bulgarian communists picked it up and gave it great prominence during the first post-war decade. At its core, the idea of shock work was masculine, particularly as related to manual work. The early post-war press was full of images of shirtless young men who were usually volunteering at a construction project. Men with less physical strength and women were supposed to catch up and even surpass the norms but to not necessarily be the norm setters.[47] However, the Bolsheviks, and later the Yugoslav and Bulgarian communists, invested much effort in showing that women could participate in shock work.[48] For example, in the first years after the war, Yugoslav communists organized large volunteering projects in which hundreds of thousands of young people constructed railroads, highways, dams, factories, and entire cities. Some of the largest volunteering projects were located in Bosnia in majority-Muslim settings, where young people from all over Yugoslavia constructed the Brčko–Banovići and Šamac–Sarajevo railroads in 1946 and 1947. Muslim youths were also encouraged to join and become shock workers (figure 4.2). The youth press published texts on Muslim girls from Bosnia who were surprised that other girls of their age were working on the same volunteer jobs as boys. They were also amazed that those young women were equally good at these jobs, even singing, studying, and resting together with the men. This new equality was presented as so attractive that the Muslim girls also planned to join them.[49]

During these early volunteering projects, a lot of effort was placed on changing the meanings of being a young Muslim man or woman. For example, volunteers not only worked hard but also studied, organized cultural events, and participated in sports. The party wanted to show that the new, socialist sports were open to everyone, and so they published important articles in which they praised Muslim girls who were outstanding at this new, physical "sports culture," and who

Figure 4.2. Citizens of Zenica assisting young workers in the construction of the Šamac–Sarajevo railroad, 1947. The scene shows unveiled women in the foreground, and veiled women in the background.

Source: Archives of Yugoslavia, f. 215 SSOJ.

also became shock workers doing physical work. The party showed that these young women successfully practised sport with men from other social backgrounds, although it was their first opportunity to participate in sports themselves. Consequently, they were allowed to show off their skills at the central youth rally in the capital. Their example was designed to encourage other girls to accept this sign of modernity, together with other policies that the party intended for minorities.[50]

Bulgarian communists did not organize such large projects in their first years in power, but they developed significant industrialization and urbanization projects in majority-Muslim areas. The idea of shock work was absolutely the same, with the same rhetoric, imagery, and expectations, and it was designed to be transformative for individuals and communities. Women shock workers were promoted in Bulgaria as in Yugoslavia. The regime tried hard to show that women could enter previously closed professions, and it featured stories about successful women – from tractor drivers to scientists.[51] Just as in Yugoslavia new socialist physical culture and sports initiatives were also envisioned as transformative for Muslim youth. In 1951, the politburo devised a plan that mandated the central sports authority to coordinate training courses for sports leaders and coaches within Turkish communities, as well as to facilitate the establishment of sports organizations. Local government councils were urged to allocate resources for the development of playgrounds and amenities. Crucially, the politburo's resolution explicitly advocated for the widespread inclusion of Turkish youth and emphasized the importance of recruiting women in these efforts.[52]

Besides showing the apparent successes of the socialist project, the idea behind promoting notable shock workers in the newspapers was to improve women's self-confidence. The usual practice was to name one woman and set her as an example for others to follow. For instance, Sherife Hasanova, a woman from a small village named Robovo in southeastern Bulgaria, dared to work at the hydro-dam, despite village members gossiping about her, and her being the only woman taking the daily bus to the construction site.[53] Slowly, the entire community was supposed to change, assisted by electrification, industrialization, and active socialists like Hasanova. The rural Muslim community could no longer remain isolated from the wider Bulgarian socialist project. After all, the article explained that even though Hasanova worked the entire day, she could easily shop in a new well-stocked store. This new urban, technical way of life was coming to the remotest areas, and it helped socialist gender equality along the way.

Socialist labour was directly contrasted with the old oppression of Muslim women by their communities. Newly built industries in the Rhodope region supposedly broke "the rusty chains of economic oppression," destroying traditions that "kept the women in complete subordination and slavery."[54] The press praised young Pomak and Turkish women who unveiled and joined the industry, thus creating new dreams and aspirations for her and the entire community. One article from *ZHenata dnes* vividly described that there were still "men who walk the Rhodope roads, riding their donkeys, and after them, their wives can barely catch up with them on foot; they hide their faces under black veils."[55] Nevertheless, the author was sure that the new generation would "bury the old one." The article also featured a story about a Fatime, a "shy" Turkish woman who became a great worker and regular shock worker. She was awarded additional money and books for her shock work, and could afford to buy herself a radio. Fatime also received an apartment from the company, and she invited her older parents to come and live with her. She then explained that many Turkish men looked on women as slaves, and that her own father had had to change thanks to her mother, who joined the party, and Fatime's own labour success. Now he did not dare to scold her when she went dancing after work.[56] Traditional family relations flipped, and work permitted Fatime to become the head of the household.

The Bulgarian press repeated that a woman could be independent only if she was economically independent, and they often named and praised such successful shock workers. Sometimes, the press would mention women from a Muslim background, such as Nahida Abdulova, as one of many women who broke production quotas.[57] Women who received the shock worker medals could also hope to feature in the newspapers and be invited to participate in one of the numerous political meetings of the Fatherland Front or the Communist Party. The most successful would be delegated to be on the party list for the national parliament, and in 1954 the first three Turkish women were elected.[58] Nevertheless, it seems that achieving awards was harder for Bulgarian women from Muslim backgrounds than for Yugoslavs. For example, in 1951, there was not a single Muslim woman among the Dimitrov award laureates.[59]

Similar stories occupied the media space in Yugoslavia. Becoming a shock worker was imagined as a transformative process for individuals and communities. Their jobs were usually in the textile industry, but occasionally articles would feature Muslim women in traditionally male-dominant fields such as construction. These stories always had a transformative function. For example, a certain Halima Redžep, who previously worked in tobacco, quickly learned a new trade, unveiled, and joined other women on the construction site. The press praised these women for "removing obstacles of obsolete understandings, shame, and the ever-present [saying] 'that is not for a woman.'"[60] These women proved to be just as good as men at creating plaster and cement, and they were ready to become proper masters and assistants. Taken together, however, the number of Muslim women in such jobs was negligible. A greater number worked in the textile industry, often in enterprises that hired hundreds of women. Since some of them hired only women, it was also easier for them to unveil, at least during the workday (figure 4.3). The issue of unveiling at this time was approached gradually, the communists expecting labour to solve what they considered a problem. The unveiling campaign discussed in the next chapter was also supposedly encouraged by emancipated, employed Muslim women.[61]

The relationship between the workers and the party, personified by their leader, was also supposed to be personal. Workers often sent a letter to Josip Broz Tito, promising to work more. For example, women from the Ključ sock factory in Sarajevo promised Tito that they would reduce their quantity of wasted material and sewing mistakes, and that they would break fewer needles and clean the machines better. Then

Figure 4.3. In 1950, Habida Jeretović unveiled herself and was recognized as a three-time shock worker at the Ključ sock factory in Sarajevo

Source: Archives of Yugoslavia, f. 112 Novinska agencija "TANJUG."

the individual workers, many with traditional Muslim names, promised Tito that they would work additional shifts to exceed the quotas and produce more socks.[62] Bulgarian communists, who evidenced the supposedly deep connection between ordinary workers and the party leadership, promoted the same kind of patronizing relationship.

Male shock workers from a Muslim background in Yugoslavia were more common. In fact, the most famous Yugoslav shock worker, Alija Sirotanović, was a Bosnian miner from a Muslim family. He was a Yugoslav version of Stakhanov, promoted in all media and even on banknotes. He became a hero of socialist labour, but also of many local stories and anecdotes.[63] The difference was that the press did not discuss men's gender and suitability for shock work. It was taken for granted, while their (former) religious background was understood as an example of successful post-war integration into the Brotherhood and Unity framework.

In general, men benefited more from the shock-work paradigm in both countries, but women's participation should not be neglected. The insistence on paid labour outside the home helped many women to create identities around their careers. The journalism professor Miglena Sternadori discusses a survey from 1969 in Bulgaria, showing that 85 per cent of women would not leave their job if they could afford to do so.[64] There is no particular information on Muslim communities, but scattered evidence shows that many used the new opportunities for social mobility and careers. As the state was organized to value labour, the importance of such self-fulfilment and identities cannot be overstated. Finally, besides secure employment, social and health benefits, and pensions, the workers' state also provided further smaller benefits. For example, workers could also obtain affordable or free vacations at newly built resorts, and at least some Muslim women made use of these advantages.[65]

Collective Farmers

Vast political, economic, and social transformations affected the Muslim populations in the countryside even more so than those in urban centres. In both Yugoslavia and Bulgaria, approximately three-quarters of the population lived in the countryside at the end of the war, and except for a few smaller cities, most Muslims lived in the countryside as well. For example, in Bulgaria only about 13 per cent of Turks lived in cities by late 1956.[66] Both countries aimed to involve the countryside in the socialist economy by following the Soviet model, and both attempted to collectivize agricultural production. This was led by the belief that collectivization would yield improved economic output and facilitate new social relations in the countryside. In practice, collectivization policies hit Muslim communities hard, dispossessing them and bringing the party to their homes. However, even before collectivization, both communist regimes passed land reform policies, limiting property sizes and distributing land to the peasants who farmed it. The remaining large farmlands were liquidated. This affected not only rich peasants but also the Muslim landowners who had retained properties after the collapse of the Ottoman Empire.[67]

Collectivization drew on Stalinist theory and was supposed to solve the countryside's backwardness and bring about a socialist transformation that would lead to the same level of socialist modernity as found in the cities. In Yugoslavia, aggressive collectivization started in late 1948, which led to significant violence against the peasantry and often open resistance. This resistance was sometimes led by women who engaged in the destruction of property and farms.[68] Over just a few years about 50,000 peasants were fined or arrested. Nevertheless, by 1951 some 20 per cent of all arable land had entered the collectivization process. The peasantry was alienated and chaos ensued, which resulted in clashes, beatings, torture, and even shootings as peasants were unwilling to hand over their products and to join the collective farms. The party slowed the process down in 1951, and eventually allowed peasants to leave collective farms in 1953 because of the farms' poor economic results. By 1955 the number of collective farms in Yugoslavia had returned to the 1948 level, and collectivization ultimately failed.[69]

Collectivization in Bulgaria was more successful, with more long-term consequences, although the initial trajectory was the same as in Yugoslavia. As Gruev demonstrates, Bulgarian collectivization started in 1948 as well, leading to massive increase in the number of farms and peasant resistance by 1951. However, Bulgarian communists did not give up on the collective farms, and recommenced aggressive collectivization in 1956; they had completed the process by 1959, even in the remote regions.[70]

As for the functioning of collective farms, the Yugoslav Zadruge, and the Bulgarian TKZS (Trudovo-kooperativni zemedelski stopanstva) were supposed to be economic but also social institutions that brought radical changes to the countryside. They were supposed to provide health services and kindergartens to ease women's work. Together with mechanization, these services were supposed to help women achieve full equality and transform both their personal lives and the economy.[71] During the Yugoslav collectivization drive, the AFŽ invested a great deal of effort in creating services such as seasonal kindergartens and in organizing medical visits on the farms. These efforts were never entirely successful as the social aspect of Yugoslavia's collective farms was always underfunded.[72]

Just as in industry, Bulgarian women were more present than Yugoslav women in the state-controlled agricultural economy. After the Yugoslav collectivization drive had ended by the mid-1950s, only state-owned farms remained until the end of the socialist period, but they were few in number. Individual peasants were allowed to retain their small plots. Instead of waging war against them, Yugoslav communists hoped that the transformation of the countryside would come through industrialization and private mechanization. In practice, the lives of peasants who did not move to cities did not change much until urbanization touched their villages. During the brief collectivization period, the AFŽ had the idea of including more Muslim women, and of fostering socialist competition among them.[73] They tried to promote notable collective farms with a Muslim background, although they were not easy to find. The AFŽ were more successful in organizing Muslim women in towns and cities in various cooperatives, such as a rug-weaving cooperative,[74] than in bringing them in to collective farms even when they were dealing with tobacco growing, in which a significant number of Muslim women were involved.[75] In Bulgaria, in contrast, collectivization affected the lives of Muslim communities to a much greater extent.

Although Muslim women were generally promoted less in the Bulgarian press than in Yugoslavia, the leading Bulgarian newspapers featured more articles on collective farmers from Muslim backgrounds. For example, *ZHenata dnes* reported from the Conference of the Leading Collective Farmers, where a certain Dzhemile Ibrahimova from Zmeitsa talked about her successful crops. She presented the results of her brigade, praised the shock worker Emine Karaosmanova from her brigade, and explained their work methods. In the end, she promised to work even harder while guarding the border from some enemies, and she ended her speech with an exclamation to the Bulgarian communist leader, Valko Chervenkov. The article also featured her picture while delivering a speech. She wore a white headscarf with half of her hair visible, which seems to have been the case for at least half of the women pictured with Chervenkov in the middle.[76]

At the same congress, Chervenkov acknowledged that women were having a hard time climbing the hierarchy of the collective farms. At the meeting with collective farmers, he criticized men for not promoting women to managerial posts. He also criticized the "horrific conservativism" present among many men, who disregarded women's labour and capabilities. Chervenkov called upon women to fight for their rights to participate and to assume the most important roles in the farms. He called upon a struggle against conservativism, which was supposed to help women obtain responsible posts, including opening more spaces at special schools for party leaders. He also recognized the struggles of many women to find free time for managerial duties amid childcare and domestic chores.[77]

During his keynote speech, Chervenkov talked of a new peasant woman who was free from capitalist exploitation – a hero of socialist labour. By working in collective farms, the women supposedly became active, independent, and equal members of society. Finally, in front of these new women lay a "wide and unlimited path to all leadership and responsible posts" in the economy and the state.[78] Despite such promises, in 1955 only twenty-eight women were presidents of the collective farms, while 3,174 were members of the ruling and control committees, out of 2,735 farms and 62.5 per cent of all arable land. It is unclear how many were Muslims, but for example, all seven of the published names of "women heroes of socialist labour" were Bulgarian.[79]

Despite obvious issues in practice, the newspapers regularly wrote about the old Muslim women whose lives were nothing but "slavery and excruciation" before 9 September, while the socialist Bulgaria had created a new life for them where they could visit cinemas and read the press. The socialist transformation resulted in the older generation's wisdom being recognized. For example, Hadzire Abadova supported her daughter, Hamide, who decided to be a milkwoman on a collective farm. Hadzire told her that there is no shameful labour in their new country. Hamide proved to be a hard-working farmer, who was very caring towards her cows, learning their names and characters. The only letdown, the article stated, was that she was not aware of the "Michurinian science."[80] Eventually, Hamide was invited to the Third Congress of the Fatherland Front, where she even delivered a speech in front of Chervenkov. Hamide explained that 9 September brought freedom to the entire Bulgarian people and to "women Mohammedans of the Rhodope region." As she explained, "our" women (she did not use the word *Muslim*) were free to work, learn, attend meetings, visit cinemas and theatres, and "elevate themselves to be equal to other women." In this short story, Hamide represented a new generation of Muslim women who fully participated in the socialist project and enjoyed all its benefits. They were hard-working and ready to learn. However, even in this story, where the heroine is a Muslim woman from a small village in southern Bulgaria, Muslim women were patronized and subjugated in relation to non-Muslim women. Supposedly, despite all these successes, there was still a long way to go in terms of "socialist elevation" before Muslim women would be equal to their "more advanced" sisters. Even when Hamide's speech was printed in *ZHenata dnes*, it was printed as the last one after those of two non-Muslim women.[81] Finally, Muslim women's success mattered only when men from the village approved of their work, and ultimately when the party leader applauded them.

Muslim women in Bulgaria who grew tobacco were particularly targeted to join the cooperatives. Stories were published about successful Muslim women who had found real happiness and recognition for their work once they had joined. Such texts did not attack their religion, and often the only connection to their Muslim background was their names. Nevertheless, even if hard-working Muslim women were the heroes of such stories, it was usually men who had to approve their work and acknowledge their success, and who were generally in a position of power.[82]

It is often impossible to determine whether these stories were fictional. They still served the purpose of mobilizing readers and activists, telling them what was expected of them. Narratives of successful Muslim women served to legitimate the regime's policies. The new, unveiled socialist women from Muslim backgrounds were presented as embodying the success brought by socialist modernism and gender equality in the countryside. They were supposed to demonstrate the contrast with the old social order. Thanks to the "caring state" led by the party, they developed welfare policies and actively fought against "backward" traditions: the new Muslim woman was able to live the socialist dream. However, that dream depended on socialist men, be it the party leader, or as one photograph from a *ZHenata dnes* article on the role of female collective farmers vividly depicted – a man reading the party newspapers to a group of women on a collective farm in Plovdiv. The man was in the centre around the gathered women, and according to the photo description, he was explaining the decree about the upcoming tasks for the autumn, and about the organizational, economic, and political strengthening of the TKZS.[83] The women wore headscarves and traditional clothing but were all unveiled. However, if the system failed to produce enough kindergartens, job opportunities, or protections from daily aggression and harassment, one could imagine that these women had very few options for complaints.

In practice, collectivization, industrialization, and the accompanying urbanization brought visible changes to rural communities. In his study of a Pomak community of Breznitsa, Darakchi shows that many women found jobs in the newly opened factories. Yet these changes challenged the patriarchal order only to a certain degree, as newly employed women remained the only people who took care of the children and household chores, besides active participation in agricultural activities.[84] The same was true in the Yugoslav countryside, where the household's gender dynamic was often not changed in women's favour. As Sternadori argues with regard to Bulgaria, and the same was the case for Yugoslavia, women were encouraged to feel and act as if they were fully equal to men, through financial and labour independence. At the same time, this did not mean that broader patriarchal structures were really shaken, with ideas about women as wives and mothers remaining equally strong.[85] Taken together, the expectations placed on Muslim women were similar to those placed on all other women – to become tireless fighters for socialism through their labour and their "correct" political stances. The difference was that because of the paternalizing understanding present, directed at Muslim communities, the communist leaders had lower expectations of Muslim women and expected them to lag behind or to never catch up due to their religious and cultural backgrounds.

High Politics: A Man's Playground

The legal transformation of Yugoslavia and Bulgaria and women's enfranchisement did not mean that more Muslim women would be able to participate in politics. The highest-level political posts were closed even to non-Muslim women. For example, for years, the Yugoslav Communist Party did not have a single woman in the politburo, while the Bulgarian Communist Party had only Tsola Dragoycheva. Women who made it to the Central Committee were those who had been active communists before the war, and only these select few held ministerial posts. In the Yugoslav case, these were Vida Tomšič, Spasenija Babović, Anka Berus, Mitra Mitrović, and Vera Aceva, but none of them made the most important political or economic decisions. Nor were any of them from a Muslim background. Both parties ruled through a very hierarchical system, massively dominated by men. Generally, women were sidelined, given the remit of dealing with social and labour issues,[86] and in Yugoslavia it would take another generation of women communists to penetrate the top of the party's hierarchy in the late 1960s and 1970s.

Despite this exclusion, the party was keen to gain support from Muslim women and to show that they participated in political processes from the early days. After all, such support was important to show the correctness of the party's decisions, particularly as Muslim women were considered to be "the most backward" and "the most downtrodden." If Muslim women were voting or being elected, this would mean that the party had managed to overcome their "backwardness" and include them in the socialist project. The space for some political activities on the part of Muslim women was open, but the limits for vertical mobility were much stricter than for non-Muslim women. By analysing the communist press, one can observe how this political space was constructed. It defined Muslim women as important, but ultimately only as an auxiliary political force.

No Muslim women found their way to the candidate list at the first Yugoslav elections in late 1945, but the communist press invested a lot of effort in showing that Muslim women voted in large numbers. After all, these elections for the constitutional assembly were supposed to change the structure of the entire state and its relation to the Muslim communities. The AFŽ's magazine for Bosnia, *Nova žena*, featured several articles and numerous short interviews with Muslim women from Sarajevo who voted for the party. In an extensive report from the polling stations, one article notably played with religion and traditions to show massive support for Tito and his politics. Muslim women were named and quoted, saying that some devoted prayers to Tito every night. Others were mentioned for using religious and Turkish phrases to bless the elections. Reports also claimed that some Muslim women came to polling stations despite being old and ill, and many Muslim women said that they decided to vote in order to pay respect to their dead sons and daughters. Some voted despite being illiterate, while often not understanding the election process. Since most of the population was illiterate, the voting was done by placing stones, walnuts, or balls in boxes. One older woman asked for thirty balls so she could put them all in Tito's box. Other women, supposedly, publicly exclaimed that they were voting for Tito. Many came to vote veiled, thanked "dear Allah" for the opportunity to vote for Tito, and for the opportunity to vote for the first time in their lives. Religion was also used when the article explained that many Muslim women called on Allah to protect Tito and give him good health. Even veiling was used to show a strong desire to support the party. In some of the more impoverished villages, Muslim women lent one another a veil when going to vote. Finally, one of the reports claimed that a 112-year-old Muslim woman insisted on being brought to the polling station to vote for Tito. Among these stories, there were pictures of veiled women walking in columns to the polling stations, carrying flags and slogans.[87] Since the opposition boycotted the election because of intimidation, only the communist-led People's Front participated and won. Nevertheless, this mobilization of Muslim people was repeated at all later elections. Yet it would take some time for the party to have Muslim women as candidates for higher-level posts.

In the early socialist Yugoslav period, the AFŽ played a prominent role in engaging women for various political, economic, and social campaigns. The AFŽ had a very similar hierarchy to the party. A closed circle of women actively led it before the war, supported by the various AFŽ federal and republic committees. Muslim women struggled to climb this hierarchy, and they were often relegated to work only on issues related to their communities. At every AFŽ Congress, Muslim women would talk only about other Muslim women. For example, at the first AFŽ Congress in 1945, a Muslim woman from Sarajevo, Dšehavija Nidžić, talked about Muslim women's illiteracy, the need for education, and the need for Muslim women to "breath fresh air," in a reference to the veils.[88] This pattern was repeated at the Second Congress in 1948 when a delegate from Kosovo, Bia Vokši, called for the unveiling, promising that they "will try to create new women from the women in Kosovo, especially from the Albanian women."[89] None of these women talked about broader political issues discussed at the congresses, and they were not elected to the top AFŽ institutions.

Muslim women talking at the congresses certainly exercised political agency. They internalized the party's modernizing messages and policies, and spread it further to their communities. They came under the political spotlight, even if only briefly and in a very controlled setting. Women's magazines printed their speeches, and one can assume that this was all a transformative experience, even though it uncovered the limits of political mobility via the party's women's section. Furthermore, some of them, like Safeta Nimani at the Fourth AFŽ Congress in 1954, conveyed a message that rallied against domestic violence, the undervaluation of women's work, and the patriarchy that existed in both men and women's consciousness. She used terms such as "bonds" and "slavery," calling for struggle against "backward customs" and for more women to participate in public life.[90]

In practice, the Yugoslav political sphere was almost entirely dominated by men. Some Muslim women managed to create significant political careers for themselves but they were a rarity. They climbed through various party and state institutions at the republic and federal level, and the Yugoslav federal structure meant that countless federal, republic, regional, and party institutions needed at least some women to fill posts and show that the party cared about women's representation. Furthermore, Yugoslav communist parliamentarism consisted of an ever-growing number of parliaments, and their ever-decreasing influence. Taken together, there were over thirty federal and republic parliaments by the mid-1960s, and yet the number of women remained low. The Yugoslav political structure was huge, with about 3,400 parliamentarians at federal or republic level in 1969. Yet there were only 272 women in all these parliaments. At the local level the situation was not much better, as out of 40,791 members of the municipal assemblies, only 2,821 were women. Montenegro is a good example of the slow inclusion of women in higher-level politics, since that republic was considered to be more conservative, and it had a significant Muslim population. The first women parliamentarians were all from non-Muslim backgrounds, and they never held presidential positions on any committee. They were usually members of the education, the social policy and public health committees. The number of women parliamentarians passed 5 per cent only after 1963, when the parliament expanded to consist of five parliaments. The republic-level parliaments consisted of five councils, including the Educational and Cultural Council, and the Social Health Council, a place where most of the women were elected, with women representatives totalling 30 per cent of this council. The number of women was lowest on the Economic Council, and there were no women in the presidency. After a peak that saw women representatives comprising just under 16 per cent of all representatives, the number of women in the Montenegrin parliament actually decreased to under 5 per cent again in 1969, and rarely again reached double digits during the period of Yugoslav socialism.[91] The situation in the federal parliament was only slightly better, with women totalling just under 8 per cent of all representatives, and in the Bosnian (5 per cent) and Macedonian (6 per cent) parliaments.[92] The situation had only slightly improved by the late 1980s, with the number of women in federal and republic parliaments usually sitting somewhere between 15 and 17 per cent.[93] The party itself also had a federal structure, which meant that there were central and other committees for the six republics and two autonomous regions. Nevertheless, women's representation was often low at about 20 per cent, while Muslim women were even less present.[94]

These numbers demonstrate the degree of women's exclusion from politics, while Muslim women had an even narrower space for progression than non-Muslim women. When Muslim women climbed the hierarchy, it was usually through a strong career in education or health. Didara Dukagjini Djordjević is a good example of such mobility. She unveiled after the war, completed AFŽ courses, and started working in a school. She was able to teach in both Albanian and Serbo-Croatian, and she slowly climbed the hierarchy as an active AFŽ member. She completed her degree in Belgrade, and then another in Skopje, and remained active in the party's women's organizations after the AFŽ dissolution. She was often tasked with visiting Albanian villages and with working on education campaigns there. Eventually, in 1968, she became a member of the federal parliament, serving for five years.[95] During all these years, Didara's work was in the field of education and social policy, and she was able to act as a bridge between the local Albanian communities and the higher-level party structures. Didara's career path was very rare.

The existence of the AFŽ, or its less powerful successor organizations, such as the decentralized Alliance of Female Societies, did not help Muslim women's political position. However, throughout its existence, the AFŽ invested a lot of effort in health campaigns, literacy courses, and other educational training in which many Muslim women participated. As discussed previously, illiteracy levels were highest in areas such as Kosovo, Bosnia, and Macedonia, where the majority-Muslim population lived, and its reduction was one of the long-lasting successes of the party and its women's section. These campaigns, however, were often tied to unveiling campaigns, as discussed in the next chapter. The abolition of the AFŽ meant that women lost a space for social activities, which in many villages was the only public space in which they had participated. Internal reports show a dissatisfaction present among many women, aware that they had lost not only reading groups or protected social spaces, and that men in the People's Front were far from interested in retaining the women's spaces and in fostering their interests.[96] The same political processes were occurring in Bulgaria, with the separate female organization that merged into the broader Fatherland Front. The reasoning behind this decision was also the same, claiming that in socialism there was no longer a need for a separate social and political organization for women. In Yugoslavia this practically destroyed women's organizing at the local level, while in Bulgaria women's activities gained traction.[97]

Yugoslav men from Muslim backgrounds had a much easier progression path into politics than women. Some, like Džemal Bijedić, reached heights unprecedented in other European countries by becoming the federal prime minister in 1971. Bijedić was a prominent Bosnian pre-war communist, and his family was an old Muslim family in Mostar. He served as prime minister for six years until he died in a plane crash. Bijedić's funeral was the first televised Muslim state funeral in Yugoslavia.[98] Men like Bijedić could utilize Yugoslav political structures – with their countless parliaments and assemblies – and the party's institutions easier than women. As discussed in the last chapter of this book, these men still had to put the party first, above all other identities and loyalties. Nevertheless, their number and power meant that interests of Muslim men were more represented and protected than in Bulgaria.

Bulgarian communists had more ambitious plans to include women in political structures, although the number of women from Muslim backgrounds that forged political careers in Bulgaria was very small throughout the socialist period. In the first Bulgarian post-war elections for local authorities, the BKP planned to have between 20 and 30 per cent of their candidate list made up of women, although this percentage was attained in less than half of all districts. The final results showed that about 16 per cent of all elected candidates were women. They also aimed to have Turkish women on their list and managed to recruit about a dozen. Yordan Mantarliev has also published data showing that the turnout rate in Muslim areas was very high, with both men and women enthusiastically voting. However, in the local elections for people's councillors in 1949, just over 5.5 per cent were Turks. These elections were heavily controlled by the BKP, and the choice was only fictitious.[99]

The politburo decided to open party schools for the Turkish minority in 1951. It aimed to recruit them for two of the three-month courses in Haskovo and Kolarovgrad, and for other party schools. The courses were supposed to be in Turkish. The politburo also directed the local party committees, including the Zhenotdels, to try to recruit loyal Turks. At the same time, they ordered the party district committees to check all members of the party organization to uncover foreign and enemy elements in the party.[100] The agitprop department was instructed to translate crucial texts such as *History of the Bolshevik Party – the Short Course* into Turkish, and the biographies of Lenin, Stalin, and Dimitrov, and translations of the most important decisions made by the party's Central Committee.[101] These efforts were relatively successful, as Georgi Burnaski shows that about a thousand Muslim women joined the party, and about 3,500 Turkish men.[102]

In the early 1950s, the Bulgarian press made an effort to promote Turkish women who were stepping into politics or activism. These texts always insisted on the transformative process that the party or its leader had instigated for a woman from a common background. For example, an article from 1952 followed Asie Mehmedova, a mother of four from Dobruja, who received an invitation to a peace congress in Sofia. Upon arrival, she was a shy Muslim woman who was used to wearing her veil and shalvari, but she was transformed by Chervenkov's presence in a large hall. When Mehmedova joined the crowd to shout out Chervenkov's name, she also became mesmerized by Stalin's portrait above them all. Thanks to these two figures, she chose to remove her veil, and she learned new things. She made a promise to Stalin's portrait that she would return to her village, gather everyone, and go door to door if necessary, telling everyone to live collectively and not allow a new war. After her personal transformation, Asie was expected to carry the party message further.[103] This article was not the end of Mehmedova's press presence. Alongside other women from the congress, she was photographed for the front page of *ZHenata dnes*. Her face was visible, but she wore a traditional long headscarf and was the only woman without a modern costume, even though some of them were also from Muslim backgrounds. Importantly, this photograph was featured immediately after the front cover, which had Stalin's image spread over it. In Stalinist Bulgaria, Muslim women were represented during this imagined transformation process. Their dress was slightly transformed, but not fully discarded.[104] Nevertheless, even such rare representations of Muslim dress disappeared after Bulgaria moved towards de-Stalinization and changed its policies towards the Muslim minorities, shifting towards assimilation rather than transformation.

In practice, both Bulgarian Muslim women and men had a hard time climbing the political hierarchy. The lack of federal structures meant that Muslims in Bulgaria had fewer political posts that they could climb. Even becoming a local deputy in the cities or villages proved hard, and often there were no Muslim women at all.[105] Burnaski shows that even Muslim women who completed the party schools and courses were usually blocked from progressing their political careers, often ending up as delegates of the district organizations and rarely participating in more than one or two local congresses. Only the most extraordinary women, such as Myusein Yuseinova Dorgudova, progressed further to become members of the parliament. However, even during her career, when she was appointed chairperson of the Front's district committee, she was in charge of a committee that worked with women. Only a handful of other women managed to reach these posts.[106]

Burnaski also offered important data on the representation of Turks in the Bulgarian parliament, showing that in the 1960s there were five women members of parliament, and as many as seven in the 1970s and 1980s. Many of these women served multiple mandates.[107] Although this number was small amid the four hundred parliamentarians in total, it was still more than in socialist Yugoslavia. The number of all women in the Bulgarian parliament and the local assemblies was constantly higher than in Yugoslavia, and it reached about 21 per cent at the end of the socialist period.[108] Women's representation from other backgrounds was also never equal to men in the party hierarchy, but with women totalling about 30 per cent of its ranks, the BKP still fared better than their Yugoslav counterparts.[109]

Limits on women's political engagements came from the top of the party leadership in both Bulgaria and Yugoslavia. This limit related to the idea of the imagined social hierarchy that disadvantaged Muslim women, but also to views on women's role in society in general. Womanhood was always tied to motherhood, and not to having a shining political career. Both communist parties always insisted that women should have children, even when the newspapers aimed at women exclaimed that there was a growing number of female workers, including the leaders of various brigades in factories and collective farms, directors, scientists, and administrators.[110] In Yugoslavia, the limits to women's social and political engagements were quickly established in the first years after the Second World War. Tito himself reminded the AFŽ activists at their congress that having children was also "socially useful work," and that women with many children were also working towards building socialism. He also reminded the AFŽ delegates not to forget their duties towards the home and family.[111] Bulgarian political leaders sent the same message, but as this chapter has shown,[112] there was a heavy bias against Muslim families with many children. At the First Congress of the BNZhS, Georgi Dimitrov announced that women must be the strongest agitators for the nationwide cause, with their "motherly, sisterly, and patriotic love."[113] It was up to the women, as a separate group, to show that they are the force behind the new socialist government. Women were called on to be not only builders of socialism but also mothers. As Marcheva shows, Dimitrov insisted on a rapid increase in the population and tried to build a cult of motherhood for women who would be loyal to the new socialist state.[114]

The discourse that was imposed on the BNZhS was also very similar to the discourse that Tito imposed onto the AFŽ. The alliance was supposed to provide a political and civic education for women, and to contribute to women's cultural and everyday elevation. The BNZhS forced all previous feminist organizations to merge with them or disappear, and it quickly set up an organization that resembled the party at the local and national levels.[115] The Bulgarian National Women's Alliance was dissolved, and the party organized the Committee of Democratic Bulgarian Women (Komitet na demokratichnite balgarski zheni, KDBZ) as part of the Fatherland Front. The committee permitted even less social mobility for Muslim women than the party had. The organization was firmly ruled by Dragoycheva and other prewar communists, who used the organization to influence politics, but also to have a platform to travel abroad as part of the Women's International Democratic Federation. Recently, there have been scholarly attempts to revalue this organization, and to show that it was a voice for women within the party, somehow separated from it, and even independent.[116] This interpretation would mean that socialist women who engaged in the women's section did not believe in party politics and only used them for their own agenda. Not only is such a stance ahistorical, but there is not a single historical source that can confirm it. The idea that socialist women just used Marxist language to justify certain programs is unfair towards these activists. At the same time, Valiavicharska shows that socialist women active in these organizations did not advance the interests of Turkish, Pomak, Roma, and other minority women. Instead, they also orientalized Muslim women, the Ottoman past, and their religion, converging with the official narratives of the party and state.[117]

A close examination of roles at the KDBZ shows that Muslim women did not even have a secondary role in some of the numerous subcommittees.[118] The organization served as a playground for non-Muslim women, in which they could exert influence and occasionally discuss work among Turkish women.[119] Turkish women did not create these policies, but were rather the objects of interventions, and were occasionally allowed to speak at meetings, to support the dominant agenda.

The way the KDBZ envisioned work among Turkish women is also telling. They suggested that every level of the party should appoint a person responsible for working among Turkish women. This would start with the Central Committee, and it would go down to the party cells with Turkish populations and the Fatherland Front. Only at the lowest level of the Fatherland Front did local committees try to recruit Turkish women themselves. The material for political and educational work was supposed to be created by the agitprop group, in line with women's "level, way of life, tradition, and customs."[120] There was no mention of the advanced literature that the agitprop group prepared for Turkish men. Instead, the document that planned work among Turkish women was more concerned about all Turkish villages getting doctors and teachers who would transform them through their work with mothers and children.[121]

The Fatherland Front was instructed to create more female sections, and indeed organized separate meetings for Turkish women in the early 1950s. They would gather notable farmers, shock workers, and activists to discuss ongoing tasks and the spread of socialism among the Turkish population. The press emphasized that many of these women had participated in a political event for the first time, discarding their veils – those "symbols of slavery, ignorance, and religious fanaticism."[122] Instead, they happily reported that white headscarves now covered only their hair. The delegates talked about the new government's successes, such as the new hospitals and kindergartens, education, and literacy courses. Mehmedova delivered one more speech that explained how collective farms were saving the country. Other women talked about their unveiling and cultural "elevation," promising to bring this to the entire population.[123]

The Fatherland Front also organized courses for women activists from Muslim backgrounds. These courses often focused on household economics and new relations in the family. Brunnbauer shows that thousands of young Muslim women completed such training, which in fact entrenched a traditional division of labour by teaching Muslim women how to organize their households in a "modern" way.[124] It is not surprising that such courses did not educate a new generation of Muslim women who would engage in Bulgarian politics. Furthermore, the Fatherland Front's activities among Muslim women also turned towards assimilation from the 1960s onwards, with lectures attacking Islamic rituals and promoting the Bulgarian ethnicity of Muslims.[125] As Nazarska argues, the language used by the Front and KDBZ often emphasized phrases such as "Bulgarian Mohammedan women" and "Bulgarian women who have adopted the Mohammedan faith."[126]

Finally, just like their Soviet mentors, Yugoslav and Bulgarian communist women were fierce anti-feminists. Their anti-feminism went beyond simple rhetoric, as numerous women who were feminists suffered serious consequences or were sidelined. For example, Marcheva considered the case of Dimitrana Ivanova, an old president of the Bulgarian Female Alliance who was arrested for four months after the war, was barred from practising law, and was then expelled from the journalist society.[127] In Yugoslavia, being accused of feminism could be an additional charge for women to be sent to prison in early socialism, while warnings against "feminist deviation" were always present in the leaders' speeches and publications.[128] It took decades for a genuine feminist movement to reappear in Yugoslavia, without much connection with women socialist leadership. Women spearheading that movement were mostly secular, left-leaning scholars and activists from major cities of Yugoslavia.[129]

This chapter has shown that the examined communist regimes invested a lot of effort in bringing Muslim women and men into the socialist projects. This entailed accepting the new legal transformation, embracing new educational and work opportunities, and being loyal to the Communist Party. Muslim populations were called upon to use their new-found equality, and to use individual opportunities to transform their own communities, which were deemed backward.

Paid labour was one of the most important means for achieving personal and community emancipation, and the state paid much attention to fostering new socialist identities attached to work. The way this was attempted was identical in Yugoslavia and Bulgaria, with the media being used to showcase exemplary Muslim women and men – people who had broken with traditional norms and brought *modernity* into their lives.

The regimes also launched massive campaigns to eradicate illiteracy, which heavily affected all Muslim communities in the Balkans. Muslim women extensively participated in crash courses in literacy, which often had a strong ideological component. Once the regimes had stabilized, they also reformed regular education. Muslim girls received elementary schooling in non-segregated, secular classrooms. Despite the numerous challenges and community resistance, many Muslim women managed to use this schooling, continuing it further and making a career for themselves.

Finally, the new labour and educational opportunities did not translate into more Muslim women pursuing careers in politics. The political sphere remained heavily dominated by men, with Muslim women struggling to climb not only the party hierarchies but also the hierarchies of countless parliaments, assemblies, and local councils. When they succeeded in these hierarchies, they were often pushed into dealing with other Muslim women, or into working on committees that dealt with education and social policies.

Chapter Five

Unveiling and Redressing of Muslim Women

On International Women's Day in 1928, *Pravda* published a letter from Clara Zetkin to the women of the "peripheral" Soviet republics. The Bolshevik unveiling campaign in Central Asia was underway, and by that time, Zetkin not only represented communists in the German Reichstag but was also one of the most influential people in the Comintern leadership, as she was part of the Comintern Executive Committee and Presidium. Zetkin opened the letter with praise for Soviet laws and institutions that enabled women's emancipation, and she mentioned opportunities for equal work, studies, and legal rights. While listing Soviet achievements, such as new schools and universities, Zetkin explained to these "peripheral" women that Soviet law prevented women from "being traded like sheep" and also stopped the practice of polygamy. Finally, she celebrated unveiled women and framed the unveiling in terms of the struggle for freedom, and she called for international sisterhood and solidarity.[1] Every word in Zetkin's letter revealed stereotypes about Central Asian women and a prevalent centre–periphery hierarchy in which the centre established policies with no contribution from the women targeted by these policies. Even as Zetkin seemingly gave agency to Central Asian women and called on them to fight for their freedom, that agency was acceptable only if in line with the imagined road towards a brighter socialist future. Her understanding of Central Asian societies was superficial at best, yet her discourse on the needs of local woman formed the mainstream in political and intellectual circles. Once such a discourse informed practice, Central Asian women had to find a way of adapting to campaigns coming from Moscow and find the best possible strategy to negotiate them; for unveiling, this proved difficult for many.

This chapter turns attention to the unveiling campaigns in Soviet Central Asia, Yugoslavia, and Bulgaria. It shows that the methods employed by the Soviets were readily used by communists in the Balkans decades later. The unveiling campaigns were imagined as a collective effort in which an individual was transformed, bringing the community to the imaginary level of socialist modernity. The unveiling campaigns were violent and never considered the positions of targeted women. The Soviets launched their unveiling campaign in the mid-1920s once the regime felt more secure in Central Asia and ready to launch an assault on traditional society. This resulted in a backlash and violence. The Yugoslav communists were the most successful in their unveiling program; they banned the veils and eradicated them, even in the countryside. The Bulgarian communists were slower; the unveiling campaigns dragged on for many years, often due to poor party support in remote areas. Nevertheless, the Bulgarian communists' approach was no less violent. This chapter shows that the women targeted suffered from both communists and their own communities. In the Soviet Union, many were murdered, raped, and bullied. In Yugoslavia and Bulgaria, Muslims were equally under pressure, although the level of communal violence was directed more outwards. The targeted women eventually adapted to the situation by altering their clothes and bodily practices in all these cases.

Global Discourse

A negative, orientalizing discourse on veils, and on Muslim women's position in society, the family, and gender relations, was not a socialist novelty. When Bolsheviks started writing about these issues in the early 1920s, images of backward and enslaved Muslim women already occupied the imagination of the press, political discourse, and academic literature in Europe. For example, a negative discourse on veils was omnipresent in the writings of British and French colonizers, and this affected how colonized societies saw themselves too. Leila Ahmed points to the debates on veiling that arose in the late nineteenth century in the era of British imperialism; she suggests that these debates would give rise to the early twentieth century's unveiling movement across Muslim societies.[2] Joan Scott has discussed how, in the same period when French women had no political rights, an imperial discourse of the "barbaric" mistreatment of "native" women conflated race and religion in the figure of the Arab Muslim. Muslim women were placed at the centre of a debate about "civilizational inferiority," and the "civilizing mission" was justified as a means of elevating Arab and Muslim women's status, which was portrayed as degraded in contrast to French women.[3] By the late nineteenth century, the narrative of Islam as degrading to women was well established, and the veil was presented as the symbol of that degradation and inferiority.[4] This narrative lasted throughout the twentieth century, and, as Neil MacMaster has demonstrated, the veil came to symbolize either support for or opposition to Islamic values in Algeria.[5]

As this study has shown so far, the Bolshevik discourse was equally Othering, and it resembled colonial discourses. There were, however, key differences in actions and intents. Pan-European ideas about veils as symbols of enslavement circulated, to which the Bolsheviks added a Marxist discourse of class struggle. They expected local populations to become Bolsheviks and Marxists at the end of the liberation process. Bolsheviks from Moscow established a clear power hierarchy through which they operated; in theory, however, policies towards Muslim populations were supposed to eliminate differences rather than perpetuate them. Moscow was the centre where the leadership assembled and where policies were crafted. These policies were then disseminated everywhere else through the networks of state and party institutions. In that sense, as Adrienne Edgar has also pointed out, since the Soviet state seemed alien to many Central Asians, the situation was similar to the colonized countries of North Africa and the Middle East. Yet colonial rulers did little to change the laws and veiling practices, and few were interested in mobilizing and educating women. Edgar shows that the patronizing colonial discourse negatively affected women's education in these places, and they were all fields in which Soviet Central Asian republics made significant advances.[6]

Marianne Kamp and Adrienne Edgar also argue that even though there were colonial components to the Bolshevik rhetoric, it actually resembled that of the more typical modernizing Muslim states of that time.[7] They examined state-led modernizing and unveiling campaigns in Turkey, Iran, and Afghanistan, and demonstrated the drive to impose reforms in education and women's dress codes. In all these reform cases, the idea was to create citizens out of women, but as Edgar demonstrates, none of these countries aimed to make women equal to men in terms of all rights. Edgar also posited that these were the main reasons why reforms were passed more easily in Muslim countries, while there was resistance to the aggressive Soviet polices pursued during the Hujum era, which is discussed later in this chapter.[8]

Negative discourses on veils were also very much present in Kemalist Turkey and drove reforms of dress practices alongside nationalist discourse. The Bolsheviks carefully followed the Kemalist reforms; this even alarmed local Zhenotdel activists when certain female teachers in Tashkent praised the Turkish reforms in women's emancipation. The Bolsheviks could not afford to be upstaged on this issue.[9] The impacts of Kemalism were even more significant in the Balkans in the interwar period, and as Anđelko Vlašić reveals, there was a lot of media interest in Yugoslavia about the status of Turkish women. While Yugoslav women were legally, politically, and socially disempowered, Turkish women acquired the right to vote, to the envy of the Yugoslav feminist press.[10] Kemalist reforms also polarized the Yugoslav Muslim communities, as they split them in half between those who supported such reforms and those who vehemently opposed them. The Bulgarian press also regularly reported on reforms and unveiling of Turkish women.[11] Even though the reforms were not enacted in interwar Yugoslavia and Bulgaria, Kemalist Turkey was a strong centre whose policies were carefully followed. After the war, however, Yugoslav communists came to lean on Soviet solutions and neglected any connections with Turkey. The same was the case in Bulgaria, which took a more hostile stance with Turkey being their NATO neighbour, and Kemalism considered a threat to the Bulgarian socialist state.[12] Instead, both Yugoslav and Bulgarian communists drew inspiration from Soviet experiences in Central Asia, as interpreted through the censored Moscow lenses.

The Soviet Hujum and Resistance

In the previous chapters, I discussed how the new Central Asian states' success was measured in terms of women's emancipation and women's participation in political and economic activities. According to Shirin Akiner, the campaign for the emancipation of Central Asian women was a strategic priority "from the earliest days of Soviet rule."[13] In his book *The Surrogate Proletariat*, Gregory Massell argues that, when faced with the lack of a native proletariat in Central Asia, the Soviet government turned to women as the group they perceived to be the most oppressed section of Central Asian society in order to mobilize their subversive potential and garner support for the new Soviet state.[14] Following Massell's argument, Akiner claims that the act of creating a surrogate proletariat was not only a political imperative but also marked by a genuine concern for the conditions of women's lives and the necessity of drawing women into economic production.[15]

Several interventions into the norms of Central Asian communities occurred prior to unveiling. As Keller asserts, they could all be categorized in two major areas – "freeing women from Muslim social and religious structures" and moving women into the agricultural and industrial workforce.[16] As discussed in previous chapters, the first point of intervention was at the legal level. Soviet laws in Central Asia differed slightly with each republic, but they were based on the same foundational principles. Changes were gradual until the mid-1920s, when the situation in the country as a whole stabilized. The Bolsheviks did not abolish sharia courts immediately, and they remained in operation in the early years of Soviet rule. The legal transformation was profound, however, and laws were passed between 1921 and 1923 that banned polygamy, the payment of kalym, and underage marriage. New Soviet laws set the minimum age for marriage as eighteen for men and sixteen for women, which challenged existing practices.[17] Civil marriage and the possibility of divorce were also new, and many Muslim people took up this opportunity. However, as Keller notes, many women who brought charges against violent men faced great difficulties in getting any support from their families and communities. From 1926 to 1927, Uzbekistan also included "social crimes" in the penal code, which included targeting the payment of a bride price, and forcing women to marry against their will.[18]

The new Soviet laws had their limits regarding what they could change in practice. *Kommunistka* was full of instructions to activists on how to fight for the Bolshevik social order, but many articles also lamented the inability of Soviet power to impose their own laws. Ljubimova and other leading Zhenotdel activists repeatedly warned that they had no evidence that old customs had ceased to exist, or that they had been replaced by Bolshevik laws and a Bolshevik way of life.[19] Keller writes that even the outlawing of polygamy in Turkmenistan proved to be a contested issue, as the party was too weak and support for polygamy too strong. She notes that polygamy was not banned in Uzbekistan until 1931. Furthermore, certain practices, including polygamy, were popular among party members as well. During these years, the legal codes were modified to criminalize the prevention of women from participating in society, such as through girls not going to school.[20]

Other Bolshevik interventions also had limited success in the early 1920s. For example, Bolsheviks attempted to include more women in education and in labour activities. In theory, new secular schools were opened to all, and parents were encouraged to send girls to schools as well. In practice, many girls were barred from education by their community. Furthermore, the school network was insufficiently developed, leaving many areas without any schools, and there were shortages of local teachers in general. The Bolsheviks invested a lot of effort in remedying these issues, but female illiteracy was improving only slowly.[21] Women were also called upon to enter new socialist industries, and many did make use of these new opportunities. But as the country was recovering from the wars, with a socialist economy, new opportunities for women were few and far between. Zhenotdel activists often complained that land reforms and socialist agriculture meant little for women when Soviet power was not strong enough to break the old norms that disenfranchised them. Job opportunities in industry or trades were even harder to obtain, although the party and the press used any opportunity to promote women who made successful careers for themselves. This issue was even more important because of the idea that women's engagement in organized production was the main precondition for socialist emancipation.[22] Muslim women were, therefore, targeted out of a genuine – although very paternalizing – belief that they needed to be emancipated, while the emancipation campaign was one of the primary weapons against Islam as a whole. Keller argues that the Bolsheviks never passed up a chance to declare that Islam must be eliminated because it oppressed women. Yet such rhetoric was also used to generate rifts and divisions within the community.[23] Zhenotdel activists regularly blamed the clergy for all the failures in their political campaigns. Yet in the mid-1920s, they still advised their local women's sections against direct and forceful methods of work and anti-religious propaganda, as such methods supposedly harmed their work's reputation and efficiency.[24]

While gradually introducing new legislation and waging war on the clergy, the Bolsheviks fostered a very negative discourse on veils from the very beginning of their rule. As in the case of legal transformation to improve women's rights, and in advocating for women's employment and education, the Zhenotdel was the most vocal organization on the topic of Muslim women's unveiling. The Zhenotdel leadership considered veils – in all their forms – to be not only signs of backwardness but also a physical barrier to women's participation in new socialist life.[25] Veils supposedly hindered women's ability to participate in the economy, while the goal was to create a mobile and loyal population in which women would have economic independence from men.[26] More than that, Adrienne Edgar observes, the Soviet discourse on women's emancipation in Central Asia used veils as a potent symbol of women's oppression and Muslim backwardness, and as a convenient target of emancipation work.[27] Another reason was that veils did not simply disappear after the revolution, and local women did not became such a revolutionary force as initially presented.[28] Instead, veils occupied the imagination of Bolshevik activists over the following two decades.

The paranja and chachvon, however, were not worn universally across Central Asia. What the Soviets considered full veiling was practised primarily in urban areas of territories that became delineated as Uzbekistan and Tajikistan in the 1920s by settled populations who self-identified as Uzbek, Tajik, Sart, Turk, Jewish, and, to a lesser extent, Tatar. Full veiling was also practised in settled rural areas but mainly among the wealthy. Full veiling in a paranja and chachvon was not practised by the nomadic populations of what became Turkmenistan, Kyrgyzstan, and Kazakhstan.[29] Nevertheless, the Bolshevik press would often confuse these different local practices, and activists would follow policies on women's dress crafted in Moscow, with little to no nuances.

The Zhenotdel did have a solid network of offices in Central Asia, which it developed as soon as the new Soviet state established control. The organization opened clubs that offered women "a range of medical, legal and educational services."[30] Despite these developments, the Zhenotdel in Central Asia was led by Serafima Ljubimova under the umbrella of Sredazburo.[31] Many of their activists came from the European parts and brought with them Eurocentric notions of what was modern, and what was backward. Within this patronizing approach, local activists often struggled to climb the organization's hierarchy, while the Zhenotdel's magazine, *Kommunistka*, struggled to define the situation in Central Asian societies. It orientalized and blamed them, tried to place them in a more general discussion of capitalist exploitation and imperial colonialism, and sometimes did all of the above.[32] Activists were initially told to ground their work in "the working element" among women. They tried to bring women into the new trade unions, which indicates how detached the Moscow organizers were from the reality of Central Asian women.[33] Ljubimova also often lacked nuanced views of Central Asian societies, or she was at the very least unable to reconcile the local situation with the messages Moscow desired. For example, Keller suggests that when Ljubimova insisted on women entering the workforce, she implied Western assumptions and ignored how seclusion was associated with wealth, status, and virtuous modesty in Uzbek society.[34]

Initial unveiling attempts by Zhenotdel activists were sporadic and focused on trying to persuade women to lift their veils once they had contacts with the new Soviet state. *Pravda, Kommunistka,* and other publications lauded women who unveiled, while local party cells were told to encourage such women's promotion within the party or state apparatus. These women were expected to become agitators themselves, and to hold public speeches in support of new policies.[35] Most Zhenotdel activities were centred around the 8 March (International Women's Day), when they would gather more resources and at least some attention from male party members. Women would usually gather at mass public meetings, read resolutions, organize rallies, and some would also publicly unveil. Nevertheless, it became apparent – from the early days of Soviet rule – that Zhenotdel priorities regarding unveiling were not shared universally among the male party members.[36]

These initial unveiling efforts had very limited effects. Zhenotdel activists impacted only a small number of women, and even the wives and daughters of party members continued to wear their veils. The frequency of appeals to these men to be exemplary communists demonstrated the Zhenotdel's powerlessness to change cultural norms. Zhenotdel magazines were full of criticisms of local communists for displaying Soviet ideals only in public, while at home they stuck to traditions and forced women to cover.[37] Zhenotdel activists also reported that unveiling impoverished women was an easier task than unveiling the wives of party functionaries. In some cases, they even reported party officials who sent fake wives to unveil publicly while actually ignoring the party orders.[38]

It seems that the Zhenotdel was more successful when they had the resources to organize women's clubs at which women could gather, receive medical consultations, and learn new skills. Some of the women visiting clubs would occasionally unveil, but they would also be exposed to more Soviet ideas, and would have at least some benefits from the Soviet state. Women's clubs were an important novelty in the region; they were places where women could socialize, learn, and build networks. Women's clubs, however, were far from available to everyone, and were usually located in more urban areas.[39]

Once the regime had stabilized its power more, the Bolsheviks opted for a more radical approach to attacking the veils and traditional clothing practices, with a set of policies that became known as the Hujum (assault). The Hujum was launched on International Women's Day in 1927, amid public rallies and unveiling events. The Bolsheviks tried to make unveiling as public as possible, which would demonstrate the power of the party and entice other women to unveil. The first wave targeted primarily cities of Uzbekistan where the wearing of the paranja and chachvon was most commonly practised. The first mass public unveiling took place in Tashkent on 8 March. According to Akiner, "The organisation and preparatory propaganda work was delegated to specially constituted regional party committees, but the overall strategy continued to be formulated and directed by the central authorities."[40] Kamp observed that unveiling was a ritual act with personal and political significance for the women involved. According to Kamp, the gender subversion present in public unveiling ceremonies was a declaration of loyalty to the state and the Communist Party. She considered these unveilings and the backlash they produced as "the crucible within which women became Uzbek citizens."[41] The number of local women who actively supported Soviet policies was small, but Kamp convincingly argues that their actions contributed considerably to social change and the eventual decline of veiling.[42]

Once the Hujum started, the Moscow-based *Pravda* was surprisingly silent on the issue. The feature article on 8 March mentioned only that female workers must march forwards and lead the way for "backward" women of the East,[43] while the longer article addressed working women in capitalist countries.[44] Aleksandra Artyukhina, the then leader of the Zhenotdel, published a long article focused on women's labour and elections to various Soviets, while the article featured a picture of "three sisters" – three communist women from Russia, Uzbekistan, and Kyrgyzstan.[45] Only the following day, buried among other news from the Soviet republics, *Pravda* reported that some women in Uzbekistan had lifted their veils and asked the Uzbek Central Executive Committee to ban the paranja.[46] *Pravda* actually devoted more space to unveiled women only a few years later, with the ascent of Stalinism.

As the paranja came to symbolize the Hujum, much of the research on the Hujum has focused on Uzbekistan, where it was most prevalent. The Hujum campaign incited turmoil. It challenged the boundaries of Soviet authority to transform local societies, and also presented a quandary for numerous Uzbek women. Shoshanna Keller contends that Uzbek women who sought to partake in the initiative were torn between adhering to government mandates and remaining faithful to their families, communities, and traditions. The personal aspirations of these women were also important, and they saw opportunities emerging. Their agency must also be acknowledged.[47] In this context, significant societal resistance, which could be construed as opposition to Soviet colonialism, was present, but it was neither unified nor all-encompassing. Women's interests were multifaceted as well. For instance, the Hujum spurred the ulema to preach against unveiling. Furthermore, efforts targeting women were often led by mullahs' wives to adhere to segregation norms.[48]

The Hujum incited violence against women who chose to unveil or participate in activities associated with the Soviet emancipation campaign. Scholars such as Douglas Northrop, Marianne Kamp, and others have highlighted the widespread rape and murder of Uzbek women, often perpetrated by their own family members or their husband's family. This wave of violence persisted for several years.[49] Soviet attempts to transform Central Asian societies and challenge men's roles in families and communities frequently served as a unifying force. *Kommunistka* reported on fierce resistance in the Tashkent region, which resulted in activities ceasing because of cases of the murder and raping of unveiled women shortly after the campaign started.[50] Northrop posited that in

Uzbekistan, veiling was primarily linked to the urban and upper-class populations, but the Hujum transformed it into a symbol of men's resistance and Uzbek identity. He also suggested that the assault on veiling contributed to the spread of veiling practices in rural areas. Marianne Kamp, however, demonstrated that the complexity of unveiling as a unifying element runs even deeper. Unveiling was not entirely foreign to Central Asia, as pre-Soviet Muslim reformist traditions such as the Jadids already existed. Kamp revealed that disagreements among Uzbeks about unveiling were prevalent, and Uzbeks existed who advocated for unveiling without being members of the Soviet foreign elite. It was these people who the party aimed to win over to communicate with Uzbeks and translate ideas from the Moscow centre to the Central Asian periphery.[51]

The Hujum had a widespread impact across Central Asia; it even affected areas where veiling was not a common practice. In these regions, Soviet activists targeted specific customs, especially those related to marriage, and they positioned the Hujum as a comprehensive assault on the traditional social order.[52] In Turkmenistan, where face veiling was uncommon, *byt* (way of life) crimes took on increased significance as key components of the Hujum. Edgar contended that the absence of veiling made the Zhenotdel's mission to emancipate women more challenging. First, some believed that since Turkmen women did not veil, they were less oppressed, and so their emancipation was deemed less urgent. Second, without the conspicuous symbol and target that veiling represented in Uzbek and Tajik areas, organizing a campaign proved more difficult. Edgar's work also uncovered how the emancipation campaign was influenced by local factors in various Central Asian republics and occasionally led to a practice being outlawed in one region while remaining legal in another. Edgar argues that the lack of veiling, which Soviets identified as a symbol of women's oppression, allowed indigenous communists in Turkmenistan to resist top-down pressures to transform gender relations and family life more effectively than in neighbouring Uzbekistan. For instance, Turkmenistan initially refrained from banning bride wealth and imposed greater restrictions on divorce than Uzbekistan. Edgar asserted that "by framing the veil as the consummate symbol of female oppression, Zhenotdel activists had undermined their ability to be advocates for Muslim women who did not wear the veil."[53]

Assessing the extent to which Bolsheviks and international revolutionaries were cognizant of the nuances surrounding the Hujum is challenging. *Pravda* reported on the campaign's resistance using the typical rhetoric of wealthy elites and clergy attempting to keep the masses oppressed,[54] but occasionally acknowledged that the resistance ran deeper, admitting that even party members upheld the old social order by, for example, having multiple wives.[55] *Kommunistka* received more localized reports from Zhenotdel activists and frequently wrote about resistance. It attributed blame to local religious leaders, men, and even party members for insufficiently promoting the cause. The paper was also aware of the fact that many women who unveiled ultimately re-veiled because of pressure from their local communities.[56] Confronted with this resistance, Arthyukina even reported that not only were rank-and-file communists unsupportive, but they also re-veiled their wives while assaulting other unveiled women.[57] Despite being aware of this resistance and of the struggles faced by local women, neither the party nor the Zhenotdel leadership ever questioned the correctness of the unveiling campaign. Instead, they expressed disappointment that the movement did not receive more robust support from specific groups.

Despite the terror inflicted upon women by men, not only did the Soviet state fail to protect them, but Soviet courts also fell short in delivering justice afterwards. Keller notes that the Commissariat of Justice did not categorize acts against women's liberation, including murders and rapes, as counter-revolutionary crimes, and instead left them to local courts to handle. These courts often demonstrated leniency, and many men who killed women were never even brought to trial.[58] Regarding resistance, women who re-veiled after a public unveiling were frequently pressured by their own communities with threats of violence. Kamp asserted that the widespread violence, killings, and rapes perpetrated by Muslim men should not be viewed as a form of resistance against the Soviet state, but rather as an attempt to (re-)establish gender hierarchy. Women were punished for violating patriarchal norms. In this sense, women who re-veiled were pragmatically trying to survive. They resisted the party in the same way that women who unveiled resisted the communities that threatened them.[59]

Another challenge for the Zhenotdel was that the party did not ban wearing the veil, opting instead to focus on propaganda efforts and both direct and indirect coercion. Demands for a ban persisted throughout the period, and often originated from activists working in the field who encountered resistance from communities. The People's Commissariat of Justice opposed a legal ban and interpreted veiling as an everyday habit. Discussions also took place regarding whether veils should be prohibited in schools and other public institutions, as locations that were certainly easier to regulate.[60] Those advocating for the ban argued that the veil should be prohibited because of its detrimental impact on women's health and on girls' physical development. They also maintained that women could not unveil themselves, as they feared murder or disgrace from their husbands and relatives.[61] Over the following years, *Kommunistka* featured more articles in which local activists urged the party to take legal action. Even Ljubimova contended that a decree was necessary to safeguard the campaign's accomplishments by protecting unveiled women. She also believed that the ban would create an atmosphere of empathy and support for local women, while identifying those against unveiling as enemies.[62] Nadezhda Krupskaja also joined the debate but argued against a law that could incite further resistance and "fanaticism." Instead, she advocated for more economic measures to encourage unveiling rather than an outright ban.[63] The debate continued for years, but veils were never legally banned. The Moscow centre remained resolute that change would come through the campaign and "persuasion," rather than through legal measures.[64]

By 1929, widespread resistance contributed to the party's decision to scale back the Hujum, although the party's efforts towards women's emancipation and an end to violence against women did not cease entirely. Forced unveiling campaigns became less prominent in the 1930s, even as the Soviet Union pursued radical social transformations through collectivization and industrialization. Through both of these ambitious projects, the Soviet state aimed to alter and Bolshevize the targeted communities. As Keller argues, veiling continued to be viewed as oppressive, but collective farm work or employment in a factory was now considered the most effective means for women's liberation. Moreover, she suggested that collectivization and industrialization brought more changes to the lives of people of all genders than all the previous efforts undertaken by the Zhenotdel and party activists.[65] Collectivization and industrialization were so vast in scale that no community was left untouched. Stalinism penetrated areas that Bolshevik power had struggled to reach. Large population movements, repression, and the annihilation of entire groups of people meant that organized local resistance to any policy was not only more difficult, but often impossible, and it could result in death. Kamp demonstrated that women still suffered; she cited archival material indicating that women were still "occasionally murdered by their families for unveiling or activism in 1930 and 1931," although at a lower frequency than in previous years.[66]

Although the aggressive unveiling campaign was abandoned, the Stalinist transformation of society as a whole led to more radical changes. Unveiling was conducted via the surveillance of party members and then of wider society. Douglas Northrop argues that in the late 1920s and 1930s, gender relations within families were significant indicators of someone's loyalty, and were often crucial for surviving Stalinist purges. Party members were particularly at risk if they engaged in bride price practices, polygamy, or underage marriages. The unveiling of their family members was also monitored.[67] While veils were not officially banned, other practices were made illegal. For instance, a legal reform in Uzbekistan led to people being prosecuted for bride price, polygamy, or underage marriage as *byt* (way of life) crimes. In this sense, Northrop suggested that the Hujum persisted for decades and attacked customs through various, often indirect means.[68]

The violence of the Stalinist regime, along with the expansion of collective farms and women's agricultural labour, resulted in a much higher number of women unveiling than during the original Hujum. Women's employment rose rapidly throughout the 1930s. Kamp also highlighted that the ever-expanding network of collective farms resulted in more schooling and new pressures to send girls to secular schools in which veiling was not allowed.[69] The all-encompassing nature of Stalinism penetrated the homes of communities previously resistant to the party. *Pravda*, adopting a new militant Stalinist style, featured more articles about successful Central Asian women than ever before. Women collective farmers were now leading farms, setting new productivity norms, and breaking old stereotypes about women's labour. Unveiled women were learning new skills, gaining professional qualifications, and becoming happier every day while writing exalted letters to Stalin.[70] International revolutionaries were taking note.

The Yugoslav Unveiling Campaign

The Yugoslav communists' approach towards the issue of women's veiling bore a striking similarity to the Hujum, and it was embedded within the sweeping Stalinist societal transformation. The backbone of this campaign was the network of AFŽ activists who led the initiative. Mimicking the rhetoric used to denounce veiling and advocate for unveiling, they also orchestrated public unveiling events using the same tactics as Bolsheviks. This unveiling campaign, however, unfolded alongside Yugoslavia's industrialization and collectivization processes, with the local modernist Islamic Religious Community (Islamska vjerska zajednica, IVZ) extending their support to the Yugoslav communists. One significant departure from Soviet arrangements was the further step taken by the Yugoslav communists – they outright banned the veil when the initial campaigns did not yield the desired results. The profound influence of Stalinism in Yugoslavia was underscored by these events occurring *after* the Yugoslav-Soviet split of 1948. This highlighted the pervasive nature of Stalinist ideology, which endured even amid geo-political tensions.

The Yugoslav communists held a firm belief that the practice of veiling was incompatible with the principles of a socialist society. Interestingly, as revealed in chapter 2, during the Second World War, they used veils pragmatically for protection. In the initial elections of 1945, they reported on veiled women participating in the voting process, viewing the veils as a curiosity while simultaneously highlighting that even veiled women were supporters of the party. Not long after, more articles underscored the suffering that veils inflicted on Muslim women.[71] The AFŽ press was at the forefront of critiques against veiling, and they exhibited no awareness of nuance in their portrayal of different local veiling practices. They indiscriminately labelled all traditional face coverings in identical terms and did not acknowledge any variations.

AFŽ congresses and gatherings served as platforms on which the negative discourse on veils became firmly established and was later disseminated through a myriad of women's magazines. At the First Congress of the AFŽ in 1945, a Muslim woman from Bosnia depicted veils as a "black rug." She cautioned against "reactionaries" intent on confining women to the domestic sphere and enforcing veiling.[72] Another Muslim woman from Sarajevo equated unveiling with the liberty to breathe freely, and she also promoted a collective effort to promote literacy among Muslim women.[73] Later, regional AFŽ conferences were organized in each republic with a Muslim population. Efforts were made to include Turkish and Albanian women, who expressed their thoughts on unveiling at the Congress of the Macedonian AFŽ, at which they also offered their gratitude to Tito "for leading their peoples to victory."[74] The narrative remained consistent across these meetings. The AFŽ leaders would invite a select few Muslim women to share personal accounts of their unveiling, and they would then insist on community efforts to encourage the same. These women seldom ventured into discussions of broader issues, unlike the AFŽ leaders, who all came from non-Muslim backgrounds. For example, Alija Morina from Kosovo and Metohija shared her experience; she applauded local *hodžas* for supporting unveiling, an initiative that resulted in over 20,000 women casting off their veils. The AFŽ magazine underscored how the visiting Soviet comrades at the congress enthusiastically applauded Muslim women who chose to unveil during the congress. As the Soviet visitors spoke, the AFŽ activists rose and fervently invoked "Generalissimus Stalin."[75]

Initial endeavours to persuade Muslim women to unveil were far from triumphant. Yugoslav activists employed tactics that mirrored those of their more experienced Soviet counterparts. They attempted to convince women to remove their veils during rallies, conferences, and meetings. The campaign, which gained momentum in 1946, became a primary focus for the AFŽ in 1947 after their Second Congress. The congress issued a resolution against veils. It described them as symbols of a harsh past and indicators of women's unequal status. For the AFŽ leadership, veils were barriers that prevented women from engaging in the social, political, and economic life of the nation. Activists were charged with implementing this mandate, with the promise of support being extended to Muslim women contemplating unveiling.[76]

The methods deployed were strikingly consistent across the country, with variations arising only from the creativity of local activists. Commonly, activists would deliver speeches and reiterate the notion that veils represented darkness and oppression, and they encouraged women to embrace the future. Activists ventured into villages, arranged public rallies, and even visited people's homes.[77] Some local activists showcased greater creativity and strove to secure backing from local religious leaders.[78] Others curated lectures on topics likely to pique the interest of Muslim women, such as health and child-rearing, and they used these as incentives to encourage Muslim women's participation in meetings.

The AFŽ encountered significant difficulties in understanding the reality that the initial campaigns to encourage unveiling had been less successful than anticipated. Their reports greatly exaggerated the figures, which were in contrast to an abundance of grievances from local activists struggling to convince women. These activists acknowledged that women would choose to re-veil as soon as the activists had departed from their village. The AFŽ's official 1947 report made claims of progress in Bosnia's unveiling movement, and they also noted that 24,675 women in Kosovo had chosen to lift their veils. The report further claimed that Albanian women called persistently for legislation to ban the veil; this demand originated from the AFŽ conference in Peć.[79] Spasenija Babović reiterated this figure in her congress speech, touting it as "the strongest example how the people's government truly elevates and brings into the country's public life even the most backward masses."[80] But during closed-door meetings, activists conceded that the unveiling movement was not widely popular in any republic. An additional challenge in Kosovo and Macedonia was that most activists had a Slavic background, and there was a severe shortage of individuals fluent in Albanian.[81] Internal reports from the Bosnian AFŽ also expressed frustration over the "considerable resistance" displayed by Muslim women who had previously been affiliated with the AFŽ. This resistance was attributed to "religious fanaticism, cultural backwardness, and, frequently, the wishes of husbands."[82] Women who formed the focus of these campaigns told the activists that they did not feel adequately protected at unveiling events.

The reality on the ground did not mirror the rhetoric of the AFŽ speeches at congresses, and the situation even prompted criticism from Avdo Humo, a high-ranking Bosnian politician. Humo argued that the act of unveiling represented "a revolutionary shift in Muslim women's lives," but conceded that progress had stalled after the initial AFŽ campaign. His critique was not directed at the campaigns or methods per se, but rather at their lack of potency in driving fundamental change.[83] Failures were ascribed to the perceived "limited cultural level" of Muslim women, and the attitudes of their communities. Yet the underlying issues were considerably more profound and paralleled those found in the Soviet case. When attending local AFŽ conferences, Muslim women cautioned that unveiling could be successfully accomplished only if men – brothers or husbands – were involved in the process.[84]

Some men, particularly those within the IVZ's leadership, voiced support for the unveiling movement (figure 5.1). In his inaugural address as the IVZ's reis-ul-ulema, Ibrahim Fejić emphasized the importance of "modernizing Muslim women." He articulated that this necessity stemmed from Islamic teachings that confer upon women the same rights and responsibilities as men. Fejić maintained that, even within the framework of sharia law, women were entitled to fulfil all public duties, sign contracts, manage businesses, take care of older people and the disadvantaged, and even defend the country in times of need. Women also bore the responsibility for raising children alongside all of the above. Fejić contended that women could effectively perform these multifaceted roles only if they were well educated and free of veiling. He argued that obliging women to wear the veil, while simultaneously providing them with equal legal rights to men, would be deeply unjust and hypocritical. To strengthen his stance, he referenced the Qur'an and the viewpoints of various international Islamic scholars.[85] The government also convened a conference of ulema who lent their support to the cause of unveiling.

The AFŽ, however, continued to encounter significant resistance. During the AFŽ plenum in September 1948, the high-ranking AFŽ official Ljubomirka Tomić disclosed that out of 50,000 Muslim women in Macedonia, only 1,592 had chosen to discard their veils. In the southern Serbian district of Bujanovac, a mere 10 out of 28,000 women chose to unveil, while in eleven districts in Kosovo, out of 40,000 Albanian women, 5,473 opted to unveil, but 4,196 later decided to veil again. The AFŽ levelled blame at the People's Front and Youth Organization for

Figure 5.1. In 1947, Sulejman Kemura, director of Waqf and later reis-ul-ulema, called on Muslim women to unveil

Source: Archives of Yugoslavia, f. 215 SSOJ.

their lack of participation in the campaign. They accused them of making no efforts to deter young women from taking up the veil. Tomić further noted that in Bosnia, the number of young women choosing to start wearing the veil exceeded those who decided to unveil. Activists also reported that some women working in factories would unveil while on the job, but would then choose to wear veils again upon returning home.[86]

By late 1948, the AFŽ had started to recognize that public campaigns and declarations were not always the most effective approach. They acknowledged in their publication that numerous women had chosen to veil again, and that even some AFŽ activists, otherwise committed to the cause, remained veiled. Nevertheless, they faced difficulties in finding innovative methods of engagement. Instead, they proposed more reading groups (incorporating literature examples from the Soviet Union), community volunteer work, and extended assistance for women who had unveiled.[87] The AFŽ continued to arrange conferences, pass resolutions, and make declarations. They endeavoured to persuade Muslim women to unveil, but with minimal backing from other party organizations.[88] Their strategies proved inadequate in dealing with the feedback their activists received: that women frequently reverted to veiling due to societal pressures, and that attempts to unveil women during public lectures and conferences led to women boycotting these events out of fear of being coerced into unveiling. What was particularly disconcerting for the AFŽ was the fact that even local party members did not encourage or permit their family members to unveil.[89] The calls from the IVZ leadership did not prove persuasive for many.

As the campaign trudged along with limited success, calls to ban the veil grew louder. Debates over introducing a law to ban the veil commenced in 1946. Reports often suggested that local women advocated such a law, asserting that it would offer them added protection. In April 1946, a group of local Albanian women from Kosovo, along with Fazil Hodža, a Kosovo representative in the Serbian parliament, put forth one such proposal. While the parliament declined to pass the proposed law, the president of the parliament, Blagoje Nešković, articulated the government's endorsement of unveiling. He extended "moral support to Muslim women in Kosovo and Metohija" and admonished those hindering women from unveiling. Instead of enacting a law, the Serbian parliament issued a resolution of support.[90]

By 1950, it had become apparent that the campaigns conducted solely by the AFŽ lacked the clout to yield significant results in the unveiling movement. The government had already launched its comprehensive collectivization program, in addition to the five-year industrialization plan announced in 1947. As in the Soviet Union, society as a whole was mobilized for these projects, and few communities were left unaffected. With the government's interventions proceeding at full tilt on multiple fronts, the issue of veiling became a focal point. In the autumn of 1950, the press mobilized the voices of various Muslim women's groups that called for a law to ban veils.[91] The reis-ul-ulema, Ibrahim Fejić, also endorsed the ban, articulating his support in both modernist and religious terms.[92] This media campaign served as a precursor to the legislation that would outlaw the wearing of veils. This law was to be implemented in each republic individually, although the wording was uniform. The law was initially announced in Bosnia, and later in other republics with Muslim populations.

The law's preamble outlined the rationale behind the veil ban, claiming it aimed "to eliminate the age-old symbol of dependence and backwardness of Muslim women, and facilitate the full use of rights secured through the People's Liberation Struggle and the construction of socialism in this country, and to ensure complete equality and more extensive participation in the social, cultural, and economic life of the country."[93] Those who persisted in wearing a veil faced penalties of up to three months in prison or a substantial fine. The law applied not only to women but also to family members exerting pressure on them to wear a veil, or compelling them to do so. If a man coerced a woman into wearing a veil through force, intimidation, or blackmail, the punishment was two years of corrective labour or an even larger monetary fine.

The press widely reported on the law. Veils were portrayed as symbols of humiliation and backwardness, remnants of religious prejudices that had historically inhibited Muslim women's participation in public life, and signs of the most abhorrent forms of subjugation.[94] The IVZ also expressed their support, and in their bulletin, they published views staunchly in favour of the law and the unveiling process, which they considered essential for achieving gender equality and putting an end to segregation.[95] Artists, too, were mobilized and enlisted to assist the unveiling movement. For example, their poetry was featured in handbooks for agitators, presumably to be used in local newspapers. The Macedonian writer Vančo Nikoleski penned a poem denouncing veils, which he likened to chains and a darkness that obscured one's face, life, sun, and personal freedom. He implored his "Turkish sisters" to dismantle harmful customs, to learn to read and pursue science, and to struggle for their lives.[96]

The unveiling campaign was no longer solely reliant on the AFŽ activists' zeal, as other organizations such as the People's Youth of Yugoslavia and the People's Front were also compelled to respond. All party cells were mobilized as well. Party secretaries were provided with guidance that favoured persuasion over punishment, although the secretaries of larger political units held meetings with the police and devised "tactics" for dealing with women who resisted unveiling. Džemal Bijedić was particularly insistent on preventing excessive force and the humiliation of Muslim women. He also cautioned activists to exercise particular patience with the mothers of fallen Partisans, recommending that experienced communists personally converse with them.[97]

Once the law was publicly promoted and both the political and police apparatus were mobilized, the campaign was prompt and comprehensive, across the entire country. The youth organization faced heavy criticism for deliberately neglecting Muslim women, often driven by personal interests in "not unveiling their wives." It was only after an "energetic intervention" from the party that the youth organization incorporated unveiling into its annual plan.[98] The youth organization was directed to establish more flexible criteria for Muslim girls, and to arrange more home-based courses, reading groups, and casual meetings. In practice, however, they found it challenging to engage many young Muslims, which they frequently attributed to a conservative parental influence.

The attitudes of young men towards women did not aid the cause either, with the youth organization often resembling a boys' club.[99] Simultaneously, a health campaign was initiated, with a focus on Kosovo's Muslim-majority areas.[100] The government mobilized health care professionals, the Red Cross, students, and the AFŽ, forming teams that visited villages and screened nearly the entire population. Activists arranged lectures, organized travelling exhibitions on health, and completed activities such as house painting and educational courses on healthy cooking and child hygiene. The Ministry of Health also organized vaccinations, with activists notably encouraging women to undergo gynaecological examinations. The health campaign also served as a tool to monitor unveiling, as activists were granted access to homes without prior permission under the guise of health.[101]

The legislation on veiling marked the beginning of a comprehensive assault on traditional ways of life. In certain locales, such as the Montenegrin town of Bijelo Polje, activists went to extreme lengths. They demolished tall fences and the gates of private Muslim homes, broadened streets that extended into formerly secluded yards, and even enlarged the windows of old houses. For the activists, Muslim women had previously been "like ghosts, only permitted to venture outside under the cover of darkness in their veils," but now they and their children could enjoy fresh air and sunshine. Activists also relished being able to observe families at home to ensure the absence of domestic violence. They reported witnessing happy family relationships with portraits of Tito adorning the walls.[102] These numerous examples often juxtaposed "primitive" Ottoman customs with modern ways of living. As one journalist noted upon entering the home of an unveiled woman in Skopje, one room still bore traces of old Ottoman decor, while the other was "completely westernized."[103]

Analysing resistance in this case is challenging. It requires a nuanced reading between the lines and a critical analysis of documents to glimpse opposition by women whose voices were not recorded by surviving sources. Nevertheless, party organizations and activists expressed concerns for years that women were not venturing outside after being coerced into unveiling. Reports from across the country echoed the same issue, and at times women simply did not have suitable outdoor clothing once they had abandoned their veils, a revelation that both highlighted the level of poverty and revealed a socialist misunderstanding of the practice of veiling.[104] The veils gradually vanished from Yugoslav streets, although occasional resistance was still reported as late as January 1954, eliciting calls for government intervention.[105] Gradually, many women adapted by wearing headscarves, while the government shifted its focus to other priorities, primarily to incorporating Muslim communities into universal health care and education.[106]

Unveiling and Redressing in Bulgaria

The Bulgarian discourse on veils bore similarities to the Soviet and Yugoslav cases and also included a continuity that dated back to the pre-communist era. The Bulgarian discourse frequently depicted veils as vestiges of a gloomy Ottoman history. Scholars like Neuburger and Nahodilova have argued that this stems from specific forms of Orientalism. Neuburger contended that Bulgarians forged their own conceptions of masculinity, femininity, and nationalism through their interactions with Muslim communities.[107] The Bulgarian socialist press expanded on already established notions; it wrapped them up in Marxist rhetoric and framed the veil as a symbol of subjugation and enslavement for women – a recurring motif found in various contexts and analysed in this book.[108]

The Bulgarian discourse, however, had a slight difference in that it often underscored the "beauty" of Muslim women, more so than in Yugoslavia. *ZHenata dnes* regularly published pieces about beautiful Turkish women who had discarded their veils, frequently implying that their beauty should be the primary incentive for unveiling. Furthermore, researchers like Nahodilova have highlighted how the politics of communist aesthetics were used to illustrate the correlation between beauty and the emancipatory and modernizing aspects of communism, all embedded within an Orientalist discourse.[109] These elements were absent from Yugoslav discussions, which instead concentrated on the impracticality of veils for work and potential health hazards. This probably stems from unveiling starting earlier in Yugoslavia, when middle-class beauty norms had not yet permeated the press as they had by the mid-1950s. As Nahodilova aptly puts it, "The veils of 'Pomak' women were from point of view of communist atheism politically incorrect, from point of view of emancipation doctrine not ethical and from the point of view of the 'civilizing process' aimed at individualization not aesthetical."[110]

In practice, the Bulgarian redressing process was considerably lengthier than the Yugoslav one, primarily because of the Bulgarian Communist Party's weaker influence in rural areas compared with their Yugoslav equivalents. For instance, even in the summer of 1948, the Kardzhali region's secret service lamented their lack of sway among the Pomaks and their inability to challenge religious leaders.[111] Yet by 1948, the Yugoslav communists maintained strict control over all religious activities. Bulgarian attempts at unveiling also commenced slightly later, with one of their earliest measures to address veiling being the implementation of "passportization," which obligated citizens to carry photo identification. This policy stipulated that women must be photographed without veils, which led to considerable opposition. Secret service agents reported on this issue. They attributed the resistance to foreign influences and advocated the use of more propaganda and the potential engagement of female photographers to capture images of women with headscarves in such a way that their faces would be visible. Despite these attempts, the process uncovered a profound distrust between the authorities and the Muslim communities, with policies being enforced and implemented without Muslim women being involved or having any input.[112]

Resistance to photographing women and issuing passports occasionally escalated to violence, with incidents alarming the top echelons of the party. In the Pomak village of Valkosel, a collective of women disrupted a gathering and assaulted a party member who arrived with a team of photographers. Roughly twenty women resorted to using sticks and stones, which compelled the party member and his crew to seek shelter in a restaurant. Similar incidents occurred when women uncovered attempts to photograph them in private residences. This led to further confrontations and women charging into houses to assault party members. One party member ultimately sustained a knife injury to his leg. In response, the party arranged a substantial delegation, which included regional party dignitaries, the chairwoman of the women's organization, and three *hodzhas*, to pacify the situation. Only then were they able to photograph approximately one hundred women, while those identified as leaders of the resistance were arrested.[113]

Nevertheless, the party members' difficulties were far from concluded, as confidential, top-secret reports revealed that protests linked to unveiling emerged in numerous areas populated by Pomak and Turkish communities. Women were at the vanguard of these protests. At times their numbers swelled into the hundreds, and they threw stones at the windows of local government buildings. They primarily protested against being compelled to identify as Turks and being forced to pose for photographs without veils. Local party functionaries retaliated with heightened repression. They attempted to restrict villagers from leaving the village or going to work without passports, from purchasing flour and other commodities, and from using public wells. Ultimately, they intruded into homes to inspect passports. Those without passports were given a two-day deadline to procure them and cautioned not to venture outside their homes without them. Heavy fines were later imposed on those people still without passports.[114]

In the late 1950s, the Bulgarian Communist Party continued their campaign to challenge traditional female garments as part of their broader "cultural revolution." With de-Stalinization underway, and feeling increasingly secure in their power, the party aimed to enforce a modernist agenda with "unveiling" (*razferedzhavane*) a pivotal aspect. This term frequently included the modification of traditional attire, such as the shalvari, *shamii*, or fez for men.[115] The dichotomy of modern versus traditional lay at the heart of the party's messaging and was propagated through media and public conversation. Artistic production was also harnessed to bolster this agenda. For instance, a painting by Elza Goeva, *A Teacher in the Village*, illustrated a young woman, dressed in a stylish skirt and jacket with a book tucked under her arm, striding confidently through the village. Children trail behind her while four veiled Muslim women gaze at her with insecurity. Two gossip behind her back as the teacher walks forwards. The corresponding article in *ZHenata dnes* was even more direct, clarifying for readers that this woman was a youthful, dynamic teacher who arrived in a remote Rhodope village and succeeded in "weeding out the ignorance ingrained in the souls of the people in that secluded village" by sharing her knowledge, experience, and faith in life with the eager and curious children.[116] With the children at her side, she steers them away from the influence of the veiled women. The painting and the article depict the traditional attire and indigenous lifestyle of Muslim women as a "weed" or "darnel" (*plevel*) that the young teacher intends to uproot and eliminate. The secondary message is that the older women, steadfast in their attire, may be apprehensive, but the young boy and girl accompanying the teacher are also venturing down a new path. Finally, beside this picture in the magazine, and linked to the analysis in chapter 3 regarding pro-natalist policies, was a painting titled *Maternal Glory*. It celebrated a mother with a medal for bearing numerous children, but the family depicted in the painting is neither veiled nor Muslim.[117]

These seemingly banal images in fact lay at the heart of the Bulgarian communists' concept of modernity and backwardness. As Neuburger articulated, Bulgaria, "insecurely teetering on the edge of the continent, went to extreme lengths to express its Marxist modernity in European terms, which by definition necessitated a negation of Bulgaria's five centuries under Ottoman rule."[118] Savova-Mahon Borden posits that communists, in theory, aspired to improve the lives of everyone loyal to communist ideals. This also implied the eradication of differences, or what communists perceived as differences associated with specific communities.[119] The unveiling campaign turned into an endeavour to obliterate differences and forge a uniform Bulgarian socialist nation on the one side, while the targeted communities attempted to protect tradition and lifestyle on the other, with clothing becoming a highly politicized domain.

The idea of changing everyday life was intrinsically linked with the assault on Muslim communities. As in the Soviet Union where activists initiated campaigns to transform the *byt* in Bulgaria, the idea of modifying "bitova kultura" also took hold.[120] The goal was to revamp ordinary families' everyday life and primarily bring about technological and hygienic improvements to people's homes. It was an effort to regulate and standardize everyday life and reshape the domestic sphere. In terms of altering Muslim communities' everyday life, Bulgarian publishing houses translated Soviet pamphlets, often immediately after their publication in Moscow, in addition to producing their own publications. These pamphlets called for education and the eradication of the remnants of "feudal attitudes towards women."[121] Mary Neuburger showcased how this novel concept was employed to infiltrate Muslim communities and prescribe how individuals should dress, eat, and organize their homes.[122] Nikolova and Ghodsee examined some of these programs, arguing that they were welcomed by women, although they did not investigate the imperialist nature of such initiatives. They correctly contended that women may have seen culinary or domesticity courses as an opportunity to learn something new and step outside the house, but one must question the alternative.[123]

Unveiling and redressing were the core of this concept. The unveiling campaign began by targeting the Pomak population in the late 1950s, and it expanded to encompass Turkish and other Muslim communities in the early 1960s. Scholars like Myuhtar-May have scrutinized local party documents that show detailed numbers of veiled and unveiled women, particularly among the Pomak population.[124] While the figures reported by party officials may have been exaggerated, there is evidence of traditional garments worn by all genders being aggressively targeted. In numerous smaller communities, there were heightened campaigns, and women who continued to wear veils or shalvari were harassed. These intimidations included refusing service to these women in local shops, mock trials intended to scare them, and even the application of force by special commissioners to remove traditional clothing deemed non-Bulgarian. Women who were employed could not receive their wages unless they donned Bulgarian attire, and in some villages, their veils were confiscated.[125]

Declassified documents from the secret service reveal local attempts to unveil Pomak women as early as in the late 1950s. In January of 1959, local communists in the village of Filipovo initiated a campaign to unveil women. The leader of the local collective farm distributed money and other rewards to men who unveiled their wives, which provoked further resistance from others. The secret service meticulously documented the protest organizers, particularly as some protesters travelled to Sofia to request an official explanation for the unveiling campaign from the party. They complained about the withholding of flour unless they unveiled, and questioned whether this was merely a decision taken by local leaders. At that time, they were informed that unveiling was strictly voluntary, and they forced local officials to halt the campaign.[126] This attempt at unveiling, however, was not an isolated case, as other reports show similar campaigns and resistances, with secret service agents reporting that women would rather engage in physical confrontation or commit suicide than unveil.[127] Local officials were often pressured to take action, and to serve as an example to other men and veiled women, but those loyal to other issues often resisted. Some returned the party membership, and some even hid in the forest so as not to receive the order from the party committee to unveil their wives.[128] Some Turks also tried to leverage institutional protections: they wrote to the president of the Bulgarian parliament, the party's Central Committee, and the prime minister's office. They cited Stalin's work on the national question and the Bulgarian constitution, requested a stop to forceful unveiling, and advocated gradual evolution.[129]

The voluntary nature of unveiling, even as early as in 1959, depended on local authorities and often turned into violent abuse. The secret service reported on campaigns around the town of Ardino in which the local authorities prohibited women from working when veiled, forcefully unveiled them, and barred them from visiting doctors. Men were also not allowed to work until their wives unveiled. After such resistance, the local party committee was notified and halted such practices,[130] but these early attempts in the late 1950s served as a trial run for much larger campaigns in later decades. In some villages, local communists went as far as to confiscate and burn veils.[131] Also, it is questionable whether local authorities would have attempted such measures were they not encouraged by the central authorities. It is more likely that the higher party levels reacted when the resistance were too intense, and they would have attributed the excesses to local authorities.

Myuhtar-May notes that the unveiling campaign often involved public humiliation and the mockery of Muslim women. They were denied access to essential services, such as shops, post offices, and health care, if they did not wear the approved clothing. Local committee members would enter homes, confiscate traditional clothing, and impose fines. In some instances, women were forcibly redressed in public, while entire villages were cordoned off and intimidated with firearms. Additionally, Muslim party members were pressured to inspect the homes of their subordinates and check for veils. Those whose own family members still wore veils could face expulsion from the party.[132]

Resistance to unveiling was, however, concealed in the Bulgarian press. *ZHenata dnes* reported on successes in many regions, with the number of unveiled Turks rapidly increasing. Their reports also focused on the beauty of unveiled Muslim women, as recognized by others or by themselves.[133] As they unveiled, they were also perceived to be embracing a new life, not just externally through their attire, but also internally, with a renewed, joyful life full of work opportunities. *ZHenata dnes* even went so far as to describe this as an end to slavery.[134] Occasionally, they would also turn to translated Soviet articles on successes from Central Asia to demonstrate that their approach aligned with the Soviet one, resulting in a radical transformation that would only benefit women.[135]

Over the following decade, the local population resisted and frequently reverted to traditional attire. Nahodilova argues that this entire process was perceived as oppressive and violent, with unveiled women experiencing feelings of shame and exposure.[136] Nonetheless, Muslim communities underwent change and adaptation. According to Muratova, after the unveiling campaigns of the 1960s, it became uncommon for women to wear full veils. Instead, most continued to wear shalvari trousers and headscarves. While shalvari trousers also came under scrutiny, it seems that initially the party was more focused on addressing veils.[137] The campaign against shalvari gained momentum during the 1980s when local governments issued decrees banning the wearing of shalvari in public spaces, offices, and institutions. Furthermore, those who defied the ban and continued to speak Turkish were denied service in commercial establishments and faced penalties. Despite these efforts, shalvari trousers persisted on Bulgarian streets, experiencing a revival after the regime's collapse.[138]

The unveiling campaigns conducted by the Bolsheviks in Central Asia served as both an inspiration and a model for Yugoslav and Bulgarian communists. Under the belief that they were eradicating backwardness, the Bolsheviks initiated an all-encompassing assault on veils, and this sparked significant resistance within Muslim communities. The harshest repercussions of this campaign were borne by local women, who local men murdered, attacked, and abused. The intensity of the opposition forced the Bolsheviks to temporarily retreat; however, with the advent of Stalinism and comprehensive projects such as collectivization and industrialization, along with widespread political violence primarily targeting men, veils gradually disappeared from the streets.

Yugoslav and Bulgarian communists used remarkably similar rhetoric on veils and conducted similar campaigns. But unveiling in Yugoslavia proved more successful than in Bulgaria for several reasons. The Communist Party of Yugoslavia established more solid structures within Muslim communities, especially in regions where the Partisans had strongholds during the Second World War. The federal system in Yugoslavia allowed for more significant Muslim participation at all levels of government. For example, political institutions in Bosnia, Kosovo, and other regions were populated with local Muslims, and so the system adhered to the Stalinist model of nationality policies. As a result, Muslim men in Yugoslavia had more to lose by opposing unveiling than their counterparts in Bulgaria, where Muslim men were largely excluded from political processes. Finally, Yugoslav communists likely had a more effective party organization in rural areas, while the Bulgarian unveiling campaign struggled for years. The speed of the Yugoslav unveiling campaign was crucial in preventing veils from becoming a symbol of resistance against the regime. Initial unveiling efforts in Yugoslavia were largely unsuccessful, as not many Muslim women chose to abandon their veils. In response, the Yugoslav communists implemented a ban on veils, which led to the entire state apparatus joining the campaign and the rapid disappearance of veils from Yugoslav streets until the 1990s. Muslim women became increasingly engaged in the Yugoslav socialist economy, with their identities shaped by labour and the secular Muslim nation in Bosnia, on the one hand, and global Islamic revivalism, on the other. Turks and Albanians maintained connections to their respective nations, although the former experienced significant waves of immigration, which will be discussed in the next chapter.

Because Muslims were more excluded from Bulgarian politics, there was limited genuine support for unveiling. Rather than being part of a "modern and unified socialist nation," Muslim women often organized resistance that sometimes escalated into violence, and this resulted in unveiling efforts being prolonged. In cases where the government quelled such resistance, communities under constant pressure from other policies – such as renaming – retreated inwards. This response mirrored the resistance seen in other colonial projects, where the external or material sphere was dominated by colonizers, and the internal or spiritual sphere served as a refuge for the subjugated.[139] Muratova demonstrated that the Muslim community began to lead a dual existence – one public and another private – in which they preserved their names, traditions, and clothing practices. When women were not actively rioting, they silently protested by abstaining from attending meetings organized by the party to discuss changes in women's attire. When prohibited from wearing shalvari, they opted for tracksuits or trousers with a band on the back.[140]

Gendered Interventions and Challenges to Masculinities

In the autumn of 1950, Muslim communities across socialist Yugoslavia found themselves embroiled in fervent debates and disputes over an impending law that would prohibit the wearing of veils. The issue was the talk of the streets, polarizing opinions and even leading some to attribute a recent earthquake to divine retribution for the proposed legislation. While women were at the heart of the debate, men too found themselves in the spotlight, their views ranging from endorsement to vehement opposition. Hivzija Zelihić, a modest Muslim man from Sarajevo in Bosnia, was among those ardently opposed to the change. Newspapers reported that upon hearing the official announcement of the law, he was so overcome that he fainted and fell gravely ill. These reports also painted a grim picture of his domestic life, describing his wife Elfa as having been "enslaved" to his violent tendencies for over two decades. Elfa, who was the sole breadwinner of the family, working as a cleaner to support her husband and seven children, reached her breaking point. Driven to desperation, she appealed to the People's Front for assistance, telling them that she would rather kill her husband, serve the sentence, and then be free than still be veiled. In a dramatic turn of events, Behija Krkbešić, an activist and a figure from the very beginning of this book, intervened. She visited the Zelihić household to address the issue head-on. Hivzija initially dismissed the likelihood of the law being enacted, asserting that Tito would never put his signature to such a measure. Behija countered by reminding him that Tito had fought alongside the very women who were now advocating for this law. She also cited her own transformation, having abandoned traditional veils and shalvari in favour of contemporary attire. Behija sternly warned Hivzija of the repercussions he would face if he continued to obstruct Elfa's right to unveil. Recognizing Behija's newfound authority as a member of the local government, Hivzija finally acquiesced, agreeing that Elfa could go unveiled, albeit still wearing shalvari. The intervention of the party had a profound impact; Hivzija's toxic masculinity was not only challenged but ultimately vanquished, leaving him to "retreat to his bed" to recover from this significant defeat.[1]

In this chapter, I examine how a particular discourse and a series of gendered interventions conducted by the Soviet, Yugoslav, and Bulgarian communists targeted Muslim men. I show that the communists were guided by preconceived notions about Muslim men, their families, and their communities, and that the idea of socialist modernity underpinned all these notions. The Yugoslav and Bulgarian communists had been profoundly swayed by Soviet paradigms emanating from Central Asia. They constructed narratives of Muslim backwardness within the framework of Marxist discourse, and they enacted a series of policies to force these communities to engage in the socialist endeavour. Throughout this period, Muslim men were depicted as barriers to women's access to the privileges of socialism, and they frequently clung to "backward" traditions to maintain their advantageous positions. They were further held responsible for any shortcomings in communist modernization efforts, despite the divergent and often fragmented interests present among Muslim men. Some embraced socialist initiatives with zeal, while others exhibited resistance in various forms. As this chapter clarifies, Muslim men were not exempt from scrutiny or from attempts to change their attire and bodily practices. All these cases show a keen interest in the transformation of Muslim men's clothing, with restrictions or outright bans on male circumcision imposed, and changes made to the observance of public and private religious festivities. These interventions varied in how successful they were, and they encountered formidable resistance in many instances. Ultimately, when faced with dwindling alternatives, many chose to abandon their homeland and were driven away, seeking refuge in other countries with a predominantly Muslim population.

Establishing a Narrative on Muslim Men

From Soviet Central Asia to the Balkans, but also in colonial projects,[2] Muslim societies were portrayed as timeless constructs in which men exerted complete authority over the domestic sphere and family members. As early as 1920, the Soviet women's magazine *Kommunistka* depicted "Oriental" women as entities straddling the line between human and property.[3] This publication frequently described a traditional social order in which even a young boy's voice held more sway than his mother's, while education for girls was not even considered, and women were allowed to partake in meals only after the men had eaten.[4] Recurring narratives featured the motif of the "eternal slave" woman, ensnared in a world of harems and veils, and hidden from view. These narratives were a continuation of Orientalist portrayals from Tsarist Russia, injected with a new Marxist outlook. The revolution, they claimed, was transforming these women into fighters for the communist world.[5] This discourse was rehashed repeatedly in the years immediately after the revolution, which suggested that even though the revolution had brought liberation to all, Muslim women were still being held back by their husbands and other male community members.[6] *Kommunistka* invoked images of the "fat bais and aksakals" – the elders – in a state of panic because they could no longer subjugate and abuse women. These men were also vilified for their antagonism towards women who assumed leadership roles in villages and councils.[7] Of course, the focus on women's liberation was not confined to Muslim communities – it was widespread. The key point here is that these Soviet publications fostered a straightforward narrative of "backward" Muslim societies that necessitated communist intervention. As Northop observes, this discourse held significant value for activists who saw themselves as the purveyors of modern European cultural norms,[8] or, as Michaels puts it, "Russian revolutionaries donned the mantle of brave knights coming to the rescue of exploited Central Asian women."[9]

The dominant discourse in Yugoslavia and Bulgaria before communist rule was similar to colonial narratives. Scholars have pointed out that the discourse on devout Muslim men was frequently coloured by Orientalist and prejudiced views in both these regions. Muslim men were often portrayed as being emblematic of a bygone Ottoman age, acting as patriarchal figures exerting strict control over women and standing in stark contrast to what was considered a "civilized" European identity. The Orientalist and racist lens depicted these men as unyielding relics who resisted both progress and modernity.[10] For instance, mainstream Yugoslav publications like *Vreme* used terms such as "Oriental eeriness" to describe Bairam celebrations in Skopje, adding that "fanaticism still rules and religion is turning into a caste that alienates them from the rest of the world."[11] The same article also highlighted the subordinate status of women, lamented the situation, and called for their freedom. The feminist publications from the Women's Movement also pointed out how the quest for women's emancipation was often misconstrued by many Muslim men as an affront to their personal honour and religious beliefs.[12] Notably, some Yugoslav Muslim intellectuals even internalized this discourse and used it as a foundation for advocating reforms to both men's and women's attire.[13] In the case of Bulgaria, the historian Anna Mirkova has argued that Muslim men were often portrayed as "backward" to justify land and agricultural policies that seized lands from Muslim communities. The same discourse was employed to further the state's objective of "national harmonization."[14]

The communist press was often more interested in the social and class dimensions, though they did not shy away from echoing prevailing stereotypes, especially when discussing affluent Muslims. Soviet publications inspired Yugoslav and Bulgarian communists, leading to a striking similarity in the press outputs of both communist parties in the decade after the Second World War.[15] Articles touching upon the themes of "slavery" and Muslim women's harems were occasionally directly translated from Russian and featured in the party-affiliated women's magazines in both Yugoslavia and Bulgaria.[16] Publications and public speeches that described Muslim men as the oppressors were common in both countries in early socialism. Descriptions of Muslim men's oppressive behaviours were often juxtaposed with the new regime's endeavours to integrate everyone into a socialist economy and to culturally transform communities. Women's magazines led the trend, and both Yugoslav and Bulgarian communist parties printed a myriad of articles on how Muslim men intentionally kept women in backward situations. One oft-repeated criticism was that Muslim men isolated women from public life or prohibited them from participating in socialist work.[17] Such male behaviours were commonly attributed to Islamic religious customs, and this led to the portrayal of women as victims supposedly ensnared in family dynamics deeply rooted in Islam. For example, the Yugoslav publication *Nova žena* ("New woman"), issued in Sarajevo, explained that while all women in pre-war Yugoslavia faced disenfranchisement, Muslim women bore the brunt as they were relegated to "slaves in the home and [to] outdated traditions."[18] *Naša žena* ("Our woman"), published in Montenegro, repeated these ideas many times. It stated that Albanian women were constantly separated from society, while "their entire life consisted of obedient slavery to their master, be it their father, brother, or husband."[19]

The Bulgarian publication *ZHenata dnes* echoed similar themes. It wrote about "the curtains of the dark world" that held women in utter subjugation and slavery.[20] However, the Bulgarian media often went further into stereotypes of Turkish men, whom they typically portrayed as staunch opponents of their wives' external engagements. In one story, a non-Turkish wife lamented her husband's objections to her extensive work commitments. Asked whether her spouse was Turkish, she clarified that he was Bulgarian, which led the text's author to ask in surprise, "But he does not want his wife to wander around too much?"[21] Obviously, the problem of gender inequality was pervasive across various communities and depended on many factors. Nonetheless, this inequality was widely perceived as more pronounced within Turkish communities.

The press was, after all, just repeating tropes fostered by non-Muslim women activists and politicians. Records from their assemblies and symposiums, coupled with official reports, predominantly attributed policy failures to Muslim men. Many communists in both countries struggled to understand that Muslim women may dissent from the regime or disapprove of a particular campaign, initiative, or directive. When activists encountered challenges in meeting local voluntary labour targets or in achieving sufficient female attendance at political gatherings, or when women persisted in enrolling their children in a mekteb, these behaviours were ascribed to the reactionary influence of the men to whom these women ostensibly yielded.[22] Husbands and brothers were often accused of obstructing women from participating in literacy courses and other activities organized by the AFŽ. For example, in Montenegro, the AFŽ struggled to recruit local Muslim women and urged local governments and party organizations to help persuade local men to break with "harmful customs." The AFŽ activists reported that even men who were part of the communist organizations were not "flexible" towards their wives.[23] The AFŽ's leaders consistently warned about "backward people" thwarting their initiatives, while "the enemy" disseminated "his" propaganda among Muslim women, particularly discouraging the education of young girls. Even when rural women voiced their dissent against policies like wool appropriation and other agrarian directives, their grievances were not perceived as seriously adversarial, given the fundamental interpretation of women's agency.[24] Since Muslim women were understood to be at the bottom of the imagined social hierarchy, viewed as the most oppressed group in the country, it was believed that while they could be misled into opposition, they lacked the capacity to spearhead resistance autonomously.

The historian Nurie Muratova has demonstrated that both the BNZhS and the women's committees within the Fatherland Front employed similar rhetoric, often believing their inability to engage women was due to men's opposition to women's liberation. Furthermore, Muratova claims the BNZhS did not attempt to mobilize Muslim women until 1947. It was only in the early 1950s that the party intensified its initiatives, creating compulsory courses in domestic economics and literacy. Despite the emphatic discourse on the integration of Muslim women into society, however, Muratova highlights the stark reality that scarcely a single Muslim woman ascended the party ranks in Bulgaria.[25] This suggests that the frequent attribution of blame to men was just a form of systemic gatekeeping, rather than genuinely facilitating social mobility for these women.

The narrative of Muslim men cast them as backward, perilous, and potentially antagonistic to the emergent socialist society, and so the options available to them were considerably restricted. The postwar environment made it challenging for them to maintain their prewar lifestyles, also because of the drastic legal and economic changes already tackled in this book. Muslim men were asked to embrace new conceptions of masculinity and of their role within the new state, and to shun their identity anchored in Islam in favour of one rooted in socialist labour and in proclaimed equality with women in both the public and private sphere.

Eradicating "Backwardness" at Home and in Public

The discourse on backwardness meant that Muslim communities and Muslim men had to change their daily practices. This included changes in Muslim men's behaviour at home and changes in educational institutions, workplaces, and places of worship. Moreover, it also entailed changes to their attire and to how they approached their own bodies. Just like women, men found themselves at the centre of a series of gender-specific interventions that should be viewed in the context of surveillance and one group asserting control over another. Patterns of social interventions and discussed issues were similar in the Soviet Union, Yugoslavia, and Bulgaria, albeit with local variations contingent upon the degree of party involvement. Each case also uncovers the limits of party power, particularly when interventions were conducted by outsiders to the targeted community, as was the case in Bulgaria.

Each intervention was encased in a paternalistic approach towards Muslim communities. The notion of socialist paternalism has been examined by many authors, who have generally argued that the state adopted a role reminiscent of, in the words of Lewis H. Siegelbaum, a wise, stern, but also beneficent father.[26] This form of paternalism has frequently been analysed through the perspective of the welfare state, showing that the welfare model was intrinsically linked to paid employment throughout the bloc.[27] The state's paternalism was further explored through the lens of fatherhood,[28] and the general assumption is that the state and the party assumed the traditional position of father, particularly with respect to the imagined roles of authority and protection. The concept of a paternalistic socialist state was also critiqued and challenged,[29] although I posit here that the party harboured a distinct intention to establish itself, and its (male) leader, in a very paternalistic manner towards various groups in the country, often adopting divergent strategies depending on how they interpreted a specific group's "backwardness." In this instance, the party told Muslim men that a fundamental flaw in their lifestyle existed, deemed unacceptable in socialist society, while also asserting that the party possessed the blueprint for progress.

In the previous chapter I demonstrated how communist state policies on Muslim women were characterized by party paternalism and populism, and how the policies constructed a gendered and Othering hierarchical structure of protection and care. This was also the case with the concept of family. In all three cases, the family was posited as the "fundamental cell of society," albeit under special protection of the state to ensure loyalty to socialist ideals.[30] In the case of Muslim families, this often entailed heavier state intervention because of supposedly "more backward"[31] family relations rooted in Islam. Socialists often assumed that it would be harder to influence Muslim families, reach Muslim women, and persuade Muslim men to accept supposedly different gender relations.[32]

In this setting, challenges to masculinity were manifest in complex and varied ways. The party's heavy interference and governance over familial life were ostensibly designed to destabilize men's *traditional* role as the primary guardians and breadwinners within the family structure, even though in all these instances, such notions were disconnected from the actual state of affairs even before the advent of communist rule. It is important to note that Muslim families, akin to other familial groups, were neither static nor homogeneous, even within a singular region. However, the socialist endeavour to alter personal convictions and enforce new gender roles incited profound fears among many men, a sentiment echoed both in Central Asia and the Balkans, and frequently documented by party officials as "rumours." These included stories about the party activists' plans to abduct wives, allegations of immoral conduct by women, and plans to separate children from their families, among others.[33] Essentially, the masculinity of numerous individuals found itself at a juncture, with men navigating a path through traditional roles, state expectations, and personal ideologies and identities, all while existing in a period marked by considerable uncertainty and shifting economic landscapes.

The changes Muslim men experienced were, arguably, more pronounced beyond the confines of their homes. As with men from other groups, new expectations for acceptable public conduct emerged. All children were expected to attend schools without gender segregation, and they received a secular education from teachers outside the community. Later, Muslim men were expected to engage in the labour market on an equal footing with women. As I have demonstrated in previous chapters, this change had a significant influence on many women, although the process was not free of aggression. The Soviet media frequently highlighted instances of Muslim men resisting women's inclusion in the workforce. They occasionally attempted to obstruct them, and at times surveilled their wives during work hours.[34] This pattern of behaviour was observed similarly among men in Yugoslavia and Bulgaria. Nevertheless, the extensive industrialization initiated across these regions altered the makeup of the workforce – it ushered more Muslims into socialist factories and facilitated greater control. A considerable number of women secured employment, which compelled men to acknowledge their presence. Nevertheless, numerous studies, including my own, have indicated that the workplace continued to be heavily skewed towards men, with women facing an uphill battle to overcome discriminatory practices on the shop floor.[35] As Valiavicharska also notes, gender equality under Stalinism "remained productivist and male-centric," while workplaces often tolerated sexist behaviours in all these countries.[36] During the phase of de-Stalinization, these practices often became further entrenched. Nonetheless, industrialization and new employment prospects certainly brought benefits to many Muslim men, facilitating improvements in their standard of living and helping them attain esteemed careers.

The promotion of secularism, however, also entailed overt religious practices, including public prayers, being either discouraged or curtailed. In chapter 2, I delineated the Bolshevik endeavours to curb public displays of religiosity, a phenomenon present in both Yugoslavia and Bulgaria, albeit with varying degrees of intensity. Amid the process of de-Stalinization and Yugoslavia's growing aspirations within the Non-Aligned Movement, which embraced numerous Muslim nations, Yugoslavia generally adopted a more lenient and less aggressive stance, compared with Bulgaria. From the late 1950s and notably in the 1960s, numerous Yugoslav Muslim men capitalized on the newly introduced educational opportunities and scholarships to pursue studies at religious hubs, including one in Cairo.[37] Merdjanova illustrated how, throughout the 1970s and 1980s, a significant number of mosques were refurbished and constructed, alongside improvements in religious education, notably marked by the re-establishment of the Faculty of Islamic Studies in 1977.[38] Such opportunities in Bulgaria were rarer.

All these states, however, tried to reconfigure the significance of holidays within familial life, which were fundamentally intertwined with Islam and regional traditions. In all three instances, the regime sought to pivot communal life towards communist celebrations, which were occasionally universal, such as May Day, while at times they pertained to locally significant communist milestones, like Tito's birthday or 9 September in Bulgaria. Despite a relative easing of religious oppression in the Soviet Union, described in chapter 2, Muslim festivities were, at best, overlooked and frequently suppressed. This suppression, however, did not always achieve its intended effect. Indeed, internal documents indicated that even in regions with established collective farms, individuals simply adjusted to the changing circumstances. For example, in 1951, the Council of Ministers in Moscow continued to receive internal updates regarding the observance of fasting and the celebration of Uraza Bairam (Eid al-Fitr). One informant expressed satisfaction that no women donned veils and that farmers were not observing the fast, yet they noted that a substantial assembly of devotees had packed out the mosque and extended across three hectares of the surrounding area.[39] Ultimately, as the political scientist Hélène Thibault suggested, the Soviet authorities were compelled to recognize the existence of a "parallel" Islam, covertly practised and closely associated with significant life events, such as circumcisions, weddings, and funerals.[40]

A similar scenario unfolded in Bulgaria. Scholars have previously highlighted the government's efforts to suppress celebrations like Kurban Bairam (Eid al-Adha) and Ramazan Bairam (Eid al-Fitr) in Bulgaria, with official prohibitions enacted. Nonetheless, the authorities found little reason to rejoice, as their surveys revealed that Muslims maintained a considerably higher degree of religiosity compared with the Orthodox populace, and that the newly propagated secular traditions were not widely embraced.[41] Conversely, Yugoslavia adopted a more conciliatory strategy, albeit with efforts made to confine celebrations within the precincts of mosques.[42]

Muslim men's attire came under scrutiny, with regional variations of traditional garments being labelled as backward. Northrop illustrates that in Uzbekistan, members of the Komsomol were dissuaded from wearing national attire such as khalats from the late 1930s onwards.[43] While traditional garments and headwear were not officially prohibited, there was a distinct preference for European-style suits and hats, particularly among men aspiring to prominent roles in public life. Similarly, in Yugoslavia, traditional attire and hats like the fez were frowned upon and deemed backward, albeit without formal bans. In certain locations, such as in Novi Pazar, old shops that had crafted fezzes for generations, situated along narrow Turkish-style streets, were demolished. In their place, party volunteers established expansive avenues adorned with parks and office buildings, supposed symbols of progress.[44] The press disseminated images of men in traditional attire, which they juxtaposed with narratives highlighting these men's supposed backwardness. This applied pressure through the Orientalist and racist discourse that accompanied these depictions.[45] The expectation was for the fez and turban to be replaced by contemporary hats, mirroring a broader shift in clothing styles. Men, now immersed in the new socialist lifestyle, were anticipated to "outgrow" the fez, along with old neighbourhoods (*mahale*), towering home fences, and traditional diminutive windows on their homes. As the press described vividly, in the evolving landscape marked by railways, construction sites, and factories, these elements were expected to become mere vestiges of a bygone era.[46] As with the Soviet Union, the federal structure of the Yugoslav state facilitated the political participation of numerous local Muslims, although attending official events in such "outdated" attire was unthinkable. The case in Bulgaria, where Muslims of all genders were less represented in politics, presented even greater challenges.

In Bulgaria, traditional male attire was cracked down on the most aggressively. As Neuburger shows, a long tradition existed of forcibly removing the traditional fez worn by Muslim men.[47] The fez, described as a relic of the Ottoman era, had been the focal point of numerous campaigns before the Second World War, although a period of grudging acceptance existed during the Bulgarian Stalinist era. This "tolerance," however, was marred by negative portrayals in the Bulgarian press, with satirical publication depicting individuals wearing fezzes as "backward," in contrast to their modern, fez-less counterparts who were often portrayed as industrious workers, public personalities, or students.[48] Such publications further caricatured Turks, among other perceived foreign policy adversaries, with depictions featuring cannon-like hats that were branded as the "new Turkish fez." They thus framed the fez as an alien, potentially perilous item, decidedly unfit for loyal citizens.[49]

The Bulgarian authorities made no efforts to conceal their objectives. The historian Iliyana Gancheva notes that Pencho Kubadinski, a member of the Central Committee, declared the intention to eradicate all markers distinguishing Muslims from Bulgarians, markers that encompassed aspects like religion, circumcision, fezzes, and veils.[50] After the period of de-Stalinization ended, the anti-fez campaign escalated from the early 1960s, although declassified intelligence documents reveal that party activists had initiated local campaigns against men wearing fezzes in the late 1950s, destroying and incinerating them along with veils and shalvari in numerous villages in the Razgrad district.[51] Myuhtar-May further illustrates that Muslim men encountered harassment and prohibitions against entering shops unless they discarded their fezzes, with clerks who defied this directive facing termination in certain smaller locales.[52]

Each instance in which the attire of Muslim men was either prohibited or discouraged, and depicted as backward, warrants consideration for its implications on individual masculinity and identity. In every case, the traditional clothing of Muslim men, as perceived by the authorities, was relegated to a subordinate power position. This diminished its political significance and overlooked its personal and cultural relevance. The regulation of men's attire also had profound implications. During the entire period, local bans and prohibitions were followed up with people's resistance. Attacks on men's hats dragged for decades in Bulgaria. Men often resisted through various means, depending on the intensity of the government pressure. Sometimes they just replaced confiscated hats, whereas on other occasions they protested by refusing to go to work in the state-owned enterprises. These instances were duly noted by the secret service, and they also noted that these protests sometimes occurred after local governments had prohibited men wearing a fez from entering buses, shopping in the stores, accessing services, or having their kids in schools.[53]

The assault on bodily customs, notably circumcision, was a significant facet of the "modernization" agenda directed at men. While the Bolsheviks refrained from outlawing circumcision, it was referred to disparagingly as a "barbaric custom." The party members and their sons were regularly observed, with some losing their posts and party membership. This scrutiny extended to Jews too, though the few accounts available suggest that circumcision remained prevalent throughout the Soviet era.[54] However, this topic remains notably underexplored. Earlier research suggested that despite its negative portrayal in Soviet propaganda, circumcision retained its significance among numerous communities in Central Asia and symbolized a festive occasion for the extended family. Binnigsen posited that this ritual was universally observed, thus encompassing even atheists and prominent figures within the communist hierarchy. To a degree, this practice was intertwined with national identity constructs related to, for example, what being an Uzbek entailed. Despite regular denunciations from the Bolsheviks, the practice was never legally prohibited.[55]

Conversations about circumcision also occurred often among Yugoslav and Bulgarian communists, although the campaign gained substantial momentum in Bulgaria alone. In Yugoslavia, deliberations began in the early 1950s within the Federal Ministry of Health, but they ended with a decision not to ban the practice. Instead, health officials advocated for circumcisions to be conducted by licensed medical practitioners. Since Yugoslavia actually had doctors with a Muslim background, the circumcision practice experienced minimal interruption. By the 1960s, the Islamic community had proclaimed male circumcision as a paramount parental responsibility.[56] Although not actively promoted or endorsed in the media, the practice was evidently tolerated. It is plausible that Muslim men within party ranks influenced the discourse, thereby safeguarding the tradition.

In Bulgaria, the party passed a ban on circumcision. Gruev and Kalionski contend that this assault on circumcision traditions was one of the most egregious infringements upon Muslim societies, given the profound significance that circumcision holds for families and the wider community. They highlighted regional disparities in the celebration of male circumcision, but the existence of abundant rituals and ceremonies intrinsically linked to this practice was universally acknowledged, establishing it as a crucial milestone in the lives of individuals and communities alike. While fundamentally a private event, as Gruev and Kalionski described, the ceremonies in the Western Rhodopes often escalated to not merely a village celebration, but a festivity encompassing multiple villages, thereby becoming integral to communal identity.[57]

The initial move against circumcision was initiated in December 1959 by the Bulgarian Ministry of Health, which circulated a directive alleging that circumcisions were being performed in "primitive" and "unhygienic" ways. The ministry demanded that circumcisions should be conducted exclusively by licensed medical professionals in hospitals. Consequently, community-led circumcisions were criminalized as acts of grievous bodily harm, with Gruev and Kalionski noting that the designated physicians were all non-Muslims.[58] Declassified files from the secret service reveal a stringent vigilance in arresting individuals conducting circumcisions, with sentences extending up to eight months of imprisonment.[59] Later, the Bulgarian government escalated their stance by completely outlawing the practice towards the end of that year.

Gancheva argues that, notwithstanding the augmented fines imposed from the mid-1960s, families remained resolute in facilitating community-based circumcisions for their children.[60] The practice progressively retreated to a more private domain, yet, as documented by Gruev and Kalionski, a significant mass circumcision event, encompassing over a hundred children, took place in the Rhodope village of Korova (now known as Draginovo) in 1964, and it caught the secret service off guard because of the extensive participation.[61] After this event, the regime intensified its efforts to eradicate the practice, albeit without stopping the practice completely. The task of regulating circumcisions proved substantially more challenging than overseeing the use of veils or fezzes. The party then mandated Muslim parents to formally pledge, via documented agreements, to abstain from circumcising their sons. Eminov provides an example of such a document in his pivotal study, which required parents to provide exhaustive information about themselves and their offspring, inclusive of identification particulars. Furthermore, they were obligated to affirm their rejection of circumcision, described as "jeopardizing the life and well-being of my son," with warnings of legal repercussions for non-compliance, as stipulated in the criminal code.[62]

Parents found in breach of this ban frequently encountered financial penalties and lost their jobs. Muratova recounted harrowing narratives of young boys subjected to humiliating inspections in educational institutions and residences, which even extended to public spaces. Notably, mothers predominantly endured the repercussions of this scrutiny and maltreatment, thus emphasizing the regime's delineation of gender roles within the realms of child-rearing and health care.[63] This campaign of harassing children and parents persisted until the end of the socialist era in Bulgaria, with the prevalence of circumcision declining only slightly.[64]

Violence, Resistance, and Resilience

The degree of violence, resistance, and eventual emigration abroad correlated directly with the extent of the party's gendered interventions. It was also contingent upon the party's capability and willingness to incorporate Muslim men into its ranks. In every instance, however, the government's endeavours to change family gender dynamics came up against limitations. Despite legal transformations that curtailed the influence of men within families, patriarchal structures largely persisted. Male-perpetrated patriarchal violence was a pervasive issue across all religious communities. As described in chapter 3, domestic violence was rampant, and the only difference was the extent to which Muslim communities were stigmatized and perceived as inherently more susceptible to domestic violence because of their perceived "backwardness." Muslim families underwent transformations akin to other families, propelled by industrialization and urbanization, and developments that facilitated increased educational and employment opportunities for women. In the context of Central Asia, Northrop posited that these transitions were most evident among the generation born into and nurtured within the Soviet Union.[65] Brunnbauer's analysis further suggested that traditional domestic structures in the Rhodopes remained unchanged until the advent of socialist modernization initiatives, with later collectivization and industrialization bringing about notable changes, particularly given that a substantial 95 per cent of the Muslim populace was engaged in agriculture.[66] A similar trajectory was observed in Yugoslavia, which underwent substantial industrialization and urbanization that mirrored the Soviet model. Nevertheless, despite these transformations, family dynamics within the Soviet sphere predominantly maintained a pronounced gender-based division of roles and duties, a trend mirrored in Yugoslavia and Bulgaria.[67] Muslim men, akin to their counterparts from other communities, very much succeeded in sustaining patriarchal norms; they adjusted marginally to the emerging socialist expectations while superficially endorsing professed principles of equality.

The manifestation of overt resistance was less universal. As examined previously, Muslim men were responsible for significant acts of violence against women, encompassing both those perceived as outsiders and those who sought to challenge established patriarchal principles. A considerable number of women faced fatal violence, sexual assault, and intimidation during the 1920s unveiling campaign within the Soviet Union. Conversely, men were subjected to substantial violence, especially during Stalin's rule, with many falling victim to purges or enduring various forms of brutality amid the collectivization and industrialization phases. Finally, in the aftermath of the Second World War, the region underwent profound transformations. These fostered the rise of a new political, social, and economic elite, a development intrinsically linked to the Soviet agenda.

In Bulgaria, the Muslim populace exhibited particular resistance – a consequence of prevalent assaults on Muslim communities and the evident scarcity of Muslim men within governmental and party structures. Turkish and Pomak men were targeted indiscriminately, with such targeting frequently culminating in violent confrontations with the state. Resistance to unveiling initiatives was quelled more easily in Yugoslavia compared with Bulgaria. These campaigns, coupled with circumcision prohibitions and assaults on religious festivities, personal names, and attire, incited opposition in rural areas, which occasionally escalated to violent clashes.[68] Each campaign posed a threat to individual autonomy and fostered both cultural dislocation and heightened vulnerability. In instances where violent resistance was absent, individuals often retained their original names within private circles and just resorted to the enforced dress codes and Christian names for official engagements. Such acts of defiance also often resulted in community isolation.[69] Myuhtar-May revealed accounts from the early 1960s that depicted instances where midwives declined to record newborns under Muslim names, or unilaterally assigned names without parental consent. In other cases, local administrative offices refused to register children. Despite these challenges, numerous parents staunchly rejected the imposed names.[70] This resistance was vividly documented within the secret service archives, and it encapsulated both overt and covert acts of defiance.[71]

Violence in Yugoslavia was also significant, albeit less intense during the unveiling of Muslim women, a matter the Yugoslav party expediently addressed, as discussed in the preceding chapter. The socialist regime in Yugoslavia initiated early and severe social interventions, yet Muslim men experienced a greater degree of integration within the Yugoslav political frameworks. Nonetheless, the Turkish populace experienced a substantial wave of emigration, and it struggled amid socio-economic policies perceived as adverse and alien to their interests.

All these aggressive actions towards Muslim communities, coupled with radical shifts in their societal standing, enacted through legislative reforms and land expropriation, spurred numerous Muslim families to relocate from Yugoslavia and Bulgaria to Turkey. Hopken contends that this Muslim migration was often a reaction to the sociocultural transformations that occurred in post-Ottoman Balkan societies. During and before the communist period, the Muslim populace frequently opted for migration as a strategy to navigate the escalating difficulties of assimilating into a setting viewed as antagonistic to their cultural heritage, religious convictions, and ethnic affiliations. Thus, Hopken theorizes, migration surfaced as a strategy to evade this friction, a dynamic he labelled a "modernization conflict."[72] This is a term I find applicable only when modernization is perceived as a value-neutral notion. However, migration perturbed the regimes only when manifest on a large scale. At the individual level, I interpret migration as a form of resistance. Predominantly, those who migrated were Turks, although in Yugoslavia, numerous Albanians, Roma, and Bosniaks also assumed Turkish identities to facilitate their departure, a trend also present among the Pomaks in Bulgaria. The early 1950s witnessed the state-endorsed migration of Turks from Yugoslavia, instigated by an agreement between the respective nations. The population movement eventually surpassed the scale anticipated by the Yugoslav government, prompting efforts to restrain it.[73]

The Yugoslav secret service documented "rumours" circulating within Muslim communities, purportedly disseminated by elusive

"Turkish agents." These rumours potentially illuminate the concerns harboured by the Muslim populace. These "agents" claimed that Yugoslavia offered no viable future for Muslims, with governmental agendas seeking to dismantle Islam. Additional claims posited that Islamic doctrines did not endorse gender equality and that literacy programs were actually designed to facilitate the conversion of Muslim women to Christianity. It remains plausible that these "agents" were simply community members dissenting against the new regime.[74] Intelligence also indicates that various party entities were vigilant in tracking any information or gossip emanating from Turkey, encompassing topics such as sharia or unveiling.[75] It is unclear how Yugoslav migrants viewed the contemporary Turkish landscape. Turkey had supplanted sharia with the civil code in 1926, which granted women voting rights considerably earlier than Yugoslavia. The Turkish modernization project had distinctive characteristics that amalgamated with nationalism and imposed definite boundaries on female autonomy. Nonetheless, Turkish society was undergoing significant transformations; it was diverging markedly from the Ottoman Empire that potentially dominated the perceptions of Yugoslav and Bulgarian Muslims.[76] Migration to Turkey most likely just stemmed from resistance to assimilation into the socialist project.

The exodus of Turks from Bulgaria was even more extensive.[77] The initial significant wave of migration occurred in the summer of 1950.[78] While some of this migration was voluntary, the regime predominantly facilitated it, either through direct state agreements or indirectly via a range of discriminatory policies. As early as the summer of 1949, the government resolved to grant exit visas to Turks seeking to depart. Most of these applicants were peasants, disenfranchised because of the collectivization policies. By the time Turkey had closed its borders in 1951, over 150,000 individuals had already left Bulgaria.[79] The Bulgarian secret service maintained a vigilance comparable to its Yugoslav counterpart, meticulously scrutinizing and documenting correspondence between Turks residing in Turkey and those remaining in Bulgaria. These exchanges unveiled the anxieties and hopes numerous families had of reuniting.[80] In their internal reports, secret service agents expressed concerns about circulating rumours stating that life in Turkey was not only more tolerable for Muslims but also had a superior standard of living.[81] A later wave of migration ensued as Bulgaria initiated a series of social interventions and aggression towards Muslim communities. This migration phase was expedited by a bilateral agreement between Bulgaria and Turkey, which facilitated the immigration of over 100,000 individuals. Hopken posited that this migration surge, spanning from 1968 to the late 1970s, was directly linked to Bulgaria's approach towards minority groups.[82]

For those who opted to remain in Bulgaria, resistance was manifest, to a certain extent, as a straightforward refusal to embrace the party's initiatives, albeit in a more subdued manner. The internal dialogues within the party are quite illuminating, even when couched in euphemisms or attributing the burgeoning "Turkish nationalism" and "deficiency of education in the spirit of proletarian internationalism" to its own flawed "cultural work" and permissiveness towards radio and press.[83] Nonetheless, Muslim people of all genders demonstrated resilience. They acquiesced to certain initiatives, adapted to others, and outright rejected the remainder, enduring further assaults in the later stages of socialism, particularly at the zenith of the "revival process."[84] Ultimately, over 300,000 Turks migrated from Bulgaria to Turkey before the imposition of a state of emergency led Turkish authorities to close the borders on 21 August 1989.[85] Shortly after, Bulgarian socialism dissolved.

The discourse of Muslim men's perceived backwardness was ubiquitous. The Soviet, Yugoslav, and Bulgarian press – including both films and political figures – cultivated an image of Muslim men who were stubborn in their endeavours to preserve patriarchal and discriminatory power dynamics in their families. Moreover, they were often framed as the main culprits for the parties' unsuccessful attempts to involve Muslim women in the socialist project. Such negative representations of Muslim men circulated with ease among the various socialist projects. They amalgamated with older stereotypes and were packed within the socialist discourse of modernity and progress.

Once Muslim men were marked as in dire need of change, the communist parties initiated a range of societal interventions, albeit with more regional nuances in these strategies compared with their approaches towards Muslim women. The extent of their intervention and safeguarding depended on the state structure, and the influence of loyal Muslim politicians capable of providing protections and steering the party's policies. However, in all these cases, the bodies and attire of Muslim men formed the focal points of scrutiny. Circumcision and traditional Muslim clothing were particularly targeted, with the Bulgarian communists adopting the most stringent and prohibitive measures. In the end, the clothing of Muslim men did change in all these cases, while customs such as circumcision and private religious ceremonies prevailed.

The resistance was most pronounced in Bulgaria, where Muslim men were largely excluded from political processes. This resistance was multilayered in other cases as well, with a lot of communal violence. Many women, too, suffered from communal violence. A considerable number of Muslim families opted to abandon their native lands and relocate to Turkey, facilitated by the government's eagerness to expedite their departure. Others, however, adapted to or resisted socialist projects until the eventual collapse of socialism. Decades of socialist intervention did alter gender and family relations, but patriarchal structures were far from broken.

Conclusions

In the autumn of 1935, the Soviet Komsomol Central Committee organized a series of congresses of young women from the "national republics" across the vast expanse of the Soviet Union, from Uzbekistan to
the Udmurt ASSR. These gatherings were not mere political formali-
ties; they were pivotal moments in the lives of many young women for
whom it was a maiden voyage beyond the confines of their neighbour-
hood, and the first instance in which they voiced their opinions in a
public forum. The delegates' speeches bore testimony to the resilience
of local customs and patriarchal vestiges that continued to subjugate
women, but also to women's determination to have their voices heard
and to offer mutual solidarity. The speeches of Marziia Rabibova and
Khalbibi Yuldasheva, among others, underscored the perilous journey
many undertook to attend these meetings. Rabibova recounted the tale
of her comrade Niiazova, whose own husband made threats on her life
for her audacity to attend the congress. Such was her determination that
she chose not to return home ever again. Khalbibi Yuldasheva's story
was even more harrowing. On the eve of her departure for the congress
in Tashkent, her husband, Tarakulov, assaulted her with a knife and left
her with five grievous wounds. He despised her association with the
Komsomol and her intent to attend the congress, which was perceived as
a moral transgression. In the same vein, many women talking about the
extent of the patriarchal pushback. Nazarova's election to the republic's
congress was met with physical violence from her husband, who locked
her in the house and beat her, after which she escaped to the Komsomol
district office and arranged for the man to face incarceration. He was
also accused of being a *kulak* and was sentenced to five years in prison.
Other delegates also recounted stories of desperate women facing daily
violence, abuses, limits on their freedom of movement, education and

work, and often suicide attempts to escape it all. The report to the congress was marked as top secret and sent to Stalin.[1]

These congresses, while carefully arranged to convey certain messages, also laid bare the deep-rooted patriarchal structures that resisted socialist interventions. Yet these patriarchal structures were irreversibly shaken by the all-encompassing nature and policies of the Soviet, Stalinist state. Collectivization and industrialization reached previously closed communities. In Uzbekistan alone, 25,000 delegates participated in district conferences, and more than 200,000 young women participated in meetings at which congress delegates were elected. In many cases, the delegates were elected not just by young women, but by all the collective farmworkers. The internal report carefully counted that a total of 2,033 people were registered as taking part in discussions at all the congresses of young women, and 1,265 of them spoke. Muslim communities across the Soviet Union were rapidly changing, and – as this example shows – that change was neither easy nor straightforward. Many resisted Soviet power, while others seized the opportunity for a new life despite dangers from their own communities. A few decades later, the same model of gendered transformation would drive gender policies applied by Yugoslav and Bulgarian communists. As I have shown in this book, these policies were based on the very same ideas about Muslim communities, which were then slightly modified to fit local needs, causing different outcomes and consequences for the targeted populations.

Muslim populations in Central Asia and the Balkans lived different lives. They spoke very different languages, had different local customs, and the geographical environments in which these people lived varied greatly. Yet this book has tried to bring them all together to show how all these peoples were marked by the same negative discourse imposed on them. Each chapter shows how ideas and prejudices about Muslim communities travelled thousands of kilometres easily, essentializing, orientalizing, and Othering them. Policies travelled, too. Laws, directives, initiatives, and campaigns attempted in one place were eagerly transferred to other places, often without any proper probing of possible consequences. Furthermore, local communists often ignored their own experiences with Muslim populations and tried to adapt to *proper* ways crafted in the socialist centres. In this sense, gender policies passed and implemented by communist leaderships were truly transnational, in theory and in practice, even though that practice was often detached from the needs of the targeted communities.

Gender policies towards Muslim minorities, from these regimes' perspective, were marked by both successes and failures, progress and setbacks, but they all left an indelible impact on the Muslim communities in these countries. As this book has shown, socialist transformations were multifaceted; they depended on the interplay of the same ideological foundations and legal frameworks, but they were applied differently, depending on local circumstances and the intentions of communist leaders, bureaucrats, activists, and secret service agents. Therefore, this book has not offered a simple narrative of success or failure, or of resistance and compliance. Muslim populations exercised agency – they adapted and negotiated policies, resisting some but eagerly participating in other cases.

The ideological bedrock of Yugoslav and Bulgarian communists was profoundly influenced by their pre–Second World War experiences and education in the Soviet Union. These foundational years were not only formative but also pivotal in shaping their perspectives on how to bring about societal change. The situations in Yugoslavia and Bulgaria were remarkably similar, allowing for a shared understanding of Marxist principles. Particularly noteworthy was how these communists managed to frame their gender policies and ideas about the Balkan Muslim populations within a Marxist discourse. They read the Soviet press, passed through Soviet schools, and learned how to apply Soviet notions to their own countries. This established narrative about the Muslim population was not an afterthought; it had been firmly established during the early years of Bolshevik rule with profound consequences. Articles and discussions written by communist leaders and activists provided a nuanced framework for social interventions, and this allows us to understand the complex struggle for power and domination in Central Asia and the Balkans.

The policies on gender, especially concerning Muslim minorities, were intricately woven into broader strategies of nation building, the "national question," and the centre/periphery dichotomy. Activists in all these countries and the newly formed republics faced the challenge of *modernizing* gender relations to avoid being classified as "backward." This modernization involved bringing women into industry and agriculture, increasing literacy rates, and encouraging women's political activities. New Central Asian republics were measured against these parameters. In Yugoslavia, the communists closely followed the Stalinist model of nation building, creating new federal units that offered protection to recognized nations. It also opened a lot of spaces in the bloated party and both the federal and republic apparatus for the Muslim population to participate politically. In contrast, Bulgarian communists initially offered "cultural" rights to Muslims but lacked the federal structures for the Pomak and Turkish populations. This absence became glaringly evident during the de-Stalinization process, when Muslims' rights were gradually revoked, and a "one Bulgarian nation" policy left no room for ethnic and gender differences. Yet in both Yugoslavia and Bulgaria, the *progressivness* of the Muslim communities was measured in the same way, in terms of their adoption of new gender and family relations.

Both Yugoslav and Bulgarian communists held Soviet laws in high regard, viewing them as the most progressive and the only correct path for building a just society. These laws, first tested in Central Asia, were not without their challenges. Zhenotdel activists knew, all too well, that local traditions often overruled Soviet laws, particularly when it came to women's rights. Despite these challenges, the legal landscape was changing, albeit gradually. Many women paid a high price, sometimes with their lives, for attempting to exercise their newfound rights. The process of legal transformation accelerated with the advent of collectivization and industrialization in the late 1920s and 1930s, when the party reached almost all communities, often inflicting immense suffering. In post–Second World War Yugoslavia and Bulgaria, the trajectory was the same because the new constitution was written on the Soviet model, and the new laws brought about immense changes, particularly for Muslim women. These laws promised equal political participation, employment rights, access to education, legal protection, divorce rights, property divisions, and an equal share of inheritance. However, the actual effects of these legal changes were harder to trace, especially in the early years of socialism. As this book has shown, the laws empowering women were far from straightforward to apply, particularly in rural areas where the state and party apparatus were either unable or unwilling to enforce this new equality.

The pathways for Muslims seeking to capitalize on new opportunities were fraught with obstacles, both from their communities and from the regime's understanding of Muslims as a "special case." The Bolsheviks drew on classical Marxist theories and believed that social mobility and the emancipation of "backward groups" would come through employed labour. Women from Central Asia who achieved social mobility often featured in Soviet publications, which were later translated and distributed in Yugoslavia and Bulgaria. Heroes such as Mamlakat Nahangova were known equally in Belgrade and in Sofia. She was supposed to be an inspiration for Muslim women to gain education, to find employment, and participate in the socialist project. Indeed, the Balkan communists also brought tremendous opportunities to Muslim women, insisting on mandatory elementary education, further schooling and eventually women's employment, which all brought about radical changes for Muslim communities. While women had worked in industry before the Second World War, their numbers grew significantly after the communist liberation. Work in industry was often seen as the pinnacle of one's achievement, and the notion of shock work was heavily promoted. Muslim women who became shock workers featured in top journals, not just as a testament to the apparent successes of the socialist project but also as a boost to women's self-confidence. Many, indeed, created enviable and well-paid careers, crafting completely new socialist identities centred around paid labour. Yet their numbers significantly lagged behind men, and I have demonstrated here that many women also suffered from daily sexist practices and workplace discrimination.

Common to all socialist projects was an attempt to redress Muslim women. The unveiling campaigns in Soviet Central Asia, Yugoslavia, and Bulgaria were fraught with violence and controversy. These campaigns were imagined as a collective effort to elevate communities to an imaginary level of socialist modernity. Yet they often resulted in backlashes and violence, particularly in the Soviet Union where many women were murdered, raped, and bullied by local men. In Yugoslavia, the unveiling campaigns were more successful and easily extended to rural areas. Yugoslav communists opted for the full ban on veils, and the swift state reaction to eradicate veils from the streets. In contrast, Bulgarian communists were slower, often because of poor party support in remote areas, which hampered unveiling attempts for decades. Nevertheless, their approach was no less violent, and the women targeted suffered from both the communists and their own communities. Each assault also entrenched the value of veiling as both a communal identity and a means of resistance.

Muslim men were not exempt from a series of gendered interventions either. The communists in all these countries targeted Muslim men with a particular discourse, too, marking them as "backward" and blaming them for the failures of socialist attempts at modernization. Muslim men were often depicted as barriers to women's access to the privileges of socialism, and as clinging to "backward" traditions to maintain their advantageous positions. Policies were then underpinned by preconceived notions about Muslim men, families and their communities, and the same ideas circulated over vast geographical regions. All these regimes tried to redress Muslim men too, trying to impose "modern European" clothing on them. This, in turn, depended on access to social, political, and economic participation. Male circumcision was disdained, marked by a negative discourse and eventual ban in Bulgaria. Men's bodies were to be "modernized" as well. These interventions were met with varying degrees of resistance and success, while, combined with other policies, ultimately led many Muslim men to abandon their homeland for countries with a predominantly Muslim population.

Regardless of whether they willingly participated in the socialist projects or tried to resist, Muslims living under socialist regimes experienced tectonic shifts. Their way of living, and the world around them, fundamentally changed. Many went through struggles, suffering, and displacements, but many seized new educational, economic, and political opportunities unimaginable before. Even though none of these communities were static before socialism, their socialist transformation was profound. And yet, with the fall of socialism came fresh uncertainties, conflicts, and hardships. New states in Central Asia and the Balkans formed, some with a majority-Muslim population, and many built on their previous socialist heritage. In some locations, such as Bosnia, Muslims' way of life, their well-being, and even their basic existence faced grave threats, even though assaults were no longer anchored in the core ideological foundations of state socialism but in revived nationalism, with far worse consequences.

Notes

Introduction

1 A form of collective farm. On Soviet collectivization, see Kamp and Zanca, "Recollections of Collectivization"; and Hughes, *Stalinism in a Russian Province*.

2 Shock workers were workers and peasants who broke production records or otherwise demonstrated mastery of their assigned tasks. This concept was exported to Eastern Europe after the Second World War, and it was very important for many people in Yugoslavia and Bulgaria as well. For the Soviet case, see Siegelbaum, *Stakhanovism*; and Buckley, *MobilizingSoviet Peasants*. For the Yugoslav case, see Simić, "Gender and Youth Work Actions."

3 Islamova, "Opravdaju doverie naroda."

4 *Feredža* (YU) / *feredzhe* (BG), along with *zar*, referred to both face and body covering. The same term was used in Yugoslavia and Bulgaria.

5 The Antifašistički front žena (Women's Anti-fascist Front, AFŽ) was the Communist Party's women's section, which was established in 1942 to further the war effort and mobilize women. It remained in operation until 1953. See Simic, *Soviet Influences*.

6 "Novi život Behije Krkbešić."

7 Today, this town is called Shumen. It was known as Kolarovgrad from 1950 to 1965, after Vasil Kolarov, one of the top officials of the Comintern and an important Bulgarian post-war politician.

8 The Fatherland Front (Otechestven front in Bulgarian) was a political and military coalition formed during the Second World War, primarily comprising communists, which played a role in the resistance against Nazi Germany and later governed Bulgaria. Yugoslavia had a similar organization called the People's Front (Narodni front), which changed its

name to the Socialist Alliance of Working People of Yugoslavia, but served the same purpose.

9 Stoynova, "Deputatka Muzafer."

10 See Fischer, "Interwar Albania."

11 A fez is a traditional hat that was popular among Muslim men in the Balkans, even after it was outlawed in Turkey following Atatürk's reforms.

12 The list is endless, but key works include Attwood, *New Soviet Woman*; and Bonnell, *Iconography of Power*.

13 Iriye, *Global and Transnational History*, 15. For reflections on how the field has changed in the first two decades of the twenty-first century, see Chamberlin et al., "On Transnational and International History."

14 Janz and Schönpflug, "Introduction," 2.

15 Also see the inspiring edited volume Midgley, Twells, and Carlier, *Women in Transnational History*.

16 Dimou, *Entangled Paths*, 6.

17 Mishkova, "Liberalism and Tradition."

18 de Haan, "Writing Inter/Transnational History." At the same time, de Haan completely misrepresents the WIDF, by taking away its communist and Stalinist foundations. See Gradskova, "Women's International Democratic Federation."

19 Valiavicharska, *Restless History*, 77–80.

20 The list of works I admire that combine gender and transnational history would be too long to list here. For some theoretical works that have influenced me, see Wiesner-Hanks, "Crossing Borders"; Janz and Schönpflug, *Gender History*; de Groot and Morgan, *Sex, Gender and the Sacred*; and Connell, "Masculinities in Global Perspective."

21 For instance, Bulgarian crimes against various civilian populations, particularly in the territories occupied during both world wars, are frequently neglected. Conversely, Bulgaria's influence in more international events is often overstated. In addition to various odd nationalistic claims, see Znepolski et al., *Bulgaria under Communism*. On the need to reassess Bulgaria's objectives in the First World War, moving beyond the simplistic narrative of national unification to explore the complex web of motivations that guided its involvement in the conflict, see Valkov, "Mezhdu natsionalno obedinenie i zavoevatelna voyna." On the round-up of almost all the Jews living in the Yugoslav and Greek territories under Bulgarian occupation between 1941 and 1944, see Ragaru, *Bulgaria, the Jews, and the Holocaust*. As an excellent work by Stefan Dechev has recently demonstrated, numerous Bulgarian historians played a part in the attacks on Muslim populations. Some were direct supporters of the government, and Dechev convincingly asserts that Bulgarian historiography at large laid the groundwork for aggressive assimilation

politics, painting romantic pictures of Bulgarian nationality and negatively stereotyping Muslim populations (Dechev, "Balgarskata istoriografiya i protoideologiyata").

22 See Avramov, *Nasilstvenata asimilatsiya na turtsite v Balgariya.*

23 Aleksandrieva and Kyuranov, "Balgariziraneto na Balgariya."

24 Kamusella, *Ethnic Cleansing*, 57.

25 Today, this town is called Shumen; see Avramov, *Nasilstvenata asimilatsiya na turtsite v Balgariya*, 12.

26 Parla, *Precarious Hope*; Mirkova, *Muslim Land, Christian Labor*; Dragostinova, "In Search of the Bulgarians"; and Dişbudak and Purkis, "Forced Migrants or Voluntary Exiles."

27 Darakchi, "Gender, Religion, and Identity"; Marcheva, "Sotsialisticheskoto ravnopravie na zhenite"; Stoyanova, "Modernization and Emancipation"; and Muratova, "Politiki na sotsialisticheskata vlast v Balgariya."

28 Stoyanova, *TSiganite v godinite na sotsializma.*

29 Daskalova, "Woman Politician."

30 Sygkelos, *Nationalism from the Left.*

31 Avramov, *Ikonomika na "Vazroditelniya protses."*

32 Mekić, *Muslim Reformist.*

33 Pezo, "Emigration and Policy in Yugoslavia"; and Pačariz, *Migrations of Bosniaks.*

34 Larise, "Islamic Community"; Lučić, "Im Namen der Nation"; Elbasani and Roy, *Revival of Islam*; Omerika, *Islam in Bosnien-Herzegowina*; and Mesarič, "Wearing Hijab in Sarajevo."

35 Hadžiristić, "Unveiling Muslim Women."

36 Ballinger and Ghodsee, "Socialist Secularism."

37 Pomaks were usually defined as a Slavic-speaking religious minority that practises Islam, and I use this term neutrally, aware of some negative connotations.

38 Myuhtar-May, *Identity, Nationalism, and Cultural Heritage.*

39 For the etymology of the term *Pomak*, see Gruev, *Mezhdu petolachkata i polumesetsa.*

40 For a history of the Communist International (1919–43), see McDermott and Agnew, *Comintern.*

1. Learning Together

1 Gorki, "Za novuju, svetluju, razumnuju zhizn'."

2 After the victory in the First World War, Serbia created the Kingdom of Serbs, Croats, and Slovenes in December 1918. The country's name was changed to Yugoslavia in 1929. For simplicity's sake, I use *Yugoslavia* throughout.

3 For a nuanced history of interwar Yugoslavia, see Djokić, *Elusive Compromise*.

4 The agrarian question in interwar Yugoslavia has been heavily studied. See Rafailović, "Agrarna reforma i industrijalizacija"; and Biondich, *Stjepan Radić*. On the KPJ's views regarding the agrarian question, see Milošević, "Komunistička partija Jugoslavije"; on the Bulgarian case, see Promitzer, "Interwar Bulgaria"; Baloutzova, *Demography and Nation*; and Avramov, *Stopanskiyat XX vek na Balgariya*.

5 Dragostinova, "In Search of the Bulgarians."

6 Bell, *Peasants in Power*; and Znepolski et al., *Bulgaria under Communism*.

7 See, e.g., Biondich, *Stjepan Radić*.

8 Znepolski et al., *Bulgaria under Communism*, 33–5; and Poppetrov, *Fashizmat v Balgariya*.

9 Dubowoj, "Schism in the Bulgarian Socialist Movement."

10 Mineva, "Reception of Marxism."

11 Sygkelos, *Nationalism from the Left*.

12 Bell, *Bulgarian Communist Party*, 37.

13 Promitzer, "Interwar Bulgaria."

14 Bell, *Bulgarian Communist Party*, 42–3.

15 Petranović, *Istorija Jugoslavije*, vol. 3.

16 Korov, *Rad KPJ u Zagrebu*, 2.

17 Miloradović, *Karantin za ideje*.

18 Goldstein, *Croatia*.

19 Kovačević, "Petko Miletić."

20 "Izjava drugarice Butorac o zverstvima Zagrebačke policije."

21 Rädle and Pisarri, *Mesta stradanja i antifašističke borbe*, 142.

22 Marcheva, "Tsola Dragoycheva," 44; and Iliyana, "Balgarskata 'Leydi Stalin' TSola Dragoycheva."

23 Vujošević and Protić, *Izvori za istoriju SKJ*, 591.

24 Jancar-Webster, *Women & Revolution*, 34.

25 Dimitrov, "United Front and Women."

26 Kecman, "Uloga žena u revolucionarnom pokretu."

27 Kecman, *Žene Jugoslavije*, 345–7.

28 "Njih je vaspitala naša Partija."

29 Bell, *Bulgarian Communist Party*, 57.

30 Tomšič, "Referat na V Zemaljskoj konferenciji."

31 Mitrovski, Glišić, and Ristovski, *Bugarska vojska u Jugoslaviji*; *Kratka balgarska entsiklopediya*, vol. 3; and *Directory of Officials of the Bulgarian People's Republic*.

32 Savova-Mahon Borden, "Politics of Nationalism," 110.

33 Slipičević-Bubić, "Žene Mostara u prvim godinama rata."

34 "1. maj"; and Nikolić, "Radne žene i Prvi Maj 1932."

35 Later in Moscow, Dimitrov had a girlfriend who was a communist from Serbia as well (Dimitrov, *Diary*, xliii).

36 Todorova, *Lost World of Socialists*, 54–5.

37 Savova-Mahon Borden, "Politics of Nationalism."

38 Kirschenbaum, *International Communism*, 3.

39 Studer, *Transnational World of the Cominternians*, 7.

40 Studer, 24.

41 McLoughlin, "Proletarian Academics or Party Functionaries?"

42 "International Lenin School: Study Notes."

43 "Uchebnye plany i programmy bolgarskogo sektora MLSh" (1936).

44 Pantov and Spichak, "New Light from the Russian Archives," 33.

45 McLoughlin, "Proletarian Academics or Party Functionaries?," 65–8.

46 Pantov and Spichak, "New Light from the Russian Archives."

47 *Istorija Svesavezne Komunističke Partije (Boljševika)*; and "International Lenin School: Study Notes."

48 Budding, "Nation/People/Republic," 94–5.

49 Sygkelos, *Nationalism from the Left*, 5–20.

50 "Uchebnye plany i programmy bolgarskogo sektora MLSh" (1937).

51 Kirschenbaum, *International Communism*, 16.

52 Studer, *Transnational World of the Cominternians*, 103–4.

53 Mladenović, *Spasenija Cana Babović*.

54 Köstenberger, *Kaderschmiede des Stalinismus*.

55 Studer, *Transnational World of the Cominternians*, 93–104.

56 Kirschenbaum, *International Communism*, 17.

57 Marcheva, "Tsola Dragoycheva."

58 Kirschenbaum, *International Communism*, 53.

59 Kirschenbaum, 54.

60 Daskalova, "Woman Politician," 68.

61 Bell, *Bulgarian Communist Party*, 42.

62 Köstenberger, *Kaderschmiede des Stalinismus*, 32.

63 Kirschenbaum, *International Communism*, 5.

64 It was also common among the Spanish revolutionaries; see Kirschenbaum, 2.

65 Studer, *Transnational World of the Cominternians*, 108.

66 Dimitrov, *Diary*, 113.

67 Studer, *Transnational World of the Cominternians*, 37.

68 Studer, 8.

69 Sygkelos, *Nationalism from the Left*, 33.

70 Belić, "Moji doživljaji u SSSR."

71 "Sećanja Pavla Pavlovića uzeta 6. oktobra 1960. godine."

72 Lenoe, *Closer to the Masses*.

73 "Mezhdunarodnyj kommunisticheskij zhenskij den'."

74 "O mezhdunarodnom kommunisticheskom zhenskom dne 8 marta."
75 Pichugina, "Sovetskaja zhenshhina."
76 Smirnova, "Radost' svobodnoj zhizni."
77 Matkaramova, "Tadzhihan"; and Gerasimova, "Raskreposhhennyj genij."
78 Shadieva spent eighteen years in prison, only to be rehabilitated in 1956. Following her rehabilitation, she was elected to the Presidium of the Uzbek Central Committee.
79 Seid-Mamedova, "Chudesnye mechty."
80 Seid-Mamedova.
81 Manujlov, "Odna iz mnogih."
82 Ibárruri, "Mezhdunarodnyj kommunisticheskij zhenskij den'."
83 "Pregled ženske štampe SSSR."
84 "Pregled časopisa 'Žena danas' organa AFŽ Jugoslavije."
85 E.g., "Pobediteli hlopkovyh polej."
86 Fomina, "Kak ukrasit' zhilishhe."
87 E.g., Safudri, "Za reformu nacional'nogo zhenskogo kostjuma."
88 Nurhat, "Ot zatvornichestva k proizvodstvu."
89 Oblova, "Ot chadry k udarnichestvu."
90 Chatterjee, "Soviet Heroines."
91 Knorin, "Borba dvaju svijetova"; and Cvetković, "Bilećki koncentracioni logor."
92 Khalid, "Backwardness and the Quest for Civilization." See also Bakić-Hayden, "Nesting Orientalisms."
93 Jayawardena, *Feminism and Nationalism*, 61.
94 Draškić, "Usvojenje i hraniteljstvo."
95 Pavlović, "Problem izjednačenja zakona."
96 Daskalova, "Women's Movement."
97 Brunnbauer, "Families and Mountains in the Balkans," 341.
98 Todorova, "Family Law in Bulgaria."
99 Kaser, *Porodica i srodstvo na Balkanu*; and Karčić, "Reform of Shari'a Courts."
100 Bebel, *Žena i socijalizam*; and Tucović, "Borba za oslobođenje žene."
101 "Direktivy dlja raboty sredi narodov Vostoka."
102 "Direktivy dlja raboty sredi narodov Vostoka."
103 "Doklad tov. Karimovoj o rabote sredi zhenshhin Tashkenta."
104 "Protokol sobranija musul'manok Poltoracka, vopros o religii."
105 "Doklad turkmenki na pervom s"ezde zhenshhin Vostoka."
106 "Doklad v KirCIK o polozhenii kirgizskoj zhenshhiny."
107 "Pis'mo o polozhenii turkmenki."
108 "Doklad v KirCIK o sozdanii Komissii po ulchsheniju byta kirgizskoj zhenshhiny."
109 "O rabote sredi zhenshhin."

110 "Vypiska iz protokola Orgbjuro."
111 Nestorova, "Between Tradition and Modernity."
112 Tucović, "Borba za oslobođenje žene."

2. Socialist (Gendered) Nation Building

1 The Komsomol was the Soviet organization for young people. It was supposed to facilitate political and social activities. For the history of the Komsomol, see Neumann, *Communist Youth League*. The Bulgarian version of the Komsomol was called the Dimitrov Communist Youth Union, and there was also the Yugoslav People's Youth.
2 Nyurina, "V Srednej Azii."
3 When Nyurina was executed in 1938, she held the high-ranking position of acting prosecutor general of the Russian Republic. See Chapaeva, *Putin's Dark Ages*, 194.
4 The phrase *the national question* meant different things in different contexts, and often turned into a nationalistic phrase used by politicians and scholars. In the Balkans, it was also used in various ways: to aim to redraw state borders; to try to gain independence; to centralize a state; or even to assimilate, displace, or kill other groups.
5 Martin, *Affirmative Action Empire*, 22; see also Kotkin, *Stalin*.
6 Smith, *Bolsheviks and the National Question*, 23–4.
7 See, e.g., Smith, *Bolsheviks and the National Question*; and Hirsch, *Empire of Nations*.
8 Brandenberger and Zelenov, "Stalin's Answer to the National Question."
9 Edgar, "Bolshevism, Patriarchy, and the Nation."
10 Martin, *Affirmative Action Empire*, 24.
11 Smith, *Bolsheviks and the National Question*, 78–84.
12 Khalid, *Making Uzbekistan*, 13–14. Marlène Laruelle shows that during this process various local actors, and entire villages, attempted to exercise their agency and impact new territorial organizations (Laruelle, *Central Peripheries*, 20).
13 See Khalid, *Making Uzbekistan*.
14 Gradskova, *Soviet Politics of Emancipation*, 9.
15 Martin, *Affirmative Action Empire*, 29.
16 Torskaja, "Protiv paradnyh deklaracij."
17 Khalid, *Making Uzbekistan*, 204.
18 Kasparova, "Zhenskoe dvizhenie na Vostoke"; and Sudakov, "Devushka Vostoka i komsomol."
19 Nyurina, "V Srednej Azii."
20 Ljubimova, "Rabota sredi zhenshhin v Kirgizii."
21 Ljubimova, "Robota sredi zhenshhin v Turkestane."

22 Kasparova, "Formy i metody raboty sredi zhenshhin vostochnyh narodnostej."
23 Northrop, *Veiled Empire*; Edgar, "Emancipation of the Unveiled"; Northrop, "Subaltern Dialogues"; and Keller, "Trapped between State and Society."
24 Khalid, *Making Uzbekistan*, 156–7, 205.
25 Tineva, "Rabota sredi zhenshhin Kirgizii."
26 Zavar'jan, "Rabota na Sovetskom Vostoke."
27 Keller, "Trapped between State and Society," 20–1.
28 Drieu, "Cinema, Local Power and the Central State."
29 Ro'i, *Islam in the Soviet Union*, 58.
30 Smolkin, *Sacred Space*, 47–50.
31 The destruction of the Orthodox Church and other religious communities has been well researched. See Smolkin, *Sacred Space*.
32 The interwar spiritual boards are under-researched in English-speaking scholarship. On their activities, see Arapov and Kosach, *Islam i sovetskoe gosudarstvo*.
33 See also Keller, *To Moscow, Not Mecca*.
34 Khalid, *Islam after Communism*, 78.
35 Tasar, *Soviet and Muslim*.
36 Khalid, *Islam after Communism*, 67–8.
37 The Chief Mufti Office in Bulgaria was guaranteed by international agreements, and was first subordinated to the Ottoman Shaykh al-Islām, based in Istanbul. The chief mufti functioned more or less as a mediator between the regional muftis' offices and Muslim religious communities and the Shaykh al-Islām. Also see Evstatiev, "Milletic Secularism."
38 Kandiyoti, "Politics of Gender."
39 See, e.g., Bemporad, "Behavior Unbecoming a Communist."
40 Yusufjonova-Abman, "State Feminism"; and Tursunova, "Women's Narratives."
41 Northrop, *Veiled Empire*.
42 "Uchebnye plany i programmy bolgarskogo sektora MLSh" (1937).
43 Brandenberger and Zelenov, "Stalin's Answer to the National Question."
44 Burg, "Political Integration," 12.
45 Giomi, *Making Muslim Women European*, 229–34.
46 Hopken, "Yugoslavia's Communists and the Bosnian Muslims."
47 Grgić, "Kingdom of Diversity and Paternalism," 236–7.
48 Pearson, "Muslims' Nation-Building Process," 435.
49 Pearson, 435–6.
50 Ramet, "Primordial Ethnicity or Modern Nationalism," 175.
51 Hopken, "Yugoslavia's Communists and the Bosnian Muslims," 219.

52 Todorova, *Imagining the Balkans*; Neuburger, *Orient Within*; and Merdjanova, *Rediscovering the Umma*, 9.

53 Dragostinova, "In Search of the Bulgarians," 107–12.

54 Dragostinova, 114.

55 Merdjanova, *Rediscovering the Umma*.

56 Promitzer, "Interwar Bulgaria."

57 Dechev, "Balgarskata istoriografiya i protoideologiyata," 17.

58 Myuhtar-May, *Identity, Nationalism, and Cultural Heritage*, 32–3.

59 Dragostinova, "In Search of the Bulgarians," 119.

60 Dragostinova, 120.

61 Cvijić, "O iseljavanju bosanskih muhamedanaca."

62 Giomi, *Making Muslim Women European*, 60.

63 Promitzer, "Interwar Bulgaria."

64 Merdjanova, *Rediscovering the Umma*.

65 Mirkova, *Muslim Land, Christian Labor*, 238.

66 Promitzer, "Interwar Bulgaria."

67 Hristov, *Stranitsi ot balgarskata istoriya*, 59–60. Silence on the BKP's interwar approach is also visible in other crucial official publications, including Mizov, *Islyamat v Balgariya*; and Mizov, *Islyamat v minaloto i dnes*.

68 See, e.g., *Nasha zemya*.

69 Batinić, *Women and Partisan Resistance*.

70 Znepolski et al., *Bulgaria under Communism*, 44.

71 Bell, *Bulgarian Communist Party*, 59.

72 Stanev, *SHumat ot debri i Balkani*.

73 Dudić, *Dnevnik 1941*.

74 Jancar-Webster, *Women & Revolution*, 48–9.

75 *Fočanski propisi*.

76 Beoković, *Žene heroji*, 188–227.

77 Bubić-Slipčević, "Borbe i otpori u Mostaru."

78 Marašović, "Stanodavke jedne ilegalke."

79 Slipičević-Bubić, "Žene Mostara u prvim godinama rata."

80 Kamberović, *Džemal Bijedić*.

81 Hopken, "Yugoslavia's Communists and the Bosnian Muslims," 226.

82 Bougarel, *Islam and Nationhood*, 55.

83 Pearson, "Muslims' Nation-Building Process," 436.

84 Bougarel, *Islam and Nationhood*, 74–5.

85 Pearson, "Muslims' Nation-Building Process," 436.

86 Ramet, "Primordial Ethnicity or Modern Nationalism," 175.

87 Pearson, "Muslims' Nation-Building Process," 438.

88 For a general overview of the Bulgarian de-Stalinization process, see Gruev, "Politicheskoto razvitie na Bylgariya prez 50-te-80-te godini na XX vek."

89 On the Yugoslav-Soviet split, see Perović, "Tito-Stalin Split."
90 Miller, "Between Faith and Nation"; and Bougarel, *Islam and Nationhood*. Also see Henig and Razsa, "New Borders, Old Solidarities."
91 Pearson, "Muslims' Nation-Building Process," 440.
92 Ramet, "Primordial Ethnicity or Modern Nationalism," 176.
93 Ramet, 186.
94 Pearson, "Muslims' Nation-Building Process," 441.
95 Pezo, "Emigration and Policy in Yugoslavia."
96 *Statistički Godišnjak Jugoslavije 1991*, 132.
97 Fejić, "Naša prva riječ."
98 "Maršal Tito primio pretstavnike Islamske vjerske zajednice."
99 Šećeragić, "Bratstvo i jedinstvo jugoslovenskih naroda."
100 Talić, "Islam i prosvjeta."
101 "Rezolucija Vrhovnog vakufskog sabora Islamske vjerske zajednice u FNRJ."
102 Eminov, *Turkish and Other Muslim Minorities*, 99–111.
103 Darakchi, "Gender, Religion, and Identity."
104 Myuhtar-May, *Identity, Nationalism, and Cultural Heritage*, 13.
105 Giomi, *Making Muslim Women European*.
106 Stoyanova, *TSiganite v godinite na sotsializma*, 33.
107 Hopken, "Po-slozhno ot 'etnicheskoto prochistvane'"; and Dişbudak and Purkis, "Forced Migrants or Voluntary Exiles."
108 Dechev, "Balgarskata istoriografiya i protoideologiyata," 21.
109 Gruev, *Mezhdu petolachkata i polumesetsa*, 18.
110 Stoyanova, *TSiganite v godinite na sotsializma*, 33.
111 Myuhtar-May, *Identity, Nationalism, and Cultural Heritage*, 97.
112 Bates, "What's in a Name?," 207.
113 Quoted in Eminov, *Turkish and Other Muslim Minorities*, 5.
114 Pomak, "Julvie."
115 *Hodzha* in Bulgarian is the same as *hodža* in Serbo-Croatian, *hoxha* in Albanian, *hoca* in Turkish (with another meaning – "teacher"), etc. Communist press and officials often used terms such as *hodzha* interchangeably with *imam*, particularly when they attached negative connotations to them or declared their activities hostile to the people.
116 Pomak, "Julvie," 6.
117 Pomak, 7.
118 Urdea, "Enacting Culture."
119 Stoyanova, *TSiganite v godinite na sotsializma*, 34.
120 Myuhtar-May, *Identity, Nationalism, and Cultural Heritage*, 97.
121 Gruev, *Mezhdu petolachkata i polumesetsa*, 18.
122 Savova-Mahon Borden, "Politics of Nationalism," 18.
123 Bates, "What's in a Name?"

124 Marinov, "Ot internatsionalizam kam natsionalizam," 502.

125 Stoyanova, *TSiganite v godinite na sotsializma*, 34.

126 Parla, *Precarious Hope*, 21.

127 Gruev, *Mezhdu petolachkata i polumesetsa*.

128 Savova-Mahon Borden, "Politics of Nationalism," 18; see also Ivanov and Önsoy, "From Integration to Assimilation and Forced Migration."

129 Erken, "Identity, Nationhood and Migrations to Turkey."

130 Mahon, "Turkish Minority," 149.

131 Quoted in Myuhtar-May, *Identity, Nationalism, and Cultural Heritage*, 98; and Eminov, *Turkish and Other Muslim Minorities*, 6.

132 Myuhtar-May, *Identity, Nationalism, and Cultural Heritage*, 98.

133 Stoyanova, *TSiganite v godinite na sotsializma*, 35.

134 Eminov, *Turkish and Other Muslim Minorities*, 6. For more details on policies towards Macedonians in Pirin, see Marinov, "Ot internatsionalizam kam natsionalizam."

135 Savova-Mahon Borden, "Politics of Nationalism," 41.

136 Bates, "What's in a Name?"

137 Aleksandrieva and Kyuranov, "Balgariziraneto na Balgariya," 80.

138 Myuhtar-May, *Identity, Nationalism, and Cultural Heritage*, 111.

139 Gruev, *Mezhdu petolachkata i polumesetsa*, 17.

140 Eminov, *Turkish and Other Muslim Minorities*, 191.

141 Eminov, 192.

142 Eminov, 193.

143 Eminov, 194.

144 Myuhtar-May, *Identity, Nationalism, and Cultural Heritage*, 68.

145 Aleksandrieva and Kyuranov, "Balgariziraneto na Balgariya," 80.

146 Eminov, *Turkish and Other Muslim Minorities*, 106.

147 Dechev, "Balgarskata istoriografiya i protoideologiyata," 27.

148 Myuhtar-May, *Identity, Nationalism, and Cultural Heritage*, 100.

149 Eminov, *Turkish and Other Muslim Minorities*, 106.

150 Mahon, "Turkish Minority," 155.

151 Stoyanova, *TSiganite v godinite na sotsializma*, 36.

152 Silverman, "State, Market, and Gender Relationships."

153 Scarboro, "Living Socialism," 24–5; also see Valiavicharska, *Restless History*, 14.

154 Bates, "What's in a Name?"

155 Mahon, "Turkish Minority," 156.

156 Kamusella, "Dimute imat znachenie," 89.

157 Metodiev, "Za nyakoi kosveni," 113.

158 Mahon, "Turkish Minority," 156.

159 Kamusella, *Ethnic Cleansing*, 4.

160 "Stanovishte na Politbyuro na TSK na BKP."

161 Dechev, "Balgarskata istoriografiya i protoideologiyata," 21.
162 "Protokol za saveshtanie na otdel 'Propaganda i agitatsiya.'"
163 Dechev, "Balgarskata istoriografiya i protoideologiyata," 28.
164 Eminov, *Turkish and Other Muslim Minorities*, 18.
165 Savova-Mahon Borden, "Politics of Nationalism," 21.
166 Znepolski et al., *Bulgaria under Communism*, 335.
167 Savova-Mahon Borden, "Politics of Nationalism," 36.
168 Kamusella, *Ethnic Cleansing*.
169 Suad, "Moeto sartse ostava tuk," 17.
170 Gruev, "Komunizam i homoseksualizam u Bugarskoj," 12; and Simic, *Soviet Influences*.
171 Also see Darakchi, "Bulgarian LGBTQI Movement"; Veronica Dimitrova, "Nakazatelni praktiki spryamo homoseksualnite v Balgariya"; and Gruev, "Dve marginalni grupi."
172 Neuburger, *Orient Within*.

3. Communist Enfranchisements

1 Dragoycheva, "Osem godini ravnopravni i shtastlivi."
2 Tomšič, "Ko je pokazao put ženama Jugoslavije."
3 Ljubimova, "Na puti k raskreposhheniju."
4 "Žene Sovjetskog istoka."
5 Tomšič, "Ko je pokazao put ženama Jugoslavije."
6 It was not a coincidence that as early as 1945, Grigoriij Markovich Sverdlov's book on maternity, marriage, and family in Soviet legislation was translated into Serbo-Croatian (Svjerdlov, *Materinstvo, brak, porodica u sovjetskom zakonu*).
7 McShane, "Bringing the Revolution," 70.
8 Kislova, "Zapiska o rabote turkmenskogo oblastnogo otdela rabotnic."
9 McShane, "Bringing the Revolution," 79.
10 Butuzova, "Zhenskie lavki v Uzbekistane."
11 Northrop, "Subaltern Dialogues."
12 Zahar'jan, "Brachnoe i semejnoe pravo na Vostoke."
13 McShane, "Bringing the Revolution," 96.
14 Zahar'jan, "Brachnoe i semejnoe pravo na Vostoke."
15 See Simić, "Soviet Model."
16 Beljaeva, "Zhdut vesnu."
17 Golubev, "Danka."
18 E.g., Čolaković, "Novi Sovjetski ustav."
19 "Uchebnye plany i programmy bolgarskogo sektora MLSh" (1937).
20 On the Yugoslav case, see Simić, "Soviet Model"; on Bulgaria, see Yordan Mantarliev, "Izborite za narodni saveti v NR Balgariya prez 1949 g."; and Staar, *Communist Regimes*, 35–6.

21 "Žene poslanici ustavotvorne skupštine."

22 *Zasedanje Ustavotvorne Skupštine*, 313.

23 Hasan Rebac held several significant administrative roles in Yugoslavia. In the 1920s, he worked for the Ministries of Religious Affairs and Justice. In the 1930s, he directed the Waqf Directorate in Skopje and, by 1934, managed a madrasa there. In 1936, he became a senior official in the Ministry of Education. His activities in the interwar period are also covered in Giomi, *Making Muslim Women European*.

24 *Zasedanje Ustavotvorne Skupštine*, 631.

25 Giomi, *Making Muslim Women European*, 177–8.

26 *Zasedanje Ustavotvorne Skupštine*, 544–5.

27 Jovanović, "Preslikana ili samobitna društvena izgradnja."

28 *Ustav Federativne Narodne Republike Jugoslavije.*

29 Scheide, "'Born in October.'"

30 Ananieva and Razvigorova, "Women in State Administration."

31 Ananieva and Razvigorova, 31–2.

32 "Konstitutsiya na Narodna republika Balgariya"; and *Ustav Federativne Narodne Republike Jugoslavije*. Also see Marcheva, "Sotsialisticheskoto ravnopravie na zhenite."

33 Avramov, *Annotated Legal Documents*, 3:1–2.

34 Ina Merdjanova has shown that the sharia courts were not abolished in Bulgaria, but their jurisdiction decreased; see Merdjanova, "Administering Islam."

35 "Naši novi zakoni."

36 "Osnovni zakon o braku."

37 *Zakon za litsata i semeystvoto.*

38 For other Eastern European contexts, see Haney, *Inventing the Needy*; and Alsop and Hockey, "Women's Reproductive Lives."

39 Iliev, "Pravata na maykata i deteto u nas."

40 Gradskova, "Opening the (Muslim) Woman's Space."

41 Simić and Simić, "'Who Should Care about Our Children?'"

42 "Sovetskij Turkmenistan"; and Sazonova, "Kolhoznym jasljam okazhem prakticheskuju pomoshh'."

43 Kamp, *New Woman in Uzbekistan*; and Wood, *Baba and the Comrade*.

44 Valiavicharska, *Restless History*, 93–4; and Nenova, "Retraditionalization Thesis."

45 Bogdan, "Cold War Entanglements."

46 Simic, *Soviet Influences*; and Bogdan, "Cold War Entanglements."

47 The author's own grandmother died from a botched abortion in the countryside.

48 Sternadori, "Heroines under Control," 147; and Valiavicharska, *Restless History*, 100.

49 Marcheva, "Sotsialisticheskoto ravnopravie na zhenite."

50 "Maychina gordost."
51 M.B., "Slava i chest na mnogodetnite mayki."
52 Brunnbauer, "'Most Natural Function of Women.'"
53 Anachkova, "Women in Bulgaria," 63; and Ghodsee and Bernardi, "Starting a Family at Your Parents' House," 444.
54 "Seljačka žena kao ekonomski faktor."
55 Drezgić, "From Family Planning to Population Policy."
56 "Izveštaji o izvršenoj anketi po domaćinstvima na selu"; "Sastanak aktiva Glavnog odbora AFŽ Srbije."
57 "'Protokol № 103.'"
58 Syarova, "Bezplatnata meditsinska pomosht."
59 Božinović, "Izveštaj o radu komisije za porodične odnose na selu."
60 "Imovinski odnosi u Braku."
61 *Statistički Godišnjak FNRJ 1955*, 78; for Bulgaria, see *Statisticheski godishnik na Narodna republika Balgariya* (1961), 20–1.
62 Ekmečić, "Skamenjena prošlost."
63 Velev, "Edin den v zala 13."
64 Aleksandrova, "Sartseto na Rifat."
65 Dobreva, "V otgovor na chitatelkite"; and Velev, "Edin den v zala 13."
66 Zdravković, *Posledice razvoda braka.*
67 "Brakovi u sudskoj arhivi."
68 See, e.g., Galevska, *Poremećena porodica i deca.*
69 Gruev, "Demografski tendentsii."
70 Darakchi, "Muslim Marriages."
71 Lončar, "Propitivanje pristupa istraživanju neredovnih oblika predbračnog i bračnog života na primjeru krivog puta." Also see Kurtić, "Život romkinja."
72 Meurs and Giddings, "Decline in Pre-school Use," 158; and Muratova, "Muslim Women," 143.
73 S.G., "Mnoge navike djeca stiču u roditeljskom domu."
74 Brunnbauer, "'Most Natural Function of Women.'"
75 "Svetal praznik."

4. Crafting Socialist Identities

1 Gurvich and Vajnberg, "Inzhener Kemar Ragimova"; and "Pis'mo Stasovoj v CK s prilozheniem iz knigi Shaburovoj 'Zhenshhina Vostoka v bor'be za novuju zhizn'.'"
2 Rakovskij, "Zhenshhina vostoka."
3 See Kamp, *New Woman in Uzbekistan*, 237–9.
4 Goldman, *Women at the Gates.*
5 "V pervyh rjadah."

6 Rubcova, "Gotovim kadry"; and Enukidze, "Vazhnaja zadacha sovetov."

7 "Pobediteli hlopkovyh polej."

8 "Mamljakat."

9 See, e.g., Idiceanu-Mathe and Carjan, "Architecture for the New Man."

10 Božić, "Šta ženama osigurava ustav."

11 Todorova, "9 septemvri i balgarskata zhena."

12 Dragoycheva, "Osem godini ravnopravni i shtastlivi."

13 "Devoyki-turkini – sestri v TKZS."

14 "Devoyki-turkini – sestri v TKZS."

15 Rusev, "Sakrovishtnitsa na nesmetni bogatstva," 13.

16 *Priča o fabrici; Danka*; Stoyanova, "Kam modernizatsiya i emantsipatsiya."

17 *Jezero.*

18 *Zenica.*

19 *Rebro Adamovo.*

20 Ragaru, "Symbolic Time(s) of Violence."

21 Rizel', "Zhenshhiny sovetskogo Vostoka."

22 Bykova, "Smelee vydvigat' zhenshhin na nauchnuju rabotu."

23 Grgić, "Kingdom of Diversity and Paternalism," 217.

24 Stoyanov, *Turskoto naselenie v Balgariya.*

25 Mimica, "Analfabetski tečajevi."

26 Prodanović, "Šta sve naša organizacija može da učini u pomoći majci i detetu."

27 See, e.g., Jayawardena, *Feminism and Nationalism.*

28 "Sličice sa analfabetskih tečajeva"; and "Za svoje prosvećivanje."

29 N.H., "Žene Srbije za svoju domovinu"; and "Uspesi i novi zadaci Antifašističkog fronta žena Makedonije."

30 Tsoneva, "Zhenskite druzhestva i neformalnoto obrazovanie v Balgariya."

31 "'Protokol № 103,'" 103.

32 "Zapisnik sa sastanka u Upravi za propagandu i agitaciju CK KPJ sa drugovima iz Sreskog komiteta Mostar."

33 "Izveštaj o stanju na selu."

34 Valiavicharska, *Restless History*, 84.

35 "Sastanak plenuma Glavnog odbora AFŽ Srbije"; and "Zapisnik sa savjetovanja rukovodilaca sreskih sekcija žena sa sarajevske oblasti."

36 Merdjanova, *Rediscovering the Umma*, 50.

37 Sokolović, *Dužnosti i obaveze roditelja prema djeci.*

38 *Statistički Godišnjak FNRJ* (1961), 87.

39 *Statisticheski godishnik na Narodna republika Balgariya* (1962), 62. For general overview of Bulgarian economic policies, see Vachkov, "Ikonomikata na Komunisticheska Bylgariya (1944–1962)"; and Ivanov, "Ikonomikata na Komunisticheska Bylgariya (1963–1989)."

40 Sternadori, "Heroines under Control," 145.
41 Aleksandrov, "Gordost na zavoda."
42 Rowley, "Spreading the Bolshevik Message?," 119.
43 Mezenina, "Gibnet proshloe – rastet novoe."
44 Pantieleva, "Pereplav."
45 F.R., "Iz otstalyh v peredovye."
46 Gorki, "Vtoromu vselagernomu sletu kanaloarmeek Dmitrovskogo lagerja."
47 O.J., "Ko je udarnik taj ne sustaje."
48 For the Soviet case, see Randall, "'Revolutionary Bolshevik Work.'"
49 Ilić, "Zajedno ćemo graditi prugu."
50 B.C., "Nosimo mladost, polet i snagu …"
51 Nikolov, "Priyatelki."
52 "'Protokol № 103,'" 4.
53 Garvanov, "Kray Arda."
54 Milanov, "Parvite svetlini."
55 Milanov, "Parvite svetlini."
56 Milanov, "Parvite svetlini."
57 "Mezhdunaroden den na zhenata."
58 "Nashi deputatki." The details on the number of MPs are presented in Burnaski, "ZHenite sred elita na turskata obshtnost v Balgariya."
59 "Laureatki na Dimitrovski nagradi."
60 "Na radu za plan."
61 D.V., "Radnice prvog industriskog preduzeća u Sandžaku"; and Šantrić, "Ćilimarska zadruga u Peći."
62 "8 mart 1946."
63 "Istaknuti udarnik Alija Sirotanović postigao najveći učinak u istoriji rudnika."
64 Sternadori, "Heroines under Control," 145.
65 Krapacheva, "Fakti, koito sgryavat."
66 *Statisticheski godishnik na Narodna republika Balgariya* (1959), 28.
67 See Gudac-Dodić, *Agrarna politika FNRJ i seljaštvo u Srbiji*; and Gruev, "Collectivization and Social Change."
68 Simić, "Building Socialism."
69 Bokovoy, *Peasants and Communists*; Gudac-Dodić, *Agrarna politika FNRJ i seljaštvo u Srbiji*; and Simic, *Soviet Influences*.
70 Gruev, "Collectivization and Social Change."
71 "Mezhdunaroden den na zhenata."
72 "Ocena rada sekretarijata Glavnog odbora AFŽ-a Makedonije."
73 "Provodićemo u život zadatke Petog kongresa naše Partije."
74 Šantrić, "Ćilimarska zadruga u Peći."
75 "Godišnji izveštaj za rad Glavnog odbora AFŽ-a Makedonije."

76 "Maystorki na visoki dobivi."

77 "Rolyata na zhenite v ukrepvane na TKZS."

78 "Rech na drugarya Valko Chervenkov."

79 Balgarova, "Edinadeset godini narodna vlast"; and *Statisticheski godishnik na Narodna republika Balgariya* (1962), 213.

80 Stancheva, "Kravarkata Hamide," 14–15. Michurinian science related to works of the Soviet scientist Ivan Vladimirovich Michurin.

81 "Tretiyat kongres na otechestveniya front," 4–5.

82 Voynov, "Nefise."

83 "Rolyata na zhenite v ukrepvane na TKZS."

84 Darakchi, "Gender, Religion, and Identity," 3.

85 Sternadori, "Heroines under Control."

86 "Zapisnik komisije za rad sa ženama Saveznog odbora SSRNJ."

87 "Sa birališta."

88 Nidžić, "Govor na I Kongresu."

89 Vokši, "Govor na II Kongresu AFŽ."

90 Nimani, "Govor na IV Kongresu AFŽ."

91 Drobnjak, *Ženska strana parlamenta*.

92 *Statistički Godišnjak Jugoslavije 1973*, 76.

93 *Statistički Godišnjak Jugoslavije 1988*, 115.

94 *Directory of Officials of the Socialist Federal Republic of Yugoslavia*.

95 Malešević, *Didara*.

96 "Materijal za referat IV Kongresa AFŽ Jugoslavije."

97 Muratova, "Muslim Women," 131–2.

98 Kamberović, *Džemal Bijedić*.

99 Mantarliev, "Izborite za narodni saveti v NR Balgariya prez 1949 g."

100 "'Protokol № 103,'" 103.

101 "'Protokol № 103,'" 5.

102 Burnaski, "ZHenite sred elita na turskata obshtnost v Balgariya," 34.

103 Yosifova, "Delegatkata Asie Mehmedova."

104 [Untitled article], *ZHenata dnes*, no. 12 (1952): 1.

105 See "ZHenski deyatelki," 3.

106 Burnaski, "ZHenite sred elita na turskata obshtnost v Balgariya," 44.

107 Burnaski, 57.

108 *Statisticheski godishnik na Narodna republika Balgariya* (1988).

109 Sternadori, "Heroines under Control," 146.

110 M.B., "Slava i chest na mnogodetnite mayki."

111 Simic, *Soviet Influences*, 54.

112 Sternadori, "Heroines under Control."

113 Quoted in Marcheva, "Sotsialisticheskoto ravnopravie na zhenite," 268.

114 Marcheva, 269.

115 Nazarska, "Muslim Women and the Women's Movement."

116 Nikolova and Ghodsee, "Socialist Wallpaper," 320.
117 Valiavicharska, *Restless History*, 81–2.
118 "Korespondentsiya s TSK na BKP."
119 "Predlozhenia za podobrenie rabotata vsred turkinite."
120 "Predlozhenia za podobrenie rabotata vsred turkinite."
121 "'Protokol № 103,'" 5.
122 "Sreshta na turkinite ot Kolarovgradski okrag."
123 "Sreshta na turkinite ot Kolarovgradski okrag."
124 Brunnbauer, "Making Bulgarians Socialist," 60.
125 Brunnbauer, 60.
126 Nazarska, "Muslim Women and the Women's Movement."
127 Marcheva, "Sotsialisticheskoto ravnopravie na zhenite," 269.
128 Tomšič, "Rad i zadatak Antifašističkog fronta žena"; and Mimica, "Pod rukovodstvom partije."
129 Lóránd, *Feminist Challenge*.

5. Unveiling and Redressing of Muslim Women

1 Zetkin, "K zhenshhinam okrainnyh respublik," 3.
2 Ahmed, *Quiet Revolution*, 19.
3 Scott, *Sex and Secularism*, 37–8.
4 Ahmed, *Quiet Revolution*, 33.
5 MacMaster, *Burning the Veil*, 62.
6 Edgar, "Bolshevism, Patriarchy, and the Nation."
7 Kamp, *New Woman in Uzbekistan*.
8 Edgar, "Bolshevism, Patriarchy, and the Nation."
9 Ljubimova, "Bor'ba na ideologicheskom fronte."
10 Vlašić, "Modern Women," 68–90.
11 E.g., "Oblekloto na turskata zhena," 2; and "Feredzhetata va Turtsiya," 2.
12 Paraskevov, "Insecurity and Control."
13 Akiner, "Between Tradition and Modernity," 268.
14 Massell, *Surrogate Proletariat*.
15 Akiner, "Between Tradition and Modernity," 268.
16 Keller, "Trapped between State and Society," 21.
17 Akiner, "Between Tradition and Modernity."
18 Keller, "Trapped between State and Society," 23.
19 Ibragimov, "Iz obsledovanij Semipalatinskoj gubernii"; and Ljubimova, "Vsesojuznyj s''ezd rabotnic i krest'janok i rabota sredi zhenshhin Vostoka."
20 Keller, "Trapped between State and Society," 21.
21 "O rabote sredi devushek na Vostoke"; and Zavar'jan, "Nekotorye momenty iz raboty zhenshhin srednej Azii."

22 Sejfi, "Na pomoshh' zhenskim promyslam na Vostoke"; and Zahar'jan, "Brachnoe i semejnoe pravo na Vostoke."

23 Keller, "Trapped between State and Society."

24 Kasparova, "Zadachi partii v oblasti raboty sredi zhenshhin vostochnyh narodnostej."

25 Kasparova, "Itogi i perspektivy raboty na Vostoke."

26 Keller, "Trapped between State and Society," 22.

27 Edgar, "Bolshevism, Patriarchy, and the Nation."

28 A.K., "Poslednjaja rabynja"; and Putilovskaja, "Rabota kommunisticheskih partij sredi zhenshhin narodov vostoka."

29 Akiner, "Between Tradition and Modernity," 266; Edgar, "Emancipation of the Unveiled," 132; and Keller, *To Moscow, Not Mecca*, 65.

30 Akiner, "Between Tradition and Modernity," 269.

31 Keller, "Trapped between State and Society," 22.

32 Kasparova, "Zhenskoe dvizhenie na Vostoke."

33 Putilovskaja, "Rabota kommunisticheskih partij sredi zhenshhin narodov vostoka."

34 Keller, "Trapped between State and Society," 22.

35 Sejfi, "Zhenshhiny vostoka."

36 Ishkova, "Rabota mest."

37 E.g., Ljubimova, "Na Vostoke"; and F.M., "Sredi turchanok."

38 Nikolaeva, "Pervye itogi."

39 Nyurina, "V Srednej Azii"; and Ljubimova, "Zhenskie lavki v Srednej Azii."

40 Akiner, "Between Tradition and Modernity," 270.

41 Kamp, "Pilgrimage and Performance," 264.

42 Kamp, 278.

43 "Zhenshhina truzhenica i revoljucija."

44 "K trudjashhimsja zhenshhinam vseh kapitalisticheskih stran."

45 Artyukhina, "Vos'moe marta 1927 goda."

46 "Po SSSR."

47 Keller, "Trapped between State and Society," 20.

48 Keller, 71.

49 Northrop, *Veiled Empire*; and Kamp, *New Woman in Uzbekistan*.

50 Nikolaeva, "Pervye itogi."

51 Kamp, *New Woman in Uzbekistan*, 163.

52 Edgar, *Tribal Nation*.

53 Edgar, 149.

54 "Bor'ba s bajstvom i kul'turnoj otstalost'ju."

55 Stepanov, "Perezhitki proshlogo."

56 Ljubimova, "Dekret o chadre i obshhestvo"; and Artyukhina, "Ot 'nastuplenija' k sistematicheskoj rabote."

57 Artyukhina, "Ot 'nastuplenija' k sistematicheskoj rabote."
58 Keller, "Trapped between State and Society," 27–8.
59 Kamp, *New Woman in Uzbekistan*, 213.
60 "Nuzhno li izdat' dekret, zapreshhajushhij noshenie chadry."
61 Bogacheva, "O chadre."
62 Ljubimova, "Dekret o chadre i obshhestvo."
63 Krupskaja, "Puti raskreposhhenija zhenshhin Vostoka."
64 Northrop, *Veiled Empire*, 156.
65 Keller, *To Moscow, Not Mecca*, 200.
66 Kamp, *New Woman in Uzbekistan*, 235.
67 Northrop, "Languages of Loyalty."
68 Northrop, "Subaltern Dialogues."
69 Kamp, *New Woman in Uzbekistan*, 237–40.
70 Matkaramova, "Tadzhihan"; and "Pis'mo schastlivogo uzbekskogo naroda."
71 Hadžić, "Sarajke su glasale"; and Begović, "Prvi put na izborima."
72 Jakupović, "Govor na I Kongresu."
73 Nidžić, "Govor na I Kongresu."
74 "Kongres žena Makedonije."
75 "Gosti na našem kongresu."
76 "Rezolucija Drugog kongresa Antifašističkog fronta žena povodom pokreta muslimanki za skidanje zara."
77 "Iz osmomartovskog takmičenja."
78 "Akcija za skidanje feredže na teritoriji mjesnih odbora Plav i Gusinje."
79 "Izveštaj Centralnog odbora AFŽ-a Jugoslavije."
80 Babović, "Govor na II Kongresu AFŽ."
81 "Sastanak plenuma Glavnog odbora AFŽ Srbije"; and "Savjetovanje AFŽ-a Crne Gore."
82 "Izveštaj glavnog odbora AFŽ-a Bosne i Hercegovine."
83 Humo, "Organizacija žena."
84 "Muslimanke na konferenciji."
85 Fejić, "Govor održan prigodom primanja menšure 12 septembra 1947."
86 Tomić, "Referat održan na II Plenumu Centralnog odbora AFŽ Jugoslavije."
87 "Sprovodimo u djelo odluke Petog kongresa naše Partije."
88 "Rezolucija o narednim zadatcima."
89 "Untitled Report from the Macedonian AFŽ."
90 "Narodna skupština Srbije pozdravlja inicijativu muslimanki za skidanje feredži."
91 Lj.A., "I muslimani Kosmeta i Sandžaka"; "One se bore za ranopravno učešće u javnom i privrednom životu."
92 Fejić, "Ja dijelim mišljenje naroda, a narod je rekao svoju riječ."

93 *Zakon o zabrani nošenja zara i feredže.*

94 "Objavljen je Zakon o zabrani nošenja zara i feredže."

95 Ljubuncic, "Otkrivanje muslimanke."

96 Srećković et al., *Priračnik za kulturno-prosvetna rabota.*

97 "Zapisnik sa sastanka političkih sekretara."

98 "O prosvetnom i kulturno umetničkom radu Narodne omladine u 1950. godini."

99 "INFORMACIJA o radu organizacije Narodne omladine sa ženskom omladinom"; "Materijali od XI plenaren sostanok na Centralnoiot komitet na Naordnata mladina na Makedonija"; and "O nekim problemima u radu sa ženskom omladinom."

100 Marinčević, "Počela je borba protiv neznanja i zaostalosti."

101 "Stenografske beleške sastanka izvršnog odbora Centralnog odbora Antifašističkog fronta žena Jugoslavije"; and "Akcija zdravstvenog prosvećivanja na Kosmetu."

102 Perić, "Nepoznati znanci."

103 Radojičić, "Dole zar i feredža!"

104 "Zapisnik VI plenarnog sastanka Glavnog odbora AFŽ-a Makedonije"; "Zapisnik br 8 sa sastanka sekretarijata Centralnog odbora AFŽ Jugoslavije u 1951 godini"; and "Izveštaj ekipe koja je obradila teren sreza titogradskog."

105 Jakšić, "Pisma uredništvu."

106 Mujdović, "Govor na IV Kongresu AFŽ."

107 Neuburger, *Orient Within,* 27.

108 Aneva, "Po shirokiya kooperativen drum"; and Minchev, "Krayat na edno robstvo."

109 Nahodilova, "Experiences of Communist Modernization," 90.

110 Nahodilova, 102.

111 "Doklad na nachalnika na OU – MVR, gr. Kardzhali."

112 "Dokladna zapiska na zamestnik-nachalnika na V otdel kam Upravlenie na Granichni voyski i nachalnika na Treto upravlenie na DS."

113 "Spetsialno saobshtenie na Okrazhno upravlenie – MVR – Blagoevgrad."

114 "Doklad ot polk. Stoyan Iliev."

115 Marinov, "Ot internatsionalizam kam natsionalizam," 501.

116 Dimitrova, "ZHenata v savremennoto balgarsko izobrazitelno izkustvo."

117 Dimitrova, "ZHenata v savremennoto balgarsko izobrazitelno izkustvo."

118 Neuburger, "Veils, Shalvari, and Matters of Dress," 169.

119 Savova-Mahon Borden, "Politics of Nationalism," 43.

120 Nikolova and Ghodsee, "Socialist Wallpaper," 327.

121 E.g., Vagabov, *Otnoshenieto na myusyulmanskata religiya kam zhenata* was published just a year later after its Soviet original.

122 Neuburger, *Orient Within.*

123 Nikolova and Ghodsee, "Socialist Wallpaper."
124 Myuhtar-May, *Identity, Nationalism, and Cultural Heritage*, 114.
125 Myuhtar-May, 120–1.
126 "Spravka otnosno nastroenieto na balgaromohamedanskoto naselenie v selo Filipovo."
127 "Spravka otnosno liniyata na vrazheskata deynost," 148.
128 "Spravka otnosno liniyata na vrazheskata deynost."
129 "Molba ot turskoto naselenie na s. Gradsko."
130 "Spravka ot okrazhniya nachalnik na MVR – Kardzhali."
131 "Spravka otnosno dopusnatite izvrashteniya v razferedzhavaneto sred turskoto naselenie v Razgradski okrag, Razgrad."
132 Myuhtar-May, *Identity, Nationalism, and Cultural Heritage*, 120–1.
133 E.g., Dzhedzheva, "Pod sashtoto nebe."
134 Minchev, "Krayat na edno robstvo."
135 Danilov, "Kam svobodata, kam svetlinata."
136 Nahodilova, "Experiences of Communist Modernization," 76.
137 Muratova, "Muslim Women," 141.
138 This order is printed in full in Eminov, *Turkish and Other Muslim Minorities*, 180.
139 Chatterjee, "Whose Imagined Community?"
140 Muratova, "Muslim Women," 142.

6. Gendered Interventions and Challenges to Masculinities

 1 "Priče će biti tri dana, a slobode dovijeka."
 2 E.g., MacMaster, *Burning the Veil*.
 3 A.K., "Poslednjaja rabynja."
 4 Fabaeva, "Po Vostoku."
 5 Putilovskaja, "Rabota kommunisticheskih partij sredi zhenshhin narodov vostoka."
 6 Dushinova, "Zhenshhiny v Kirgizskoj respublike."
 7 Aktjubinka, "Perevybory sovetov v Kirgizii."
 8 Northrop, *Veiled Empire*.
 9 Michaels, *Curative Powers*, 153.
10 Anthropologists and other scholars also contributed to this discourse. See Pišev, "Između 'azijatskog' islama i 'pravoslavnog' slovenstva," 189.
11 "Bajram je prošao …" Interestingly, the same newspaper wrote about the difficult position of Muslims in Bulgaria and heavily criticized their discrimination (Ćemalović, "Muslimani u Bugarskoj").
12 Anđelković, "Nekoliko reči o muslimanki."
13 See, e.g., H., "Borba protiv fesa i feredže."
14 Mirkova, *Muslim Land, Christian Labor*, 25.

15 "Pis'mo rukovodstva BNZhS v Antifashistskij komitet sovetskih zhenshhin."

16 E.g., Arbat, "Iz ropstva harema." Yugoslav and Bulgarian magazines ackowledged the original Soviet source.

17 "Devoyki-turkini – sestri v TKZS."

18 "Žene junačke Bosne i Hercegovine."

19 "Muslimanke na konferenciji."

20 Milanov, "Parvite svetlini."

21 Stefanova, "Znatna takachka," 5.

22 "Diskusija."

23 Nidžić, "Govor na I Kongresu"; and Spasojević, "13,426 žena pojećuje analfabetske tečajeve."

24 Marašović, "Govor na Drugom kongresu Antifašističkog fronta žena Bosne i Hercegovine."

25 Muratova, "Muslim Women," 131–2. On the work of the Bulgarian Women's Union, see Marcheva, "Za opekunskoto predstavitelstvo na zhenite v Balgariya 1944 – 1958 g."

26 Siegelbaum, "'Dear Comrade, You Ask What We Need.'"

27 Varsa, *Protected Children, Regulated Mothers*.

28 Examples include Nakachi, *Replacing the Dead*; and Dumančić, *Men out of Focus*.

29 See, e.g., Thelen, "Shortage, Fuzzy Property and Other Dead Ends."

30 Pachamanova, "Aspekti na paternalizma i populizma."

31 This language was always present; see, e.g., "Zhenshhina truzhenica i revoljucija"; and Vagabov, *Otnoshenieto na myusyulmanskata religiya kam zhenata*.

32 "Slovo imeet gramotnaja zhenshhina sovetskogo Vostoka"; and Vasil'eva, "Moguchaya sila sotsializma."

33 "Doklad sekretarej CK VLKSM"; "Plenum Glavnog Odbora AFŽ-a Za Hrvatsku"; and Ilieva, "Vesti ot rodinata."

34 "Put' k stanku."

35 Simic, *Soviet Influences*.

36 Valiavicharska, *Restless History*, 87.

37 Dugonjic-Rodwin and Mladenović, "Transnational Educational Strategies."

38 Merdjanova, *Rediscovering the Umma*, 51.

39 "Informacija upolnomochennogo Soveta po delam religioznyh kul'tov pri Sovmine SSSR po Oshskoj oblasti I.G. Halimova."

40 Thibault, "Labour Migration, Sex, and Polygyny."

41 Gruev and Kalionski, *Vazroditelniyat protses*, 42–3; Ghodsee, *Muslim Lives in Eastern Europe*, 68; and Hopken, "Po-slozhno ot 'etnicheskoto prochistvane,'" 226.

42 Radić, "Islamska verska zajednica 1945–1970. godine."
43 Northrop, *Veiled Empire*, 237.
44 "Menja se lik Novog Pazara."
45 Novotni, "Naviknuće se Salih beg."
46 Frdnić, "Mahale."
47 Neuburger, "Veils, Shalvari, and Matters of Dress," 172.
48 Diavatov, "Kolarovgrad."
49 Diavatov, "Vavilonsko smehotvorenie."
50 Gancheva, "Darzhavna namesa v lichniya i kulturen zhivot na balgarskite turtsi v godinite na komunisticheskiya rezhim," 211.
51 "Spravka otnosno dopusnatite izvrashteniya v razferedzhavaneto sred turskoto naselenie v Razgradski okrag, Razgrad."
52 Myuhtar-May, *Identity, Nationalism, and Cultural Heritage*, 120.
53 "Informatsiya otnosno nastroeniya i proyavi sred balgarskite mohamedani ot Smolyanski okrag."
54 Bemporad, "Behavior Unbecoming a Communist"; and Polianski, *"Pathologia religiosa."*
55 Karklins, "Islam"; and Bennigsen, *Musul'mane v SSSR*.
56 Sokolović, *Dužnosti i obaveze roditelja prema djeci*, 20.
57 Gruev and Kalionski, *Vazroditelniyat protses*, 36.
58 Marinov, "Ot internatsionalizam kam natsionalizam," 501–2; and Gruev and Kalionski, *Vazroditelniyat protses*, 36.
59 "Spravka na nachalnika na Treti otdel na DS," 194.
60 Gancheva, "Darzhavna namesa v lichniya i kulturen zhivot na balgarskite turtsi v godinite na komunisticheskiya rezhim," 214.
61 Gruev and Kalionski, *Vazroditelniyat protses*, 37.
62 Eminov, *Turkish and Other Muslim Minorities*, 182.
63 Muratova, "Politiki na sotsialisticheskata vlast v Balgariya," 91–2.
64 Burnaski, "Prosvetnoto delo i 'kulturnata revolyutsiya.'"
65 Northrop, *Veiled Empire*, 183.
66 Brunnbauer, "Families and Mountains in the Balkans," 348.
67 McCallum, "Man about the House"; and Merdjanova, *Rediscovering the Umma*, 104.
68 Nahodilova, "Experiences of Communist Modernization."
69 Darakchi, "Gender, Religion, and Identity."
70 Myuhtar-May, *Identity, Nationalism, and Cultural Heritage*.
71 *Darzhavna sigurnost*, vol. 1.
72 Hopken, "Po-slozhno ot 'etnicheskoto prochistvane,'" 221.
73 Pezo, "Emigration and Policy in Yugoslavia."
74 "Neprijateljske parole od marta 1946."
75 "Zapisnik VI plenarnog sastanka Glavnog odbora AFŽ-a Makedonije."
76 Arat, "Project of Modernity."

77 Hopken, "Po-slozhno ot 'etnicheskoto prochistvane.'"
78 Hopken, "Po-slozhno ot 'etnicheskoto prochistvane.'"
79 Ivanov and Önsoy, "From Integration to Assimilation and Forced
    Migration."
80 "Spravka ot nachalnika na III otdelenie." On the concept of hope within
    the migration context, see Parla, *Precarious Hope*.
81 "Dokladna zapiska na nachalnika na Treto upravlenie na DS."
82 Hopken, "Po-slozhno ot 'etnicheskoto prochistvane,'" 220.
83 Ognyanov, "Iz doklad na Penyu Dokuzov."
84 On the so-called "revival process," see Gruev and Kalionski, *Vazroditelniyat
    protses*; and Kamusella, *Ethnic Cleansing*.
85 Ivanov and Önsoy, "From Integration to Assimilation and Forced
    Migration," 48.

Conclusions

1 "Doklad sekretarej CK VLKSM."

Bibliography

Primary Sources

"1. maj" [May Day]. *Proleter*, no. 5 (May 1933): 1.

"8 mart 1946" [8 March 1946]. *Žena danas*, no. 40 (March 1946): 11–14.

A.K. "Poslednjaja rabynja (K s''ezdu narodov vostoka)" [The last slave (To the Congress of the Peoples of the East)]. *Kommunistka* 1920, no. 7, 24–6.

"Akcija za skidanje feredže na teritoriji mjesnih odbora Plav i Gusinje" [The campaign to discard the veil in the territory of the local councils of Plav and Gusinje]. *Naša žena* 4, nos. 6–7 (July 1947): 7.

"Akcija zdravstvenog prosvećivanja na Kosmetu" [Health awareness campaign in Kosmet]. *Žena danas*, no. 82 (April 1951): 8.

Aktjubinka. "Perevybory sovetov v Kirgizii" [Re-election of the Soviets in Kirghizia]. *Kommunistka* 1924, no. 10, 50.

Aleksandrov, Yordan. "Gordost na zavoda" [Pride of the factory]. *ZHenata dnes*, no. 7 (1957): 2–3.

Aleksandrova, Lilyana. "Sartseto na Rifat" [Rifat's heart]. *ZHenata dnes*, no. 8 (1957): 16–17.

Anđelković, Radunka. "Nekoliko reči o muslimanki" [A few words about Muslim women]. *Ženski pokret*, October 1923, 354–60.

Aneva, Vesela. "Po shirokiya kooperativen drum" [Along the wide cooperative road]. *ZHenata dnes*, no. 1 (1958): 2–3.

Arbat, Jurij. "Iz ropstva harema" [From harem slavery]. *Žena danas*, no. 53 (1948): 44–5.

Artyukhina, Aleksandra. "Ot 'nastuplenija' k sistematicheskoj rabote (k obsledovaniju raboty v srednej Azii)" [From "offensive" to systematic work (towards an evaluation of work in Central Asia)]. *Kommunistka* 1928, no. 1, 57–63.

– "Vos'moe marta 1927 goda" [8 March 1927]. *Pravda*, 8 March 1927, 3.

B.C. "Nosimo mladost, polet i snagu …" [We bring youth, enthusiasm, and strength]. *Borba na Omladinskoj pruzi*, no. 63 (15 June 1947): 7.

Babović, Spasenija. "Govor na II Kongresu AFŽ" [Speech at the 2nd AFŽ Congress]. 1948. Archives of Yugoslavia, f. 141 AFŽ, box 2.

"Bajram je prošao …" [Bairam has ended]. *Vreme*, 16 March 1929.

Balgarova, Rada. "Edinadeset godini narodna vlast" [Eleven years of people's government]. *ZHenata dnes*, no. 8 (1955): 2.

Bebel, August. *Žena i socijalizam [Women and socialism]*. Belgrade: Socijalistička knjižara, 1909.

Begović, Radmila. "Prvi put na izborima" [First time at the polls]. *Nova žena* 1, no. 7 (October 1945): 13–14.

Belić, Stevan. "Moji doživljaji u SSSR" [My experiences in the USSR]. 1934. Hrvatski državni arhiv, fond 1753 Očak Ivan, box 83.

Beljaeva. "Zhdut vesnu" [Waiting for spring]. *Rabotnica* 1932, nos. 19–20, 12.

Bogacheva. "O chadre" [On the veil]. *Kommunistka* 1928, no. 11, 66.

"Bor'ba s bajstvom i kul'turnoj otstalost'ju" [Struggle against bays and cultural backwardness]. *Pravda*, 10 March 1928, 4.

Božić, Ana. "Šta ženama osigurava ustav" [What the constitution guarantees to women]. *Zora*, no. 2 (February 1946): 2.

Božinović, Neda. "Izveštaj o radu komisije za porodične odnose na selu" [Report of the Committee for Family Relations in the Countryside]. 1953. Archives of Yugoslavia, f. 141 AFŽ, box 5.

"Brakovi u sudskoj arhivi" [Divorce in court archives]. *Žena danas*, no. 90 (December 1951): 10.

Butuzova. "Zhenskie lavki v Uzbekistane" [Women's shops in Uzbekistan]. *Kommunistka* 1927, no. 9, 62–7.

Bykova, K. "Smelee vydvigat' zhenshhin na nauchnuju rabotu" [Nominate more women for scientific work]. *Rabotnica* 1935, nos. 14–15, 10–11.

Ćemalović, Smail Aga. "Muslimani u Bugarskoj" [Muslims in Bulgaria]. *Vreme*, 11 November 1932, 2.

Čolaković, Rodoljub. "Novi Sovjetski ustav" [The new Soviet constitution]. *Proleter*, no. 1 (January 1937): 1.

Cvijić, Jovan. "O iseljavanju bosanskih muhamedanaca" [On the immigration of Bosnian-Mohamedians]. In *Govori i članci*, 1:8–9. Belgrade: Napredak, 1921.

D.V. "Radnice prvog industriskog preduzeća u Sandžaku" [Women workers of the first industrial firm in Sandžak]. *Borba*, 15 February 1949, 2.

Danilov, V. "Kam svobodata, kam svetlinata" [To freedom, to light]. *ZHenata dnes*, no. 1 (1960): 2–3.

Danka. Sofia: Boyana Film, 1952.

Darzhavna sigurnost – smyanata na imenata – vazroditelniya protses (1945–1985 g.). Dokumentalen sbornik. Vol. 1. Sofia: Komisiya za razkrivane na dokumentite i za obyavyavane na prinadlezhnost na balgarski grazhdani kam Darzhavna sigurnost i razuznavatelnite sluzhbi na Balgarskata narodna armiya, 2013.

"Devoyki-turkini – sestri v TKZS" [Turkish girls – sisters in the TKZS]. *ZHenata dnes*, no. 9 (1956): 9.

Diavatov, Ionchev. "Kolarovgrad." *Starshel*, no. 327 (16 May 1952): 3.

– "Vavilonsko smehotvorenie" [A Babylonian mockery]. *Starshel*, no. 197 (18 November 1949): 4.

Dimitrov, Georgi. *The Diary of Georgi Dimitrov, 1933–1949*. Edited by Ivo Banac. New Haven, CT: Yale University Press, 2003.

– "The United Front and Women." In *Selected Works*, Vol. 2. Sofia: Sofia Press, 1972.

Dimitrova, B. "ZHenata v savremennoto balgarsko izobrazitelno izkustvo" [Women in contemporary Bulgarian art]. *ZHenata dnes*, no. 2 (1956): 12–13.

Directory of Officials of the Bulgarian People's Republic. Washington, DC: Central Intelligence Agency, 1965.

Directory of Officials of the Socialist Federal Republic of Yugoslavia: A Reference Aid. Washington, DC: National Foreign Assessment Center, 1979.

"Direktivy dlja raboty sredi narodov Vostoka" [Directives for work among the peoples of the East]. 21 February 1920. Russian State Archive of Sociopolitical History (RGASPI), f. 122, op. 1, d. 30, ll. 67–67ob.

"Diskusija" [Discussion]. *Nova žena*, nos. 15–16 (July 1946): 7–10.

Dobreva, E. "V otgovor na chitatelkite" [In response to readers]. *ZHenata dnes*, no. 4 (1952): 21.

"Doklad na nachalnika na OU – MVR, gr. Kardzhali do Parvi otdel na DS za nastroenieto i otnoshenieto na balgaromohamedanskoto naselenie v sektora kam pravitelstvenite meropriyatiya, Kardzhali, 17 yuli 1948 g." [Report by the head of the Kardzhali District Directorate to the First Department of State Security on the mood and attitude of the Bulgarian Muslim population in the sector to government events, Kardzhali, 17 July 1948]. In *Darzhavna sigurnost*, 1:82–3.

"Dokladna zapiska na nachalnika na Treto upravlenie na DS po izpalnenieto na zapoved № I – 224 ot 19 yuni 1962 g., Sofiya, 29 yanuari 1963 g." [Memorandum of the Head of the Third Directorate of the State Security on the implementation of order no. I-224 of 19 June 1962, Sofia, 29 January 1963]. In *Darzhavna sigurnost*, 1:196–7.

"Dokladna zapiska na zamestnik-nachalnika na V otdel kam Upravlenie na Granichni voyski i nachalnika na Treto upravlenie na DS do ministara na vatreshnite raboti otnosno sazdadenoto nastroenie sred balgaromohamedanskoto naselenie po povod pasportizatsiyata, Sofiya, 16 fevruari 1953 g." [Memorandum of the deputy head of Department V at the Border Police Directorate and the head of the Third Directorate of State Security to the minister of the interior on the attitude established among the Bulgarian Muslim population on the occasion of passportization, Sofia, 16 February 1953]. In *Darzhavna sigurnost*, 1:114–17.

"Doklad ot polk. Stoyan Iliev otnosno napravena proverka po dopusnato iz-vrashtenie sred pomashkoto naselenie vav vrazka s pasportizatsiyata, Sofiya, 23 yuni 1953 g." [Report by Col. Stoyan Iliev regarding an inspection conducted on the permitted return among the Pomak population in connection with passportization, Sofia, 23 June 1953]. In *Darzhavna sigurnost*, 1:124–7.

"Doklad sekretarej CK VLKSM Stalinu o vystuplenijah na s"ezdah zhenskoj molodezhi nacional'nyh respublik" [Report of the secretaries of the Central Committee of the Komsomol to Stalin on the speeches at the Congresses of the Female Youth of the National Republics]. 11 December 1935. RGASPI, f. 17, op. 114, d. 734, ll. 91–105.

"Doklad tov. Karimovoj o rabote sredi zhenshhin Tashkenta" [Report to Com. Karimova on work among women in Tashkent]. 23 June 1920. RGASPI, f. 17, op. 10, d. 222, l. 6.

"Doklad turkmenki na pervom s"ezde zhenshhin Vostoka" [Report by Turkmen women at the first meeting of women of the East]. 5 March 1921. RGASPI, f. 544, op. 4, d. 32, ll. 107–108ob.

"Doklad v KirCIK o polozhenii kirgizskoj zhenshhiny" [Report to KirCIK on the Position of Kyrgyz women]. 23 November 1923. RGASPI, f. 17, op. 10, d. 387, ll. 59–59ob.

"Doklad v KirCIK o sozdanii Komissii po ulchsheniju byta kirgizskoj zhenshhiny" [Report to KirCIK on the establishment of a committee to improve the life of Kyrgyz women]. 16 November 1923. RGASPI, f. 17, op. 10, d. 387, ll. 58–58ob.

Dragoycheva, Tsola. "Osem godini ravnopravni i shtastlivi" [Eight years of equality and happiness]. *ZHenata dnes*, nos. 7–8 (1952): 2–3.

Dudić, Dragojlo. *Dnevnik 1941 [Diary, 1941]*. Belgrade: Prosveta, 1957.

Dushinova. "Zhenshhiny v Kirgizskoj respublike" [Women in the Kirgiz Republic]. *Kommunistka* 1921, nos. 10–11, 44–5.

Dzhedzheva, Tamara. "Pod sashtoto nebe" [Under the same sky]. *ZHenata dnes*, no. 8 (1965): 13–14.

Ekmečić, Ešref. "Skamenjena prošlost" [Petrified past]. *Nova žena*, no. 5 (September 1955): 4–5.

Enukidze, A. "Vazhnaja zadacha sovetov" [The important task of the soviets]. *Pravda*, 8 March 1930, 4.

F.M. "Sredi turchanok" [Among turkish women]. *Pravda*, 11 March 1925, 5.

F.R. "Iz otstalyh v peredovye" [From backward to advanced]. *Rabotnica* 1936, no. 5, 3–4.

Fabaeva. "Po Vostoku. Byt i pravo gorskoj zhenshhiny" [In the East: the life and rights of a mountain woman]. *Kommunistka* 1924, nos. 1–2, 39.

Fejić, Ibrahim. "Govor održan prigodom primanja menšure 12 septembra 1947 u Gazi Husrevbegovoj džamiji u Sarajevu" [Speech delivered on the occasion of receiving the *menšura* on 12 September 1947 at the Gazi Husrev-beg Mosque in Sarajevo]. *Glasnik Vrhovnog islamskog starješinstva*, nos. 1–3 (March 1950): 20–4.

– "Ja dijelim mišljenje naroda, a narod je rekao svoju riječ" [I share the people's view, and the people have spoken]. *Žena danas*, no. 75 (September 1950): 3.

– "Naša prva riječ" [Our first word]. *Glasnik Vrhovnog islamskog starješinstva*, nos. 1–3 (March 1950): 5–7.

"Feredzhetata va Turtsiya" [Veils in Turkey]. *Borba*, 14 September 1935, 2.

Fočanski propisi [The Foča ordinances]. Foča, Bosnia and Herzegovina: Muzej Fočanskog perioda NOB, 1981.

Fomina, O. "Kak ukrasit' zhilishhe" [How to decorate a home]. *Rabotnitsa*, no. 36 (December 1935): 15.

Frdnić, Nasko. "Mahale." *Borba*, 21 June 1959, 3.

Galevska, Rahela. *Poremećena porodica i deca [Disturbed family and children]*. Belgrade: Radnički univerzitet, 1958.

Garvanov, Todor. "Kray Arda" [Near Arda]. *ZHenata dnes*, no. 10 (1956): 7.

Gerasimova, Valerija. "Raskreposhhennyj genij" [Uninhibited genius]. *Pravda*, 8 March 1937, 2.

"Godišnji izveštaj za rad Glavnog odbora AFŽ-a Makedonije" [Annual report on the work of the Head Committee of the AFŽ of Macedonia]. December 1949. Archives of Yugoslavia, f. 141 AFŽ, box 15.

Golubev, S. "Danka." *Rabotnica* 1932, no. 15, 16.

Gorki, Maksim. "Vtoromu vselagernomu sletu kanaloarmeek Dmitrovskogo lagerja. Udarnicam na strojke kanala Moskva – Volga!" [The Second All-Camp Rally of the Canal Army Women of Dmitrovsky Camp: to the shock workers at the construction site of the Moscow–Volga Canal!]. *Pravda*, 9 March 1935, 3.

– "Za novuju, svetluju, razumnuju zhizn'" [For a new, brighter, more reasonable life]. *Rabotnica* 1931, no. 30, 12.

"Gosti na našem kongresu" [Guests at our congress]. *Nova žena*, no. 30 (August 1947): 20–2.

Gurvich, Ye., and Kl. Vajnberg. "Inzhener Kemar Ragimova – chlen bakinskogo soveta" [Engineer Kemar Ragimova, members of the Baku Council]. *Rabotnica* 1935, nos. 5–6, 9.

H. "Borba protiv fesa i feredže" [Struggle against the fez and veils]. *Politika*, 28 December 1927, 8.

Hadžić, Nadida. "Sarajke su glasale" [The women of Sarajevo have voted]. *Nova žena* 1, no. 8 (November 1945): 7.

Hr. Minchev. "Krayat na edno robstvo" [The end of one slavery]. *ZHenata dnes*, no. 8 (1959): 7.

Humo, Avdo. "Organizacija žena treba da razvije mnogo širu aktivnost na izvršavanju petogodišnjeg plana" [The women's organization needs to develop much broader activity on the execution of the Five-Year Plan]. *Nova žena* 4, no. 36 (April 1948): 1–3.

Ibárruri, Dolores. "Mezhdunarodnyj kommunisticheskij zhenskij den'" [International Communist Women's Day]. *Pravda*, 8 March 1938, 2.

Ibragimov. "Iz obsledovanij Semipalatinskoj gubernii" [From surveys of the Semipalatinsk Region]. *Kommunistka* 1925, no. 10, 87–9.

Ilić, Desa. "Zajedno ćemo graditi prugu" [We will construct the railroad together]. *Borba na Omladinskoj pruzi*, no. 10 (11 April 1947): 3.

Iliev, St. "Pravata na maykata i deteto u nas" [The rights of the mother and the child in our country]. *ZHenata dnes*, no. 2 (1951): 5.

Ilieva, G. "Vesti ot rodinata. Detska mlechna kuhnya" [News from the homeland: children's milk kitchen]. *ZHenata dnes*, no. 5 (1959): 7.

"Imovinski odnosi u Braku – NR Srbija" [Property relations in marriage – NR Serbia]. 1953. Archives of Yugoslavia, f. 141 AFŽ, box 4.

"INFORMACIJA o radu organizacije Narodne omladine sa ženskom omladinom" [Information on the activities of the People's Youth Organization with female youth]. 1951. Archives of Yugoslavia, f. 114 SSOJ, box 69.

"Informacija upolnomochennogo Soveta po delam religioznyh kul'tov pri Sovmine SSSR po Oshskoj oblasti I.G. Halimova v Sovet po delam religioznyh kul'tov pri Sovmine SSSR o prohozhdenii musul'manskogo prazdnika" [Information from the authorized representative of the Council for Religious Cults at the Council of Ministers of the USSR for Osh Region, I.G. Khalimov, to the Council for Religious Cults at the Council of Ministers of the USSR on the observance of Muslim holidays]. 27 July 1951. State Archive of the Russian Federation (GARF), f. R6991, op. 3, d. 454, ll. 135–6, 139, 145.

"Informatsiya otnosno nastroeniya i proyavi sred balgarskite mohamedani ot Smolyanski okrag vav vrazka s provezhdanite meropriyatiya za premahvane na feodalnite ostatatsi v bita im, Sofiya, 25 fevruari 1982 g." [Information on the mood among the Bulgarian Muslims in Smolyan District in relation to current measures to eliminate feudal remnants in their lifestyle, Sofia, 25 February 1982]." In *Darzhavna sigurnost*, 1:355–7.

"International Lenin School: Study Notes." n.d. [1927–30]. Modern Records Centre of the University of Warwick, Papers of Harry Wicks. https://mrc-catalogue.warwick.ac.uk/records/WIC.

Ishkova. "Rabota 306mest. Rabota sredi musul'manok v Azerbajdzhane" [Work places: Work among Muslim women in Azerbaijan]. *Kommunistka* 1923, no. 5, 34–6.

Islamova, T. "Opravdaju doverie naroda" [Justify the Trust of the People]." *Pravda*, 8 March 1938, 2.

"Istaknuti udarnik Alija Sirotanović postigao najveći učinak u istoriji rudnika" [A notable shock worker, Alija Sirotanović, achieved the highest record in the mine's history]. *Borba*, 20 February 1949, 1.

Istorija Svesavezne Komunističke Partije (Boljševika) [History of the All-Union Communist Party (Bolsheviks)]. Belgrade: Kultura, 1947.

"Izjava drugarice Butorac o zverstvima Zagrebačke policije" [Statement from Comrade Butorac on the brutality of the Zagreb police]. *Proleter*, no. 17 (December 1930): 7.

"Iz osmomartovskog takmičenja" [On the 8 March competition]. *Naša žena* 4, nos. 1–2 (February 1947): 9.

"Izveštaj Centralnog odbora AFŽ-a Jugoslavije" [Report of the Central Committee of the AFŽ Yugoslavia]. 1947. Archives of Yugoslavia, f. 142 SSRN, box 1.

"Izveštaj ekipe koja je obradila teren sreza titogradskog" [Report from a team that worked in the area of Titograd]. 15 July 1952. Archives of Yugoslavia, f. 141 AFŽ, box 12.

"Izveštaj glavnog odbora AFŽ-a Bosne i Hercegovine" [Report of the Head Committee of the AFŽ of Bosnia and Herzegovina]. 1947. Archives of Yugoslavia, f. 141 AFŽ, box 2.

"Izveštaji o izvršenoj anketi po domaćinstvima na selu, izveštaj Skopskog sreza, Strumičkog sreza, i analiza o stanju ženske radne snage u NRM" [Reports on the survey conducted in rural households, the report from Skopje District and Strumica District, and the analysis on the state of the female workforce in the NRM]. 19 August 1952. Archives of Yugoslavia, f. 141 AFŽ, box 13.

"Izveštaj o stanju na selu" [Report on the conditions in the countryside]. 1954. Archives of Yugoslavia, f. 354 SŽDJ, box 4.

Jakšić, Radiša. "Pisma uredništvu: Nepoštovanje Zakona o zabrani nošenja zara i feredže" [Letter to the editor: Non-observance of the Law on the Prohibition on Wearing the Zar and Feredža]. *Borba*, 4 January 1954, 2.

Jakupović, Mevla. "Govor na I Kongresu" [Speech at the 1st AFŽ Congress]. 18 June 1945. Archives of Yugoslavia, f. 141 AFŽ, box 1.

Jezero [The lake]. Novi Sad, Serbia: Zvezda film, 1950.

Kasparova. "Formy i metody raboty sredi zhenshhin vostochnyh narodnostej" [Forms and methods of work among the women of Eastern nationalities]. *Kommunistka* 1925, no. 9, 67–75.

– "Itogi i perspektivy raboty na Vostoke" [Results and prospects of work in the East]. *Kommunistka* 1924, no. 10, 45–8.

– "Zadachi partii v oblasti raboty sredi zhenshhin vostochnyh narodnostej" [Tasks of the party in the work among the women of the Eastern peoples]. *Kommunistka* 1925, no. 7, 85–92.

– "Zhenskoe dvizhenie na Vostoke" [The women's movement in the East].
   Kommunistka 1924, no. 7, 9–12.
Kislova. "Zapiska o rabote turkmenskogo oblastnogo otdela rabotnic"
   [Note on the activities of the Turkmen Regional Department of Workers].
   Kommunistka 1923, no. 6, 34–6.
Knorin. "Borba dvaju svijetova" [The struggle between two worlds]. *Proleter*,
   no. 28 (December 1932): 1–2.
"Kongres žena Makedonije" [Congress of Macedonian Women]. *Žena danas*,
   nos. 44–5 (August 1946): 18.
Konstitutsiya na Narodna republika Balgariya [Constitution of the People's
   Republic of Bulgaria]. 1947. https://parliament.bg/bg/18.
"Korespondentsiya s TSK na BKP po chestvuvaneto na 8 mart i denya
   na deteto, rabotata sred zhenite turkini, Sesiyata na Mezhdunarodnata
   demokratichna federatsiya na zhenite (MDFZH) – Sofiya" [Correspondence
   with the Central Committee of the BKP on the celebration of 8 March
   and Children's Day, work among Turkish women, and the session of the
   International Democratic Federation of Women (IDFW) – Sofia]. 1951.
   Central State Archive of Bulgaria (TsDA), f. 417, op. 1, a.e. 1.
Krapacheva, Radka. "Fakti, koito sgryavat" [Encouraging facts]. *ZHenata dnes*,
   no. 6 (1957): 6–7.
Kratka balgarska entsiklopediya. Vol. 3, *Kvant-Opere*. Sofia: Balgarska akademiya
   na naukite, 1966.
Krupskaja, Nadezhda. "Puti raskreposhhenija zhenshhin Vostoka" [Means of
   emancipating the women of the East]. *Kommunistka* 1928, no. 12, 5–12.
"K trudjashhimsja zhenshhinam vseh kapitalisticheskih stran" [To the
   working women of all capitalist countries]. *Pravda*, 8 March 1927, 1.
"Laureatki na Dimitrovski nagradi" [Winners of the Dimitrov Awards].
   ZHenata dnes, no. 6 (1951): 8–9.
Lj.A. "I muslimani Kosmeta i Sandžaka zahtevaju donošenje zakona o zabrani
   zara" [Muslims from Kosmet and Sandžak also demand declaration of a
   law to ban the veil]. *Borba*, 26 October 1950.
Ljubimova. "Vsesojuznyj s''ezd rabotnic i krest'janok i rabota sredi
   zhenshhin Vostoka" [All-Union Congress of Working Women and
   Peasant Women, and work among the women of the East]. *Kommunistka*
   1927, no. 11, 73–7.
Ljubimova, S. "Na Vostoke (Pis'mo iz Turkestana). [In the East (letter from
   Turkestan)]. *Kommunistka* 1924, no. 3, 13.
Ljubimova, Serafima. "Bor'ba na ideologicheskom fronte" [Struggle on the
   ideological front]. *Kommunistka* 1926, no. 9, 74–5.
– "Dekret o chadre i obshhestvo 'Doloj kalym i mnogozhenstvo'" [Decree on
   the veil and the Down with the Kalym and Polygamy Society]. *Kommunistka*
   1928, no. 8, 73–8.

– "Na puti k raskreposhheniju. K 5-tiletiju raboty zhenotdelov srednej Azii"
[On the road to emancipation: To the fifth anniversary of the Women's
Departments of Central Asia]. *Kommunistka* 1924, no. 12, 36–9.

– "Rabota sredi zhenshhin v Kirgizii" [Work among women in Kyrgyzstan].
Kommunistka 1923, no. 10, 43–5.

– "Robota sredi zhenshhin v Turkestane" [Work among women in Turkestan].
Kommunistka 1924, no. 7, 19–20.

– "Zhenskie lavki v Srednej Azii" [Women's shops in Central Asia].
Kommunistka 1926, no. 7, 70–2.

Ljubuncic, Hasan. "Otkrivanje muslimanke" [Unveiling of Muslim women].
Glasnik Vrhovnog islamskog starješinstva u FNRJ 1, nos. 4–7 (1950): 117–20.

M.B. "Slava i chest na mnogodetnite mayki" [Glory and honour to mothers of
many children]. *ZHenata dnes*, no. 5 (1952): 6.

"Mamljakat." *Žena danas*, no. 37 (December 1945): 23–5.

Manujlov, P. "Odna iz mnogih" [One of many]. *Pravda*, 8 March 1937, 3.

Marašović, Olga. "Govor na Drugom kongresu Antifašističkog fronta
žena Bosne i Hercegovine" [Speech at the 2nd Congress of the Women's
Anti-fascist Front of Bosnia and Herzegovina]. 12 July 1947. Archives of
Yugoslavia, f. 141 AFŽ, box 35.

– "Stanodavke jedne ilegalke" [The landladies of a resistance woman]. In *Žene
Bosne i Hercegovine u Narodnooslobodilačkoj borbi: 1941–1945 godine. Sjećanje
učesnika* [The women of Bosnia and Herzegovina in the national libreration
struggle, 1941–4: memories of participants], edited by Rasim Hurem, 5–10.
Sarajevo: Svjetlost, 1977.

Marinčević, Marija. "Počela je borba protiv neznanja i zaostalosti" [The battle
against ignorance and backwardness has begun]. *Žena danas*, no. 83 (May
1951): 6–8.

"Maršal Tito primio pretstavnike Islamske vjerske zajednice" [Marshal Tito
received delegates from the Islamic religious community]. *Glasnik Vrhovnog
islamskog starješinstva*, nos. 1–3 (March 1950): 8–9.

"Materijali od XI plenaren sostanok na Centralnoiot komitet na Naordnata
mladina na Makedonija" [Materials from the 11th Plenary Meeting of the
Central Committee of the People's Youth of Macedonia]. 5 March 1951.
Archives of Yugoslavia, f. 114 SSOJ, box 360.

"Materijal za referat IV Kongresa AFŽ Jugoslavije" [Material for the report of
the 4th AFŽ Congress]. 1953. Archives of Yugoslavia, f. 141 AFŽ, box 4.

Matkaramova, Ljajli. "Tadzhihan." *Pravda*, 8 March 1934, 2.

"Maychina gordost" [Mother's pride]. *ZHenata dnes*, no. 5 (1957): 5–6.

"Maystorki na visoki dobivi. Izkazvaniya na delegatki na natsionalnata
konferentsiya na parventsite na TKZS" [Masters of high yields: speeches
by female delegates at the National Conference of Leaders of the TKZS].
ZHenata dnes, nos. 11–12 (1951): 16–18.

"Menja se lik Novog Pazara" [The face of Novi Pazar is changing]. *Borba*, 26 August 1950, 2.

Mezenina, Nadezhda. "Gibnet proshloe – rastet novoe" [The past dies – the new grows]. *Rabotnica* 1934, no. 1, 14–15.

"Mezhdunaroden den na zhenata – 8 mart" [International Women's Day – 8 March]. *ZHenata dnes*, no. 2 (1951): 2–3.

"Mezhdunarodnyj kommunisticheskij zhenskij den'" [International Communist Women's Day]. *Pravda*, 8 March 1937, 1.

Milanov, Asen. "Parvite svetlini" [The first lights]. *ZHenata dnes*, no. 3 (1957): 12–13.

Mimica, Blaženka. "Analfabetski tečajevi, osnov kulturnog i prosvetnog podizanja žene" [Literacy courses, the basis for the cultural and educational advancement of women]. *Žena danas*, no. 47 (October 1946): 9–10.

– "Pod rukovodstvom partije, žene Jugoslavije postale su aktivni I svijesni borci za socijalizam" [Under the party's leadership, the women of Yugoslavia have become active and conscious fighters for socialism]." *Žena danas*, no. 56 (August 1948): 2–4.

Mizov, Nikolay Mihaylov. *Islyamat v Balgariya. Sashtnost, modernizatsiya i preodolyavane* [Islam in Bulgaria: essence, modernization, and overcoming]. Sofia: BKP, 1965.

– *Islyamat v minaloto i dnes* [Islam then and now]. Sofia: OF, 1970.

Mladenović, Stanko. *Spasenija Cana Babović*. Revolucionari Šumadije. Belgrade: Rad, 1980.

"Molba ot turskoto naselenie na s. Gradsko, Slivenski okrag, do predsedatelya na Prezidiuma na Narodnoto sabranie na NRB, do TsK na BKP-otdel 'Turski' i do ministar-predsedatelya na NRB, s. Gradsko, 22 septemvri 1959 g." [Request from the Turkish population of the village of Gradsko, Sliven District, to the chairman of the Presidium of the National Assembly of the People's Republic of Bulgaria, the Central Committee of the Bulgarian Communist Party Turkish Department, and the prime minister of the People's Republic of Bulgaria, village of Gradsko, 22 September 1959]. In *Darzhavna sigurnost*, 1:153–4.

Mujdović, Zahra. "Govor na IV Kongresu AFŽ" [Speech at the 4th Congress of the AFŽ]. 1953. Archives of Yugoslavia, f. 141 AFŽ, box 5.

"Muslimanke na konferenciji" [Muslim women at the conference]. *Naša žena*, nos. 8–9 (November 1947): 12–13.

N.H. "Žene Srbije za svoju domovinu" [Women of Serbia for their homeland]. *Žena danas*, no. 54 (1948): 11–12.

"Na radu za plan" [Working towards the plan]. *Žena danas*, no. 50 (October 1947): 26–7.

"Narodna skupština Srbije pozdravlja inicijativu muslimanki za skidanje feredži" [The People's Assembly of Serbia welcomes the initiative of muslim women to take off their veils]. *Borba na Omladinskoj pruzi*, no. 6 (6 April 1946): 2.

Nasha zemya [Our country]. Boyana Film, 1952.

"Nashi deputatki" [Our parliamentarians]. *ZHenata dnes*, no. 1 (1954): front cover.

"Naši novi zakoni" [Our new laws]. *Žena danas*, nos. 41–2 (May 1946): 14.

"Neprijateljske parole od marta 1946. godine do aprila 1947. godine na teritoriji FNRJ" [Hostile slogans between March 1946 and April 1947 in the territory of the FNRY]. 14 April 1947. Archives of Yugoslavia, f. 507 CK SKJ, Ideološka komisija (VIII), box 37.

Nidžić, Dšehavija. "Govor na I Kongresu" [Speech at the 1st Congress]. 19 June 1945. Archives of Yugoslavia, f. 141 AFŽ, box 1.

Nikolaeva. "Pervye itogi (Tashkentskij okrug)" [First results (Tashkent District)]. *Kommunistka* 1927, no. 8, 52.

Nikolić, Jelena. "Radne žene i Prvi Maj 1932" [Working women and May Day 1932]. *Proleter*, no. 24 (April 1932): 3.

Nikolov, Nikolay. "Priyatelki" [Girlfriends]. *ZHenata dnes*, no. 3 (1957): 5.

Nimani, Safeta. "Govor na IV Kongresu AFŽ" [Speech at the 4th Congress of the AFŽ]. 1953. Archives of Yugoslavia, f. 141 AFŽ, box 5.

"Njih je vaspitala naša Partija" [They were educated by our party]. *Radnica*, no. 2 (September 1948): 4–5.

"Novi život Behije Krkbešić" [A new life of Behija Krkbešić]. *Nova žena*, no. 40 (August 1948): 18.

Novotni, N. "Naviknuće se Salih beg" [Salih bey will get used to it]. *Radnica*, no. 12 (December 1950): 8–9.

Nurhat. "Ot zatvornichestva k proizvodstvu" [From imprisonment to production]. *Kommunistka* 1929, no. 1, 24–7.

"Nuzhno li izdat' dekret, zapreshhajushhij noshenie chadry[?]" [Is it necessary to issue a decree prohibiting the wearing of the veil?]. *Kommunistka* 1928, no. 8, 79–81.

Nyurina, F. "V Srednej Azii" [In Central Asia]. *Kommunistka* 1925, no. 4, 78–83.

O.J. "Ko je udarnik taj ne sustaje" [A shock worker does not lag behind]. *Omladinska pruga*, no. 1 (6 May 1946): 6.

"Objavljen je Zakon o zabrani nošenja zara i feredže" [Law prohibiting the wearing of the zar and feredža is announced]. *Naša žena*, nos. 11–12 (January 1951): 22.

"Oblekloto na turskata zhena" [The attire of Turkish women]. *Borba*, 15 February 1928, 2.

Oblova. "Ot chadry k udarnichestvu" [From veils to shock work]. *Rabotnica* 1932, no. 34 (December 1932): 12.

"Ocena rada sekretarijata Glavnog odbora AFŽ-a Makedonije" [Evaluation of the work of the Secretariat of the Main Committee of the AFŽ of Macedonia]. 28 July 1950. Archives of Yugoslavia, f. 141 AFŽ, box 15.

"O mezhdunarodnom kommunisticheskom zhenskom dne 8 marta" [On International Communist Women's Day, 8 March]. *Pravda*, 8 March 1938, 1.

"O nekim problemima u radu sa ženskom omladinom" [On some problems working with female youth]. 1951. Archives of Yugoslavia, f. 114 SSOJ, box 72.

"One se bore za ranopravno učešće u javnom i privrednom životu" [They fight for equal participation in public and economic life]. *Nova žena* 4, no. 64 (August 1950): 9–10.

"O prosvetnom i kulturno umetničkom radu Narodne omladine u 1950. godini" [On the educational and cultural-artistic work of the People's Youth in 1950]. 1951. Archives of Yugoslavia, f. 114 SSOJ, box 78.

"O rabote sredi devushek na Vostoke" [On work among girls in the East]. *Kommunistka* 1924, nos. 8–9, 47–9.

"O rabote sredi zhenshhin" [On work among women]. 1923. RGASPI, f. 62, op. 2, d. 65, ll. 2–13.

"Osnovni zakon o braku" [The Basic Marital Law]. *Službeni list Federativne Narodne Republike Jugoslavije*, no. 29 (9 April 1946): 229–39.

Pantieleva, Dusja. "Pereplav." *Rabotnica* 1934, no. 1, 22–3.

Perić, Danica. "Nepoznati znanci" [Unknown acquaintances]. *Žena danas*, nos. 68–9 (March 1950): 29–30.

Pichugina, Praskovia. "Sovetskaja zhenshhina" [Soviet woman]. *Pravda*, 8 March 1938, 2.

"Pis'mo o polozhenii turkmenki" [Letter on the status of Turkmen women]. 24 September 1923. RGASPI, f. 17, op. 10, d. 441, ll. 69–70.

"Pis'mo rukovodstva BNZhS v Antifashistskij komitet sovetskih zhenshhin otnositel'no poluchenija materialov o zhizni sovetskih zhenshhin" [Letter from the leadership of the BNŽS to the Anti-fascist Committee of Soviet Women regarding the recieving of materials about the life of Soviet women]. 30 December 1946. Tsentralen darzhaven arhiv, Sofia (TsDA), f. 8, op. 1, a.e. 5, l. 21.

"Pis'mo schastlivogo uzbekskogo naroda Vozhdju narodov Velikomu Iosifu Vissarionovichu Stalinu k otkrytiju XVIII S"ezda VKP(b)" [Letter from the happy Uzbek people to the Leader of the Peoples, Great Joseph Vissarionovich Stalin, on the occasion of the opening of the XVIII Congress of the All-Union Communist Party of Bolsheviks]. *Pravda*, 10 March 1939, 2.

"Pis'mo Stasovoj v CK s prilozheniem iz knigi Shaburovoj 'Zhenshhina Vostoka v bor'be za novuju zhizn'''" [A letter from Stasova to the Central Committee with an excerpt from Shaburova's book *The Woman of the East in the Struggle for a New Life*]. 11 June 1935. RGASPI, f. 17, op. 120, d. 202, ll.1, 13–20.

"Plenum Glavnog Odbora AFŽ-a za Hrvatsku" [Plenum of the Head Council of the AFŽ for Croatia]. 16 May 1947. Archives of Yugoslavia, f. 141 AFŽ, box 35.

"Pobediteli hlopkovyh polej" [Champions of the cotton fields]. *Rabotnitsa*, no. 36 (December 1935): 8–9.

Pomak, Rustem. "Julvie." *ZHenata dnes*, no. 12 (1956): 6–7.

"Po SSSR" [Around the USSR]. *Pravda*, 9 March 1927, 3.

"Predlozhenia za podobrenie rabotata vsred turkinite" [Suggested improvements for work among Turkish women]. 1951. TsDA, f. 417, op. 1, a.e. 1.

"Pregled časopisa 'Žena danas' organa AFŽ Jugoslavije" [Inspection of the magazine Žena danas, organ of the AFŽ Yugoslavia]. September 1949. Archives of Yugoslavia, f. 507 CK SKJ, Ideološka komisija (VIII), box 26.

"Pregled ženske štampe SSSR" [Review of the women's press of the USSR]. 1948. Archives of Yugoslavia, f. 141 AFŽ, box 23.

Priča o fabrici [The story of the factory]. Novi Sad, Serbia: Zvezda film, 1949.

"Priče će biti tri dana, a slobode dovijeka" [The stories will last three days, but freedom will last forever]. *Žena danas*, no. 76 (October 1950): 5–6.

Prodanović, Mila. "Šta sve naša organizacija može da učini u pomoći majci i detetu" [What our organization can do to help mothers and chilren]. *Žena danas*, no. 53 (1948): 3–4.

"'Protokol № 103.' Protokoli na Politbyuro i TSentralniya komitet na BKP" [Protocol 103: protocols for the Politburo and Central Committee of the BKP]. 26 April 1951. TsDA, f. 1B, op. 6, a.e. 1298. http://politburo.archives.bg/.

"Protokol sobranija musul'manok Poltoracka, vopros o religii" [Minutes of the meeting of Muslim women of Poltorack: The question of religion]. 14 July 1923. RGASPI, f. 17, op. 10, d. 443, l. 14.

"Protokol za saveshtanie na otdel 'Propaganda i agitatsiya' na TSK na BKP s predstaviteli na ot okrazite" [Minutes of a meeting of the Propaganda and Agitation department of the Central Committee of the Bulgarian Communist Party with representatives from the districts]. 7 May 1959. TsDA, f. 1B, op. 5, a.e. 378.

"Provodićemo u život zadatke Petog kongresa naše Partije" [We will implement the tasks of the 5th Congress of our party]. *Radnica*, no. 3 (October 1948): 1–3.

Putilovskaja. "Rabota kommunisticheskih partij sredi zhenshhin narodov vostoka" [The work of communist parties among women of the East]. *Kommunistka* 1921, nos. 12–13, 52–4.

"Put' k stanku" [Path to the machine]. *Pravda*, 9 March 1928, 7.

Radojičić, N. "Dole zar i feredža!" [Down with the zar and feredža!]. *Radnica*, no. 11 (November 1950): 8.

Rakovskij, H. "Zhenshhina vostoka, tvoe osvobozhdenie dolzhno byt' delo tvoih ruk" [Women of the East, your liberation must be the work of your own hands]. *Pravda*, 8 March 1925, 6.

Rebro Adamovo. Boyana Film, 1956.

"Rech na drugarya Valko CHervenkov" [Speech by Comrade Valko
   Chervenkov]. *ZHenata dnes*, nos. 4–6 (1951): 22.
"Rezolucija Drugog kongresa Antifašističkog fronta žena povodom pokreta
   muslimanki za skidanje zara" [Resolution of the 2nd Congress of the Anti-
   fascist Women's Front regarding the movement of Muslim women for the
   removal of the veil]. 13 July 1947. Archives of Yugoslavia, f. 141 AFŽ, box 35.
"Rezolucija o narednim zadatcima" [Resolution on subsequent tasks]. *Naša
   žena* 5, no. 6 (May 1949): 12–13.
"Rezolucija Vrhovnog vakufskog sabora Islamske vjerske zajednice u FNRJ"
   [Resolution of the Supreme Waqf Assembly of the Islamic religious
   community in Yugoslavia]. *Glasnik Vrhovnog islamskog starješinstva*, nos. 1–3
   (March 1950): 18–19.
Rizel', F. "Zhenshhiny sovetskogo Vostoka" [Women of the Soviet East].
   Rabotnica 1934, no. 30, 27–9.
"Rolyata na zhenite v ukrepvane na TKZS" [The role of women in
   strengthening the TKZS]. *ZHenata dnes*, no. 10 (1951): 2–3.
Rubcova. "Gotovim kadry" [Prepare the cadres]. *Pravda*, 8 March 1930, 4.
Rusev, Haralan. "Sakrovishtnitsa na nesmetni bogatstva" [A treasure trove of
   untold riches]. *ZHenata dnes*, no. 9 (1956): 12–13.
S.G. "Mnoge navike djeca stiču u roditeljskom domu" [Children acquire many
   habits in their parents' home]. *Naša žena*, nos. 11–12 (December 1954): 6.
"Sa birališta" [From the polling station]. *Nova žena*, no. 8 (November 1945):
   13–19.
Safudri, A. "Za reformu nacional'nogo zhenskogo kostjuma" [For the reform
   of women's national dress]. *Kommunistka* 1929, no. 13, 42–4.
Šantrić, Ružica. "Ćilimarska zadruga u Peći" [A rug-weaving cooperative in
   Peć]. *Žena danas*, no. 62 (August 1949): 24.
"Sastanak aktiva Glavnog odbora AFŽ Srbije" [Meeting of the *aktiv* of the
   Head Committee of the Serbian AFŽ]. 4 July 1952. Archives of Yugoslavia,
   f. 141 AFŽ, box 36.
"Sastanak plenuma Glavnog odbora AFŽ Srbije" [Meeting of the plenum
   of the Head Committee of the Serbian AFŽ]. 5 April 1947. Archives of
   Yugoslavia, f. 141 AFŽ, box 36.
"Savjetovanje AFŽ-a Crne Gore" [Consultations of the Montenegrin AFŽ].
   17 July 1947. Archives of Yugoslavia, f. 141 AFŽ, box 35.
Sazonova, P. "Kolhoznym jasljam okazhem prakticheskuju pomoshh'" [We
   will provide practical assistance to collective farm nurseries]. *Rabotnica*
   1933, no. 23, 11.
"Sećanja Pavla Pavlovića uzeta 6. oktobra 1960. godine" [Recollections of
   Pavle Pavlović recorded on 6 October 1960]. 1960. Archives of Yugoslavia,
   fond 516 Memoarska građa, MG 1943/5.

Šećeragić, Murad. "Bratstvo i jedinstvo jugoslovenskih naroda" [Brotherhood and unity of the Yugoslav people]. *Glasnik Vrhovnog islamskog starješinstva,* nos. 1–3 (March 1950): 9–12.

Seid-Mamedova, Zulejka. "Chudesnye mechty" [Wonderful dreams]. *Pravda,* 8 March 1939, 2.

Sejfi. "Na pomoshh' zhenskim promyslam na Vostoke" [To help women's crafts in the East]. *Kommunistka* 1925, no. 9, 75–9.

– "Zhenshhiny vostoka" [Women of the East]. *Pravda,* 8 March 1924, 4.

"Seljačka žena kao ekonomski faktor" [The peasant woman as an economic factor]. 1953. Archives of Yugoslavia, f. 141 AFŽ, box 32.

"Sličice sa analfabetskih tečajeva" [Notes from the literacy courses]. *Žena danas,* nos. 41–2 (May 1946): 16–17.

"Slovo imeet gramotnaja zhenshhina sovetskogo Vostoka" [A literate woman of the Soviet East has a voice]. *Rabotnica* 1935, no. 2, 12–13.

Smirnova, Anna. "Radost' svobodnoj zhizni" [The joy of a free life]. *Pravda,* 8 March 1938, 2.

Sokolović, Sinanuddin. *Dužnosti i obaveze roditelja prema djeci* [Duties and responsibilities of parents towards children]. Sarajevo: 22 Oktobar, 1968.

"Sovetskij Turkmenistan. Staroe – novoe" [Soviet Turkmenistan: old and new]. *Rabotnica* 1930, no. 8, 16–17.

Spasojević, Kića. "13,426 žena pojećuje analfabetske tečajeve" [13,426 women are taking part in literacy courses]. *Naša žena,* nos. 1–2 (February 1947): 8.

"Spetsialno saobshtenie na Okrazhno upravlenie – MVR – Blagoevgrad otnosno ostra vrazheska proyava na balgaromohamedanite ot s. Valkosel, Gotse-delchevsko po pasportizatsiyata, Blagoevgrad, 6 april 1953 g." [Special message from the Blagoevgrad District Directorate of the Ministry of the Interior on an acute hostile manifestation of the Bulgarian Mohammedans from the village of Valkosel, Gotse Delchev, in relation to passportization, Blagoevgrad, 6 April 1953]. In *Darzhavna sigurnost,* 1:118–19.

"Spravka na nachalnika na Treti otdel na DS otnosno izpalnenieto na pismo № 1 – 224 ot 19 yuni 1962 g. na ministara na MVR, Sofiya, [kraya na 1962 g.]" [Reference by the head of the Third Department of State Security on the implementation of letter no. I-224 of 19 June 1962 of the minister of the interior, Sofia, [end of 1962]]. In *Darzhavna sigurnost,* 1:190–4.

"Spravka ot nachalnika na III otdelenie za polucheni danni otnosno nastroenieto za izselvane v Turtsiya na turskoto i balgaromohamedanskoto naselenie v Gotsedelchevska okoliya, Blagoevgrad, 24 april 1953 g." [Reference by the head of the Third Division on data received on the feeling of the Turkish and Bulgarian Muslim population from the Gotse Delchev Region on emigrating to Turkey, Blagoevgrad, 24 April 1953]. In *Darzhavna sigurnost,* 1:120–2.

"Spravka otnosno dopusnatite izvrashteniya v razferedzhavaneto sred
turskoto naselenie v Razgradski okrag, Razgrad, 10 noemvri 1959 g."
[Reference on the atrocities permitted during the process of unveiling
among the Turkish population in Razgrad District, Razgrad, 10 November
1959]. In *Darzhavna sigurnost*, 1:155–9.

"Spravka otnosno liniyata na vrazheskata deynost i izkazvaniya v Smolyanski
okrag vav vrazka s provezhdanite meropriyatiya po myusyulmanskoto
duhovenstvo i svalyaneto na feredzhetata i shalvarite, Smolyan, 14 yuli 1959
g." [Reference on the course of enemy activity and statements in Smolyan
District in relation to the current actions taken against the Muslim clergy
and the removal of veils and trousers (*shalwars*), Smolyan, 14 July 1959]. In
Darzhavna sigurnost, 1:147–50.

"Spravka otnosno nastroenieto na balgaromohamedanskoto naselenie v selo
Filipovo po povod reshenieto na GK na BKP – Bansko za razbulvane na
zhenite balgaromohamedanki, Blagoevgrad, 26 fevruari 1959 g." [Reference
on the mood of the Bulgarian Muslim population of the village of Filipovo
on the decision of the CC of the Bansko BCP about the unveiling of
Bulgarian Muslim women, Blagoevgrad, 26 February 1959]. In *Darzhavna
sigurnost*, 1:138–41.

"Spravka ot okrazhniya nachalnik na MVR – Kardzhali otnosno vrazheskite
proyavi i komentari vav vrazka s premahvaneto na feredzhetata,
yashmatsite i shalvarite na zhenite turkini i balgaromohamedanki v
Kardzhaliyski okrag, Kardzhali, 6 avgust 1959 g." [Reference by the head of
the Kardzhali District Directorate of the Ministry of Interior on the hostile
activities and comments in relation to the removal of veils, yashmaks, and
shalvari of Turkish and Bulgarian Muslims in Kardzhali District, Kardzhali,
6 August 1959]. In *Darzhavna sigurnost*, 1:151–2.

"Sprovodimo u djelo odluke Petog kongresa naše Partije" [We must
implement the decisions of the 5th Congress of our party]. *Nova žena* 4, no.
42 (October 1948): 2–3.

Srećković, Mirko, Vančo Nikoleski, Iljam Rifatovski, Petre Prličko, Slavko
Janevski, Srbo Ivanovski, and Nikola Soldatov. *Priračnik za kulturno-
prosvetna rabota* [Handbook for cultural-educational work]. Skopje: Sojuz na
kulturno-prosvetnite organizatsii na N.R. Makedonija, 1950.

"Sreshta na turkinite ot Kolarovgradski okrag" [A meeting of Turkish women
from Kolarovgrad District]. *ZHenata dnes*, no. 4 (1952): 6.

Stancheva, Paulina. "Kravarkata Hamide" [Cowherder Hamide]. *ZHenata
dnes*, no. 9 (1952): 14–15.

"Stanovishte na Politbyuro na TSK na BKP na nyakoi aktualni problemi na
vazroditelniya protses" [Position of the Politburo of the Central Committee
of the BCP on some current issues of the revival process]. Protokoli na

Politbyuro i TSentralniya komitet na BKP, 30 September 1989. http://politburo.archives.bg/.

Statisticheski godishnik na Narodna republika Balgariya [Statistical yearbook of the People's Republic of Bulgaria]. Sofia: Nauka i izkustvo, 1959.

Statisticheski godishnik na Narodna republika Balgariya [Statistical yearbook of the People's Republic of Bulgaria]. Sofia: Nauka i izkustvo, 1961.

Statisticheski godishnik na Narodna republika Balgariya [Statistical yearbook of the People's Republic of Bulgaria]. Sofia: Nauka i izkustvo, 1962.

Statisticheski godishnik na Narodna republika Balgariya [Statistical yearbook of the People's Republic of Bulgaria]. Sofia: SU, 1988.

Statistički Godišnjak FNRJ [Statistical annual of the FNRJ]. Belgrade: Savezni zavod za statistiku, 1961.

Statistički Godišnjak FNRJ 1955 [Statistical annual of the FNRJ 1955]. Belgrade: Savezni zavod za statistiku, 1955.

Statistički Godišnjak Jugoslavije 1973 [Statistical annual of Yugoslavia 1973]. Belgrade: Savezni zavod za statistiku, 1973.

Statistički Godišnjak Jugoslavije 1988 [Statistical annual of Yugoslavia 1988]. Belgrade: Savezni zavod za statistiku, 1988.

Statistički Godišnjak Jugoslavije 1991 [Statistical annual of Yugoslavia 1991]. Belgrade: Savezni zavod za statistiku, 1991.

Stefanova, Nevyana. "Znatna takachka" [A successful weaver]. *ZHenata dnes*, no. 2 (1958): 5.

"Stenografske beleške sastanka izvršnog odbora Centralnog odbora Antifašističkog fronta žena Jugoslavije" [Proceedings from the meeting of the Executive Committee of the Central Committee of the Anti-fascist Women's Front of Yugoslavia]. 2 February 1951. Archives of Yugoslavia, f. 141 AFŽ, box 8.

Stepanov. "Perezhitki proshlogo" [Vestiges of the past]. *Pravda*, 10 March 1928, 4.

Stoynova, Ljuba. "Deputatka Muzafer" [Councillor Muzafer]. *ZHenata dnes*, no. 1 (1955): 6–7.

Suad. "Moeto sartse ostava tuk" [My heart remains here]. *ZHenata dnes*, no. 4 (1955): 17.

Sudakov. "Devushka Vostoka i komsomol" [Girl of the East and the Komsomol]. *Kommunistka* 1927, no. 8, 22–7.

"Svetal praznik" [Bright holiday]. *ZHenata dnes*, no. 8 (1957): 1.

Svjerdlov, G.M. *Materinstvo, brak, porodica u sovjetskom zakonu* [Motherhood, marriage, and the family in Soviet law]. Belgrade: IPROZ, 1945.

Syarova, Diana. "Bezplatnata meditsinska pomosht – zalog za shtastlivo maychinstvo" [Free medical care – a guarantee for happy motherhood]. *ZHenata dnes*, no. 4 (1951): 10–11.

Talić, Husein. "Islam i prosvjeta" [Islam and education]. *Glasnik Vrhovnog islamskog starješinstva*, nos. 1–3 (March 1950): 13–17.

Tineva. "Rabota sredi zhenshhin Kirgizii" [Work among women in Kyrgyia]. *Kommunistka* 1924, no. 11, 32–4.

Todorova, Rada. "9 septemvri i balgarskata zhena" [9 September and Bulgarian women]. *ZHenata dnes*, no. 8 (1949): 1.

Tomić, Ljubomirka. "Referat održan na II Plenumu Centralnog odbora AFŽ Jugoslavije" [Report at the 2nd Plenum of the Central Committee of the Yugoslavian AFŽ]. 19 September 1948. Archives of Yugoslavia, f. 141 AFŽ, box 6.

Tomšič, Vida. "Ko je pokazao put ženama Jugoslavije" [Who showed the way to the women of Yugoslavia?]. *Radnica*, no. 2 (September 1948): 6–7.

– "Rad i zadatak Antifašističkog fronta žena" [The work and tasks of the Anti-fascist Women's Front]. *Žena danas*, no. 40 (March 1946): 2–3.

– "Referat na V Zemaljskoj konferenciji" [Report on the 5th Conference]. 1940. Archives of Yugoslavia, f. 141 AFŽ, box 10.

Torskaja, N. "Protiv paradnyh deklaracij – za delovoe rukovodstvo" [Against empty declarations – for effective leadership]. *Kommunistka* 1929, nos. 17–18, 40–8.

"Tretiyat kongres na otechestveniya front. Izkazvaniya na delegatki" [The 3rd Congress of the Fatherland Front: Speeches of the women delegates]. *ZHenata dnes*, no. 6 (1952): 4–5.

Tucović, Dimitrije. "Borba za oslobođenje žene" [The struggle for women's liberation]. *Radničke novine*, no. 109 (11 September 1910).

"Uchebnye plany i programmy bolgarskogo sektora MLSh" [Curricula and programs of the Bulgarian sector of the ILS]. 1936. RGASPI, f. 531, op. 1, d. 270.

"Uchebnye plany i programmy bolgarskogo sektora MLSh" [Curricula and programs of the Bulgarian sector of the ILS]. 1937. RGASPI, f. 531, op. 1, d. 271.

[Untitled article]. *ZHenata dnes*, no. 12 (1952): 1.

[Untitled Report from the Macedonian AFŽ to the AFŽ's Central Committee]. 14 May 1949. Archives of Yugoslavia, f. 141 AFŽ, box 6.

"Uspesi i novi zadaci Antifašističkog fronta žena Makedonije" [The successes and new tasks of the Women's Anti-fascist Front of Macedonia]. *Žena danas*, no. 56 (August 1948): 8.

Ustav Federativne Narodne Republike Jugoslavije [Constitution of the Federative People's Republic of Yugoslavia]. Belgrade: Službeni list Federativne Narodne Republike Jugoslavije, 1946.

Vagabov, Mustafa V. *Otnoshenieto na myusyulmanskata religiya kam zhenata* [The attitude of the Muslim religion towards women]. Sofia: Profizdat, 1963.

Vasil'eva, Tat'jana. "Moguchaya sila sotsializma" [The mighty power of socialism]. *Pravda*, 8 March 1936.

Velev, Dimo. "Edin den v zala 13" [One day in Hall 13]. *ZHenata dnes*, no. 3 (1955): 17.

Vokši, Bia. "Govor na II Kongresu AFŽ" [Speech at the 2nd AFŽ Congress]. 1948. Archives of Yugoslavia, f. 141 AFŽ, box 2.

Voynov, Kiril. "Nefise." *ZHenata dnes*, no. 4 (1957): 14–15.

"V pervyh rjadah" [In the first rows]. *Pravda*, 8 March 1934, 1.

Vujošević, Ubavka, and Žarko Protić, eds. *Izvori za istoriju SKJ: Klasna borba* [Sources for the history of the SKJ: Class struggle]. Belgrade: Komunist, 1984.

"Vypiska iz protokola Orgbjuro o musul'manskom religioznom dvizhenii, Zapiska E.M. Jaroslavskogo v PB VKP o vnesenii izmenenij v proekt postanovlenija Orgbjuro o musul'manskom religioznom dvizhenii" [Extract from the protocol of the orgburo on the Muslim religious movement: Note by E.M. Yaroslavsky in the PB VKP on amending the draft resolution of the orgburo on the Muslim religious movement]. 8 March 1928. RGASPI, f. 17, op. 113, d. 612, ll. 11–28.

Yosifova, Brigita. "Delegatkata Asie Mehmedova" [Parliamentarian Asie Mehmedova]. *ZHenata dnes*, no. 12 (1952): 5–6.

Zahar'jan. "Brachnoe i semejnoe pravo na Vostoke" [Marriage and family law in the East]. *Kommunistka* 1926, no. 3, 42–5.

Zakon o zabrani nošenja zara i feredže [Law prohibiting the wearing of the zar and feredža], 33 Službeni glasnik § (1950).

Zakon za litsata i semeystvoto [Law on persons and the family], 182 Darzhaven vestnik § (1949).

"Zapisnik br 8 sa sastanka sekretarijata Centralnog odbora AFŽ Jugoslavije u 1951 godini" [Minutes no. 8 from the meeting of the Secretariat of the Central Committee of the AFŽ of Yugoslavia in 1951]. 4 July 1951. Archives of Yugoslavia, f. 141 AFŽ, box 9.

"Zapisnik komisije za rad sa ženama Saveznog odbora SSRNJ" [Minutes of the Committee for Work among Women of the Federal Council of the SSRNJ]. 22 May 1954. Archives of Yugoslavia, f. 354 SŽDJ, box 7.

"Zapisnik sa sastanka političkih sekretara" [Minutes from the meeting of political secretaries]. 2 October 1950. Arhiv Hercegovačko-neretvanske županije/kantona, Obl. K. KP BiH Mostar.

"Zapisnik sa sastanka u Upravi za propagandu i agitaciju CK KPJ sa drugovima iz Sreskog komiteta Mostar" [Minutes from the meeting at the Directorate for Propaganda and Agitation of the CC KPJ with comrades from the District Committee of Mostar]. 10 April 1950. Archives of Yugoslavia, f. 507 CK SKJ, Ideološka komisija (VIII), box 2.

"Zapisnik sa savjetovanja rukovodilaca sreskih sekcija žena sa sarajevske oblasti" [Minutes from the consultations of organizers of the women's district sections from Sarajevo Region]. 18 April 1952. Archives of Yugoslavia, f. 141 AFŽ, box 35.

"Zapisnik VI plenarnog sastanka Glavnog odbora AFŽ-a Makedonije" [Minutes from the 6th Plenary Meeting of the Head Committee of the Macedonian AFŽ]. 8 December 1950. Archives of Yugoslavia, f. 141 AFŽ, box 36.

Zasedanje Ustavotvorne Skupštine: 29 novembar 1945–1 februar 1946: Stenografske beleške [Session of the Constituent Assembly: 29 November 1945–1 February 1946: Minutes]. Belgrade: Izdanje Prezidijuma Narodne skupštine, 1946.

"Za svoje prosvećivanje" [For their education]. *Žena danas*, nos. 38–9 (January 1946): 18.

Zavar'jan. "Nekotorye momenty iz raboty zhenshhin srednej Azii" [Some notes on the work of women in Central Asia]. *Kommunistka* 1926, no. 6, 66–70.

– "Rabota na Sovetskom Vostoke" [Work in the Soviet East]. *Kommunistka* 1925, no. 12, 25–31.

Zdravković, M. *Posledice razvoda braka* [Consequences of divorce]. Belgrade: Radnički univerzitet, 1959.

"Žene junačke Bosne i Hercegovine (Srpkinje, Muslimanke i Hrvatice!)" [Women of the heroic Bosnia and Herzegovina (Serbs, Muslims, and Croats!)]. *Nova žena*, no. 7 (October 1945): 1–3.

"Žene poslanici ustavotvorne skupštine" [Women parliamentarians of the Constitutional Assembly]. *Žena danas*, no. 37 (December 1945): 3.

"Žene Sovjetskog istoka" [Women of the Soviet East]. *Žena danas*, no. 37 (December 1945): 21–2.

Zenica. Belgrade: Udruženje Filmskih Umetnika Srbije (UFUS), 1957.

Zetkin, Klara. "K zhenshhinam okrainnyh respublik" [To the women of the peripheral republics]. *Pravda*, 8 March 1928, 3.

"Zhenshhina truzhenica i revoljucija" [Working women and the revolution]. *Pravda*, 8 March 1927, 1.

"ZHenski deyatelki – chlenki na gradskiya i rayonite saveti v Sofiya" [Women activists – members of the city and district councils in Sofia]. *ZHenata dnes*, no. 8 (1949): 3.

Secondary Literature

Ahmed, Leila. *A Quiet Revolution: The Veil's Resurgence, from the Middle East to America*. New Haven, CT: Yale University Press, 2011.

Akiner, Shirin. "Between Tradition and Modernity: The Dilemma Facing Contemporary Central Asian Women." In *Post-Soviet Women*, edited by Mary Buckley, 261–304. Cambridge: Cambridge University Press, 1997.

Aleksandrieva, Lilyana, and Deyan Kyuranov. "Balgariziraneto na Balgariya (1984–1985)." In *Nasilstvenata asimilatsiya na turtsite v Balgariya 1984–1989*, edited by Rumen Avramov, 69–86. Sofia: TSentar za akademichni izsledvaniya, 2019.

Alsop, Rachel, and Jenny Hockey. "Women's Reproductive Lives as a Symbolic Resource in Central and Eastern Europe." *European Journal of Women's Studies* 8, no. 4 (November 2001): 454–71. https://doi.org/10.1177 /135050680100800404.

Anachkova, Bistra. "Women in Bulgaria." In *Family, Women, and Employment in Central-Eastern Europe*, edited by Barbara Łobodzińska, 55–68. Contributions in Sociology 112. Westport, CT: Greenwood Press, 1995.

Ananieva, Nora, and Evka Razvigorova. "Women in State Administration in the People's Republic of Bulgaria." *Women & Politics* 11, no. 4 (March 1992): 31–40.

Arapov, D.Ju., and G.G. Kosach, eds. *Islam i sovetskoe gosudarstvo. Po materialam Vostochnogo otdela OGPU, 1926 g.* Islam v Rossii i Evrazii. Moscow: Izdatel'skii dom Mardzhani, 2010.

Arat, Yeşim. "The Project of Modernity and Women in Turkey." In *Rethinking Modernity and National Identity in Turkey*, edited by Sibel Bozdogan and Reşat Kasaba, 95–112. Seattle: University of Washington Press, 1997. https:// doi.org/10.1515/9780295800189-009.

Attwood, Lynne. *Creating the New Soviet Woman: Women's Magazines as Engineers of Female Identity, 1922–1953*. Basingstoke: Palgrave Macmillan, 1999. https://doi.org/10.1057/9780333981825.

Avramov, Orlin, ed. *Annotated Legal Documents on Islam in Europe. Bulgaria.* Vol. 3. Leiden: Brill, 2015.

Avramov, Rumen. *Ikonomika na "Vazroditelniya protses."* Sofia: Riva, 2020.

–, ed. *Nasilstvenata asimilatsiya na turtsite v Balgariya 1984–1989*. Sofia: TSentar za akademichni izsledvaniya, 2019.

– *Stopanskiyat XX vek na Balgariya*. 2nd ed. Sofia: TSentar za liberalni strategii, 2001.

Bakić-Hayden, Milica. "Nesting Orientalisms: The Case of Former Yugoslavia." *Slavic Review* 54, no. 4 (1995): 917–31. https://doi. org/10.2307/2501399.

Ballinger, Pamela, and Kristen Ghodsee. "Socialist Secularism: Religion, Modernity, and Muslim Women's Emancipation in Bulgaria and Yugoslavia, 1945–1991." *Aspasia* 5, no. 1 (2011): 6–27. https://doi.org/10.3167 /asp.2011.050103.

Baloutzova, Svetla. *Demography and Nation: Social Legislation and Population Policy in Bulgaria, 1918–1944*. CEU Studies in the History of Medicine 1. New York: Central European University Press, 2011. https://doi .org/10.1515/9786155211928.

Bates, Daniel G. "What's in a Name? Minorities, Identity, and Politics in Bulgaria." *Identities* 1, nos. 2–3 (November 1994): 201–25. https://doi.org /10.1080/1070289X.1994.9962505.

Batinić, Jelena. *Women and Partisan Resistance in Yugoslavia during World War II.* Cambridge: Cambridge University Press, 2015.

Bell, John D. *The Bulgarian Communist Party from Blagoev to Zhivkov.* Stanford, CA: Hoover Institution Press, 1986.

– *Peasants in Power: Alexander Stamboliski and the Bulgarian Agrarian National Union, 1899–1923.* Princeton, NJ: Princeton University Press, 1977. https://doi.org/10.2307/j.ctvd58sh4.

Bemporad, Elissa. "Behavior Unbecoming a Communist: Jewish Religious Practice in Soviet Minsk." *Jewish Social Studies* 14, no. 2 (Winter 2008): 1–31.

Bennigsen, Aleksandr Adamovich. *Musul'mane v SSSR.* Paris: Ymca-Press, 1983.

Beoković, Mila. *Žene heroji.* Sarajevo: Svjetlost, 1967.

Biondich, Mark. *Stjepan Radić, the Croat Peasant Party, and the Politics of Mass Mobilization, 1904–1928.* Toronto: University of Toronto Press, 2000. https://doi.org/10.3138/9781442680203.

Bogdan, Branka. "Cold War Entanglements and Abortion Technology: Writing Yugoslavia into the Global History of Vacuum Aspiration, 1964–1974." *Australian Journal of Politics & History* 64, no. 3 (September 2018): 407–21. https://doi.org/10.1111/ajph.12486.

Bokovoy, Melissa K. *Peasants and Communists: Politics and Ideology in the Yugoslav Countryside, 1941–1953.* Pittsburgh, PA: University of Pittsburgh Press, 1998.

Bonnell, Victoria E. *Iconography of Power: Soviet Political Posters under Lenin and Stalin.* Berkeley: University of California Press, 1997. https://doi.org/10.1525/9780520924062.

Bougarel, Xavier. *Islam and Nationhood in Bosnia-Herzegovina: Surviving Empires.* London: Bloomsbury Academic, 2018.

Brandenberger, David, and Mikhail V. Zelenov. "Stalin's Answer to the National Question: A Case Study on the Editing of the 1938 *Short Course.*" *Slavic Review* 73, no. 4 (2014): 859–80. https://doi.org/10.5612/slavicreview.73.4.859.

Brunnbauer, Ulf. "Families and Mountains in the Balkans: Christian and Muslim Household Structures in the Rhodopes, 19th–20th Century." *History of the Family* 7, no. 3 (January 2002): 327–50. https://doi.org/10.1016/S1081-602X(02)00107-0.

– "Making Bulgarians Socialist: The Fatherland Front in Communist Bulgaria, 1944–1989." *East European Politics and Societies* 22, no. 1 (February 2008): 44–79. https://doi.org/10.1177/0888325407311788.

– "'The Most Natural Function of Women': Ambiguous Party Policies and Female Experiences in Socialist Bulgaria." In *Gender Politics and Everyday Life in State Socialist Eastern and Central Europe,* edited by Shana Penn and

Jill Massino, 77–96. New York: Palgrave Macmillan, 2009. https://doi.org
/10.1057/9780230101579_6.

Bubić-Slipčević, Samija. "Borbe i otpori u Mostaru." In *Hercegovina u NOB*,
181–7. Belgrade: Vojnoizdavački i novinski centar, 1986.

Buckley, Mary. *Mobilizing Soviet Peasants: Heroines and Heroes of Stalin's Fields*.
Lanham, MD: Rowman & Littlefield, 2006.

Budding, Audrey Helfant. "Nation/People/Republic: Self-Determination
in Socialist Yugoslavia." In *State Collapse in South-Eastern Europe: New
Perspectives on Yugoslavia's Disintegration*, edited by Lenard J. Cohen and
Jasna Dragović-Soso, 91–129. Central European Studies. West Lafayette, IN:
Purdue University Press, 2008. https://doi.org/10.2307/j.ctt6wq21x.

Burg, Steven L. "The Political Integration of Yugoslavia's Muslims: Determinants
of Success and Failure." *Carl Beck Papers in Russian and East European Studies*,
no. 203 (January 1983). https://doi.org/10.5195/cbp.1983.6886.

Burnaski, Georgi. "Prosvetnoto delo i 'kulturnata revolyutsiya' v
modernizatsionnata politika na Balgarskata komunisticheska partiya
spryamo turkinite v Balgariya." *Istoriya*, no. 6 (2019): 599–624.

– "ZHenite sred elita na turskata obshtnost v Balgariya. Podgotovka za i
uchastie v politicheskiya zhivot (1944–1984)." *Anamneza*, no. 3 (2019): 31–66.

Chamberlin, Paul Thomas, Kaysha Corinealdi, Cindy Ewing, Hussein Fancy,
Arunabh Ghosh, Rebecca Herman, Raevin Jimenez, et al. "On Transnational
and International History." *American Historical Review* 128, no. 1 (March
2023): 255–332. https://doi.org/10.1093/ahr/rhad138.

Chapaeva, Dina Rafailovna. *Putin's Dark Ages: Political Neomedievalism and Re-
Stalinization in Russia*. Routledge Histories of Central and Eastern Europe.
London: Routledge, 2024. https://doi.org/10.4324/9781003438045.

Chatterjee, Choi. "Soviet Heroines and the Language of Modernity, 1930–39."
In *Women in the Stalin Era*, edited by Melanie Ilič, 49–68. Studies in Russian
and East European History and Society. Houndmills: Palgrave Macmillan,
2001. https://doi.org/10.1057/9780230523425_4.

Chatterjee, Partha. "Whose Imagined Community?" In *Nations and
Nationalism*, edited by Philip Spencer and Howard Wollman, 237–47.
Edinburgh: Edinburgh University Press, 2005. https://doi.org/10.1515
/9781474472777-022.

Connell, Raewyn. "Masculinities in Global Perspective: Hegemony,
Contestation, and Changing Structures of Power." *Theory and Society* 45, no.
4 (August 2016): 303–18. https://doi.org/10.1007/s11186-016-9275-x.

Cvetković, Slavoljub. "Bilećki koncentracioni logor." *Istorija XX veka: Zbornik
radova*, no. 2 (1961): 267–309.

Darakchi, Shaban. "Bulgarian LGBTQI Movement: Generations,
Identifications, and Tendencies." *Sexualities* 25, no. 7 (2021): 909–25. https://
doi.org/10.1177/13634607211000201.

– "Gender, Religion, and Identity: Modernization of Gender Roles among the Bulgarian Muslims (Pomaks)." *Women's Studies International Forum*, no. 70 (September–October 2018): 1–8. https://doi.org/10.1016/j.wsif.2018.07.002.

– "Muslim Marriages: Intergenerational Differences in the Notions of Marriage among the Bulgarian Pomaks." *Marriage & Family Review* 55, no. 8 (2019): 778–99. https://doi.org/10.1080/01494929.2019.1610137.

Daskalova, Krassimira. "A Woman Politician in the Cold War Balkans: From Biography to History." *Aspasia* 10, no. 1 (2016): 63–88. https://doi.org/10.3167/asp.2016.100105.

– "The Women's Movement in Bulgaria in a Life Story." *Women's History Review* 13, no. 1 (March 2004): 91–104.

Dechev, Stefan. "Balgarskata istoriografiya i protoideologiyata na taka narecheniya vazroditelen protses." In Avramov, *Nasilstvenata asimilatsiya*, 15–42.

De Groot, Joanna, and Sue Morgan, eds. *Sex, Gender and the Sacred: Reconfiguring Religion in Gender History*. Oxford: Wiley Blackwell, 2014. https://doi.org/10.1002/9781118833926.

De Haan, Francisca. "Writing Inter/Transnational History: The Case of Women's Movements and Feminisms." In *Internationale Geschichte in Theorie und Praxis / International History in Theory and Practice*, edited by Barbara Haider-Wilson, William D. Godsey, and Wolfgang Mueller, 501–36. Vienna: VÖAW, 2017.

Dimitrova, Veronica. "Nakazatelni praktiki spryamo homoseksualnite v Balgariya prez 50-te i 60-te godini na XX v." In *Balgarskiyat sotsializam. Ideologiya, vsekidnevie, pamet*, edited by Ana Luleva, Ivanka Petrova, Petr Petrov, Svetla Kazalarska, and Yana Yancheva, 132–47. Sofia: AI "Prof. Marin Drinov," 2021.

Dimou, Augusta. *Entangled Paths toward Modernity: Contextualizing Socialism and Nationalism in the Balkans*. Budapest: Central European University Press, 2009. https://doi.org/10.1515/9786155211676.

Dişbudak, Cem, and Semra Purkis. "Forced Migrants or Voluntary Exiles: Ethnic Turks of Bulgaria in Turkey." *Journal of International Migration and Integration* 17, no. 2 (May 2016): 371–88. https://doi.org/10.1007/s12134-014-0411-z.

Djokić, Dejan. *Elusive Compromise: A History of Interwar Yugoslavia*. New York: Columbia University Press, 2007.

Dragostinova, Theodora. "In Search of the Bulgarians: Mapping the Nation through National Classifications." In *Beyond Mosque, Church, and State: Alternative Narratives of the Nation in the Balkans*, edited by Theodora Dragostinova and Yana Hashamova, 105–28. Budapest: Central European University Press, 2016. https://doi.org/10.1515/9789633861356-007.

Draškić, Marija. "Usvojenje i hraniteljstvo – dobra tradicija Srpskog građanskog zakonika?" In *Srpski građanski zakonik. 170 godina*, 127–43. Belgrade: Pravni fakultet Univerziteta u Beogradu, 2014.

Drezgić, Rada. "From Family Planning to Population Policy: A Paradigm Shift in Serbian Demography at the End of the 20th Century." *Filozofija i drustvo* 19, no. 3 (2008): 181–215. https://doi.org/10.2298/fid0803181d.

Drieu, Cloé. "Cinema, Local Power and the Central State: Agencies in Early Anti-religious Propaganda in Uzbekistan." *Die Welt des Islams* 50, no. 3 (2010): 532–63. https://doi.org/10.1163/157006010X545835.

Drobnjak, Nada. *Ženska strana parlamenta*. Podgorica: Skupština Crne Gore, 2010.

Dubowoj, Sina. "The Schism in the Bulgarian Socialist Movement and the Second International, 1900–1914." PhD diss., University of Illinois, 1982.

Dugonjic-Rodwin, Leonora, and Ivica Mladenović. "Transnational Educational Strategies during the Cold War: Students from the Global South in Socialist Yugoslavia, 1961–91." In *Socialist Yugoslavia and the Non-Aligned Movement: Social, Cultural, Political, and Economic Imaginaries*, edited by Paul Stubbs, 331–59. Montreal: McGill-Queen's University Press, 2023. https://doi.org/10.2307/j.ctv37mk25j.

Dumančić, Marko. *Men out of Focus: The Soviet Masculinity Crisis in the Long Sixties*. Toronto: University of Toronto Press, 2021. https://doi.org/10.3138/9781487531843.

Edgar, Adrienne. "Bolshevism, Patriarchy, and the Nation: The Soviet 'Emancipation' of Muslim Women in Pan-Islamic Perspective." *Slavic Review* 65, no. 2 (Summer 2006): 252–72. https://doi.org/10.2307/4148592.

– "Emancipation of the Unveiled: Turkmen Women under Soviet Rule, 1924–29." *Russian Review* 62, no. 1 (January 2003): 132–49. https://doi.org/10.1111/1467-9434.00267.

– *Tribal Nation: The Making of Soviet Turkmenistan*. Princeton, NJ: Princeton University Press, 2004.

Elbasani, Arolda, and Olivier Roy, eds. *The Revival of Islam in the Balkans: From Identity to Religiosity*. London: Palgrave Macmillan, 2015. https://doi.org/10.1057/9781137517845.

Eminov, Ali. *Turkish and Other Muslim Minorities in Bulgaria*. New York: Routledge, 1997.

Erken, Ali. "Identity, Nationhood and Migrations to Turkey from the Balkans, 1950–1960." *International Migration* 60, no. 2 (2022): 95–106. https://doi.org/10.1111/imig.12865.

Evstatiev, Simeon. "Milletic Secularism in the Balkans: Christianity, Islam, and Identity in Bulgaria." *Nationalities Papers* 47, no. 1 (January 2019): 87–103. https://doi.org/10.1017/nps.2018.11.

Fischer, Bernd J. "Interwar Albania." In Ramet, *Interwar East Central Europe*, 249–71. https://doi.org/10.4324/9780429027222-8.

Gancheva, Iliyana. "Darzhavna namesa v lichniya i kulturen zhivot na balgarskite turtsi v godinite na komunisticheskiya rezhim." *Epohi*, no. 3 (2013): 210–20.

Ghodsee, Kristen. *Muslim Lives in Eastern Europe: Gender, Ethnicity, and the Transformation of Islam in Postsocialist Bulgaria*. Princeton, NJ: Princeton University Press, 2010. https://doi.org/10.1515/9781400831357.

Ghodsee, Kristen, and Laura Bernardi. "Starting a Family at Your Parents' House: Multigenerational Households and Below Replacement Fertility in Urban Bulgaria." *Journal of Comparative Family Studies* 43, no. 3 (2012): 439–59. https://doi.org/10.3138/jcfs.43.3.439.

Giomi, Fabio. *Making Muslim Women European: Voluntary Associations, Islam, and Gender in Post-Ottoman Bosnia and Yugoslavia (1878–1941)*. Budapest: Central European University Press, 2021. https://doi.org/10.7829/9789633863688.

Goldman, Wendy Z. *Women at the Gates: Gender and Industry in Stalin's Russia*. Cambridge: Cambridge University Press, 2002. https://doi.org/10.1017/CBO9780511511868.

Goldstein, Ivo. *Croatia: A History*. Kingston, ON: McGill-Queen's University Press, 2001.

Gradskova, Yulia. "Opening the (Muslim) Woman's Space – The Soviet Politics of Emancipation in the 1920s–1930s." *Ethnicities* 20, no. 4 (August 2020): 667–84. https://doi.org/10.1177/1468796820905030.

– *Soviet Politics of Emancipation of Ethnic Minority Woman: Natsionalka*. New York: Springer Berlin Heidelberg, 2018. https://doi.org/10.1007/978-3-319-99199-3.

– "Women's International Democratic Federation, the 'Third World' and the Global Cold War from the Late-1950s to the Mid-1960s." *Women's History Review* 29, no. 2 (2020): 270–88. https://doi.org/10.1080/09612025.2019.1652440.

Grgić, Stipica. "The Kingdom of Diversity and Paternalism: The Kingdom of Serbs, Croats, and Slovenes/Yugoslavia, 1918–1941." In Ramet, *Interwar East Central Europe*, 213–48. https://doi.org/10.4324/9780429027222-7.

Gruev, Mihail. "Collectivization and Social Change in Bulgaria, 1940s–1950s." In *The Collectivization of Agriculture in Communist Eastern Europe: Comparison and Entanglements*, edited by Constantin Iordachi and Arnd Bauerkämper, 329–68. Budapest: Central European University Press, 2014. https://doi.org/10.1515/9789633860489-012.

– "Demografski tendentsii i protsesi v Balgariya v godinite sled Vtorata svetovna voyna." In Znepolski, *Istoriya na Narodna republika Balgariya*, 368–94.

– "Dve marginalni grupi v 'obshtestvoto na ravenstvoto.' Sotsialno konstruirane i stigmatizirane." In *Prepodrezhdaneto na obshtestvoto – stranitsi ot sotsialnata istoriya na komunizma v Balgariya,* edited by Mihail Gruev, 299–345. Sofia: Institut za izsledvane na blizkoto minalo, 2021.

– "Komunizam i homoseksualizam u Bugarskoj (1944–1989)." *Godišnjak za društvenu istoriju,* no. 3 (2010): 7–23.

– *Mezhdu petolachkata i polumesetsa. Balgarite myusyulmani i politicheskiyat rezhim (1944–1959).* Sofia: IK Kota, 2003.

– "Politicheskoto razvitie na Bylgariya prez 50-te-80-te godini na XX vek." In Znepolski, *Istoriya na Narodna republika Balgariya,* 131–79.

Gruev, Mihail, and Aleksei Kalionski. *Vazroditelniyat protses. Myusyulmanskite obshtnosti i kommunisticheskiyat rezhim.* Sofia: Institut za izsledovanie na blizkoto minalo: Institut otvoreno obshtestvo, 2008.

Gudac-Dodić, Vera. *Agrarna politika FNRJ i seljaštvo u Srbiji, 1949–1953.* Belgrade: Zavod za udžbenike i nastavna sredstva: Institut za političke studije, 1999.

Hadžiristić, Tea. "Unveiling Muslim Women in Socialist Yugoslavia: The Body between Socialism, Secularism, and Colonialism." *Religion and Gender* 7, no. 2 (February 2017): 184–203. https://doi.org/10.18352/rg.10137.

Haney, Lynne. *Inventing the Needy: Gender and the Politics of Welfare in Hungary.* Berkeley: University of California Press, 2002. https://doi.org /10.1525/9780520936102.

Henig, David, and Maple Razsa. "New Borders, Old Solidarities: (Post-)Cold War Genealogies of Mobility along the 'Balkan Route.'" In *Socialist Yugoslavia and the Non-Aligned Movement: Social, Cultural, Political, and Economic Imaginaries,* edited by Paul Stubbs, 360–82. Montreal: McGill-Queen's University Press, 2023. https://doi.org/10.2307/j.ctv37mk25j.20.

Hirsch, Francine. *Empire of Nations: Ethnographic Knowledge & the Making of the Soviet Union.* Culture & Society after Socialism. Ithaca, NY: Cornell University Press, 2005.

Hopken, Wolfgang. "Po-slozhno ot 'etnicheskoto prochistvane.' Emigriraneto na turtsi i myusyulmani ot Balkanite v istoricheskata perspektiva." In Avramov, *Nasilstvenata asimilatsiya,* 203–40.

– "Yugoslavia's Communists and the Bosnian Muslims." In *Muslim Communities Reemerge: Historical Perspectives on Nationality, Politics, and Opposition in the Former Soviet Union and Yugoslavia,* English supplemented and translated ed., edited by Edward Allworth, translated by Caroline Sawyer, 214–50. Central Asia Book Series. Durham, NC: Duke University Press, 1994.

Hristov, Hristo. *Stranitsi ot balgarskata istoriya. Ocherk za islyamiziranite balgari i natsionalnovazroditelniya protses.* Sofia: Nauka i izkustvo, 1989.

Hughes, James. *Stalinism in a Russian Province: A Study of Collectivization and Dekulakization in Siberia*. London: Palgrave Macmillan, 1996. https://doi.org/10.1057/9780230379985.

Idiceanu-Mathe, Dan, and Roxana Carjan. "Architecture for the New Man in the 1950's in Romania. First Glimpse of Communism Build Environment." *Procedia Engineering*, no. 161 (2016): 1520–6. https://doi.org/10.1016/j.proeng.2016.08.620.

Iriye, Akira. *Global and Transnational History: The Past, Present, and Future*. Palgrave Pivot. Basingstoke: Palgrave Macmillan, 2013. https://doi.org/10.1057/9781137299833.

Ivanov, Ivo Kirilov, and Murat Önsoy. "From Integration to Assimilation and Forced Migration: An Evaluation of the Bulgarian Communist Party's Turkish Minority Policy." *Bilig*, no. 103 (2022): 31–58. https://doi.org/10.12995/bilig.10302.

Ivanov, Martin. "Ikonomikata na Komunisticheska Bylgariya (1963–1989)." In Znepolski, *Istoriya na Narodna republika Balgariya*, 303–37.

Jancar-Webster, Barbara. *Women & Revolution in Yugoslavia, 1941–1945*. Denver, CO: Arden Press, 1990.

Janz, Oliver, and Daniel Schönpflug, eds. *Gender History in a Transnational Perspective: Networks, Biographies, Gender Orders*. New York: Berghahn Books, 2014. https://doi.org/10.3167/9781782382744.

Janz, Oliver, and Daniel Schönpflug. "Introduction." In Janz and Schönpflug, *Gender History in a Transnational Perspective*, 1–24.

Jayawardena, Kumari. *Feminism and Nationalism in the Third World*. The Feminist Classics. London: Verso Books, 2016.

Jovanović, Miroslav. "Preslikana ili samobitna društvena izgradnja. Komparativna analiza ustava FNRJ (1946) i 'Staljinskog' ustava SSSR-a (1936)." *Tokovi istorije*, nos. 1–2 (2008): 280–90.

Kamberović, Husnija. *Džemal Bijedić. Politička biografija*. Mostar, Bosnia and Herzegovina: Muzej Hercegovine Mostar, 2017.

Kamp, Marianne. *The New Woman in Uzbekistan: Islam, Modernity, and Unveiling under Communism*. Jackson School Publications in International Studies. Seattle: University of Washington Press, 2010. https://doi.org/10.1515/9780295802473.

– "Pilgrimage and Performance: Uzbek Women and the Imagining of Uzbekistan in the 1920s." *International Journal of Middle East Studies* 34, no. 2 (May 2002): 263–78.

Kamp, Marianne, and Russell Zanca. "Recollections of Collectivization in Uzbekistan: Stalinism and Local Activism." *Central Asian Survey* 36, no. 1 (January 2017): 55–72. https://doi.org/10.1080/02634937.2016.1221381.

Kamusella, Tomasz. "Dimute imat znachenie. Mezhdu politikata i obektivnostta." In Avramov, *Nasilstvenata asimilatsiya*, 87–112.

– *Ethnic Cleansing during the Cold War: The Forgotten 1989 Expulsion of Turks from Communist Bulgaria*. London: Routledge, 2019. https://doi.org /10.4324/9781351062701.

Kandiyoti, Deniz. "The Politics of Gender and the Soviet Paradox: Neither Colonized, nor Modern?" *Central Asian Survey* 26, no. 4 (December 2007): 601–23. https://doi.org/10.1080/02634930802018521.

Karčić, Fikret. "The Reform of Shari'a Courts and Islamic Law in Bosnia and Herzegovina." In *Islam in Inter-war Europe*, edited by Nathalie Clayer and Eric Germain, 253–70. London: Hurst, 2008.

Karklins, Rasma. "Islam: How Strong Is It in the Soviet Union? Inquiry Based on Oral Interviews with Soviet Germans Repatriated from Central Asia in 1979." *Cahiers du monde russe et soviétique* 21, no. 1 (1980): 65–81. https://doi. org/10.3406/cmr.1980.1374.

Kaser, Karl. *Porodica i srodstvo na Balkanu. Analiza jedne kulture koja nestaje*. Belgrade: Udruženje za društvenu istoriju, 2002.

Kecman, Jovanka. "Uloga žena u revolucionarnom pokretu do 1941. godine." In *Tito i revolucija*, 177–84. Belgrade: Eksport pres, 1979.

– *Žene Jugoslavije u radničkom pokretu i ženskim organizacijama: 1918–1941*. Belgrade: Institut za savremenu istoriju, 1978.

Keller, Shoshana. *To Moscow, Not Mecca: The Soviet Campaign against Islam in Central Asia, 1917–1941*. Westport, CT: Praeger, 2001. https://doi.org /10.5040/9798216026174.

– "Trapped between State and Society: Women's Liberation and Islam in Soviet Uzbekistan, 1926–1941." *Journal of Women's History* 10, no. 1 (1998): 20–44. https://doi.org/10.1353/jowh.2010.0552.

Khalid, Adeeb. "Backwardness and the Quest for Civilization: Early Soviet Central Asia in Comparative Perspective." *Slavic Review* 65, no. 2 (July 2006): 231–51. https://doi.org/10.2307/4148591.

– *Islam after Communism: Religion and Politics in Central Asia*. Berkeley: University of California Press, 2007.

– *Making Uzbekistan: Nation, Empire, and Revolution in the Early USSR*. Ithaca, NY: Cornell University Press, 2015. https://doi.org/10.7591/cornell /9780801454097.001.0001.

Kirschenbaum, Lisa A. *International Communism and the Spanish Civil War: Solidarity and Suspicion*. New York: Cambridge University Press, 2015. https://doi.org/10.1017/CBO9781316226902.

Korov, Goran. *Rad KPJ u Zagrebu od 1931. do 1941. godine*. Belgrade: Rosa Luxemburg Stiftung SEE, 2016.

Köstenberger, Julia. *Kaderschmiede des Stalinismus. Die Internationale Leninschule in Moskau (1926–1938) und die österreichischen Leninschüler und Leninschülerinnen*. Wiener Studien zur Zeitgeschichte 8. Vienna: LIT, 2016.

Kotkin, Stephen. *Stalin*. New York: Penguin Books, 2014.

Kovačević, Jelena. "Petko Miletić (1897–1943) – od revolucionara do 'frakcionaša.'" *Tokovi istorije*, no. 1 (2017): 47–73. https://doi.org/10.31212 /tokovi.2017.1.kov.47-73.

Kurtić, Vera. "Život romkinja." In *Neko je rekao feminizam? Kako je feminizam uticao na žene XXI veka*, edited by Adriana Zaharijević, 236–45. Belgrade: Regionalna kancelarija za Jugoistočnu Evropu, 2008.

Larise, Dunja. "The Islamic Community in Bosnia and Herzegovina and Nation Building by Muslims/Bosniaks in the Western Balkans." *Nationalities Papers* 43, no. 2 (March 2015): 195–212. https://doi.org/10.1080 /00905992.2014.998186.

Laruelle, Marlène. *Central Peripheries: Nationhood in Central Asia*. Fringe. London: UCL Press, 2021. https://doi.org/10.2307/j.ctv1gn3t79.

Lenoe, Matthew. *Closer to the Masses: Stalinist Culture, Social Revolution, and Soviet Newspapers*. Russian Research Center Studies 95. Cambridge, MA: Harvard University Press, 2004. https://doi.org/10.4159/9780674040083.

Lončar, Sanja. "Propitivanje pristupa istraživanju neredovnih oblika predbračnog i bračnog života na primjeru krivog puta." *Senjski zbornik* 32, no. 1 (2005): 223–70.

Lóránd, Zsófia. *The Feminist Challenge to the Socialist State in Yugoslavia*. New York: Springer Berlin Heidelberg, 2018. https://doi.org/10.1007/ 978-3-319-78223-2.

Lučić, Iva. "Im Namen der Nation. Der politische Aufwertungsprozess der Muslime im sozialistischen Jugoslawien (1956–1971)." PhD diss., Uppsala Universitet, 2016.

MacMaster, Neil. *Burning the Veil: The Algerian War and the "Emancipation" of Muslim Women, 1954–62*. Manchester: Manchester University Press, 2012.

Mahon, Milena. "The Turkish Minority under Communist Bulgaria – Politics of Ethnicity and Power." *Journal of Southern Europe and the Balkans* 1, no. 2 (November 1999): 149–62. https://doi.org/10.1080/14613199908413996.

Malešević, Miroslava. *Didara. Životna priča jedne Prizrenke*. Belgrade: Srpski genealoški centar, 2004.

Mantarliev, Yordan. "Izborite za narodni saveti v NR Balgariya prez 1949 g." *Istoricheski pregled*, nos. 1–2 (2007): 134–67.

Marcheva, Deyana. "Sotsialisticheskoto ravnopravie na zhenite." *Godishnik na departament "Pravo"* 5, no. 6 (2016): 260–77.

Marcheva, Iliyana. "Balgarskata 'Leydi Stalin' TSola Dragoycheva." In *Balgarski Darzhavnitsi 1944–1989. Epohata na sotsializma*, edited by Mariya Radeva, 124–38. Sofia: Skorpio, 2005.

– "Tsola Dragoycheva – yarka figura ot parvite godini na Otechestveniya front." In *Istoriya na Otechestveniya front/sayuz v Balgariya*, edited by

Iskra Baeva, 2:41–47. Sofia: Universitetsko izdatelstvo "Sv. Kliment Okhridski," 2012.

– "Za opekunskoto predstavitelstvo na zhenite v Balgariya 1944–1958 g." In *Pol i prehod 1938–1958*, edited by Krasimira Daskalova and Tatiana Kmetova, 203–21. Sofia: Centar za izsledvanija i politiki za zhenite, 2011.

Marinov, Tchavdar. "Ot internatsionalizam kam natsionalizam. Komunisticheskiyat rezhim, makedonskiyat vapros i politikata kam etnicheskite i religioznite obshtnosti." In Znepolski, *Istoriya na Narodna republika Balgariya*, 481–532.

Martin, Terry. *The Affirmative Action Empire: Nations and Nationalism in the Soviet Union, 1923–1939*. Wilder House Series in Politics, History, and Culture. Ithaca, NY: Cornell University Press, 2001.

Massell, Gregory J. *The Surrogate Proletariat: Moslem Women and Revolutionary Strategies in Soviet Central Asia, 1919–1929*. Princeton, NJ: Princeton University Press, 1974.

McCallum, Claire E. "Man about the House: Male Domesticity and Fatherhood in Soviet Visual Satire under Khrushchev." In *The Palgrave Handbook of Women and Gender in Twentieth-Century Russia and the Soviet Union*, edited by Melanie Ilic, 331–47. New York: Palgrave Macmillan, 2018. https://doi.org/10.1057/978-1-137-54905-1_22.

McDermott, Kevin, and Jeremy Agnew. *The Comintern: A History of International Communism from Lenin to Stalin*. Basingstoke: Macmillan, 1996. https://doi.org/10.1007/978-1-349-25024-0.

McLoughlin, Barry. "Proletarian Academics or Party Functionaries? Irish Communists at the International Lenin School, Moscow, 1927–1937." *Saothar*, no. 22 (1997): 63–79.

McShane, Anne. "Bringing the Revolution to the Women of the East: The Zhenotdel Experience in Soviet Central Asia through the Lens of *Kommunistka*." PhD diss., University of Glasgow, 2019.

Mekić, Sejad. *A Muslim Reformist in Communist Yugoslavia: The Life and Thought of Husein Đozo*. London: Routledge, 2017. https://doi.org /10.4324/9781315525853.

Merdjanova, Ina. "Administering Islam in Bulgaria: Legal and Political Aspects." *Turkish Review* 3, no. 5 (2013): 474–83.

– *Rediscovering the Umma: Muslims in the Balkans between Nationalism and Transnationalism*. Oxford: Oxford University Press, 2013. https://doi.org /10.1093/acprof:oso/9780199964031.001.0001.

Mesarič, Andreja. "Wearing Hijab in Sarajevo." *Anthropological Journal of European Cultures* 22, no. 2 (September 2013): 12–34. https://doi.org /10.3167/ajec.2013.220202.

Metodiev, Momchil. "Za nyakoi kosveni, no trayni posleditsi ot 'vazroditelniya protses.'" In Avramov, *Nasilstvenata asimilatsiya*, 113–36.

Meurs, Mieke, and Lisa Giddings. "Decline in Pre-school Use in Post-socialist Societies: The Case of Bulgaria." *Journal of European Social Policy* 16, no. 2 (May 2006): 155–66. https://doi.org/10.1177/0958928706062504.

Michaels, Paula A. *Curative Powers: Medicine and Empire in Stalin's Central Asia.* Pitt Series in Russian and East European Studies. Pittsburgh, PA: University of Pittsburgh Press, 2003. https://doi.org/10.2307/j.ctt5vkh97.

Midgley, Clare, Alison Twells, and Julie Carlier, eds. *Women in Transnational History: Connecting the Local and the Global.* London: Routledge, 2016. https://doi.org/10.4324/9781315626802.

Miller, Brenna Caroline. "Between Faith and Nation: Defining Bosnian Muslims in Tito's Yugoslavia, 1945–1980." PhD diss., Ohio State University, 2018.

Miloradović, Goran. *Karantin za ideje. Logori za izolaciju "sumnjivih elemenata" u Kraljevini Srba, Hrvata i Slovenaca, 1919–1922.* Belgrade: Institut za savremenu istoriju, 2004.

Milošević, Srđan. "Komunistička partija Jugoslavije o seljačkom i agrarnom pitanju u periodu između dva svetska rata." *Tokovi istorije*, no. 2 (2015): 101–27. https://doi.org/10.31212/tokovi.2015.2.mil.101-127.

Mineva, Emilia. "On the Reception of Marxism in Bulgaria." *Studies in East European Thought* 53, nos. 1–2 (June 2001): 61–74. https://doi.org/10.1023/A:1011210628290.

Mirkova, Anna M. *Muslim Land, Christian Labor: Transforming Ottoman Imperial Subjects into Bulgarian National Citizens, 1878–1939.* Budapest: Central European University Press, 2017. https://doi.org/10.1515/9789633861622.

Mishkova, D. "Liberalism and Tradition in the Nineteenth-Century Balkans: Toward History and Methodology of Political Transfer." *East European Politics and Societies* 26, no. 4 (September 2012): 668–92. https://doi.org/10.1177/0888325412459310.

Mitrovski, B., V. Glišić, and T. Ristovski. *Bugarska vojska u Jugoslaviji 1941–1945.* Belgrade: Medjunarodna politika, 1971.

Muratova, Nurie. "Muslim Women in Socialist Bulgaria." *Balkanistic Forum*, no. 2 (2013): 128–49.

– "Politiki na sotsialisticheskata vlast v Balgariya kam zhenite myusyulmanki." *Arhivi na zheni i maltsinstva*, no. 3 (2011): 59–105.

Myuhtar-May, Fatme. *Identity, Nationalism, and Cultural Heritage under Siege: Five Narratives of Pomak Heritage – from Forced Renaming to Weddings.* Leiden: Brill, 2014. https://doi.org/10.1163/9789004272088.

Nahodilova, Lenka. "Experiences of Communist Modernization in a Bulgarian Muslim Village, 1945–2005." PhD diss., Charles University, 2008.

Nakachi, Mie. *Replacing the Dead: The Politics of Reproduction in the Postwar Soviet Union.* New York: Oxford University Press, 2021. https://doi.org/10.1093/oso/9780190635138.001.0001.

Nazarska, Zhorzheta. "Muslim Women and the Women's Movement in Bulgaria (1940s–1960s): Archive Documentation and Historical Problems." *Arhivi na zheni i maltsinstva*, no. 1 (2009): 123–32.

Nenova, Gergana. "Questioning the Retraditionalization Thesis: Gender Differences in Paid and Unpaid Work in Bulgaria (1970–2010)." In *Gender and Power in Eastern Europe: Changing Concepts of Femininity and Masculinity in Power Relations*, edited by Katharina Bluhm, Gertrud Pickhan, Justyna Stypinska, and Agnieszka Wierzcholska, 157–72. Cham: Springer International, 2021. https://doi.org/10.1007/978-3-030-53130-0.

Nestorova, Tatyana. "Between Tradition and Modernity: Bulgarian Women during the Development of Modern Statehood and Society, 1878–1945." *Women's History Review* 5, no. 4 (December 1996): 513–24. https://doi.org/10.1080/09612029600200132.

Neuburger, Mary. *The Orient Within: Muslim Minorities and the Negotiation of Nationhood in Modern Bulgaria*. Ithaca, NY: Cornell University Press, 2004.

– "Veils, Shalvari, and Matters of Dress: Unravelling the Fabric of Women's Lives in Communist Bulgaria." In *Style and Socialism: Modernity and Material Culture in Post-war Eastern Europe*, edited by Susan Emily Reid and David Crowley, 169–88. Oxford: Berg, 2000.

Neumann, Matthias. *The Communist Youth League and the Transformation of the Soviet Union, 1917–1932*. London: Routledge, 2011. https://doi.org/10.4324/9780203815847.

Nikolova, Miroslava, and Kristen Ghodsee. "Socialist Wallpaper: The Culture of Everyday Life and the Committee of the Bulgarian Women's Movement, 1968–1990." *Social Politics: International Studies in Gender, State & Society* 22, no. 3 (September 2015): 319–40. https://doi.org/10.1093/sp/jxv023.

Northrop, Douglas. "Languages of Loyalty: Gender, Politics, and Party Supervision in Uzbekistan, 1927–41." *Russian Review* 59, no. 2 (April 2000): 179–200. https://doi.org/10.1111/0036-0341.00116.

– "Subaltern Dialogues: Subversion and Resistance in Soviet Uzbek Family Law." *Slavic Review* 60, no. 1 (2001): 115–39. https://doi.org/10.2307/2697646.

– *Veiled Empire: Gender & Power in Stalinist Central Asia*. Ithaca, NY: Cornell University Press, 2004.

Ognyanov, Lyubomir. "Iz doklad na Penyu Dokuzov – zavezhdasht otdel na TSK na BKP, do Politbyuro – Za rabota sred turskoto naselenie, za politicheskoto, stopanskoto i kulturnoto polozhenie na turskoto naselenie v Balgariya i merkite za negovoto podobryavane – Sofiya, 19 may 1956." In *Politicheska istoriya na savremenna Balgariya. Sbornik dokumentu (1944–1947)*, 3:557–8. Sofia: Darzhavna agentsiya Arhivi, 2018.

Omerika, Armina. *Islam in Bosnien-Herzegowina und die Netzwerke der Jungmuslime (1918–1983)*. Balkanologische Veröffentlichungen 54. Wiesbaden: Harrassowitz, 2014.

Pačariz, Sabina. *The Migrations of Bosniaks to Turkey from 1945 to 1974: The Case of Sandžak*. Sarajevo: Centar za napredne studije, 2016.

Pachamanova, Ina. "Aspekti na paternalizma i populizma na balgarskiya sotsialisticheski model (darzhavnata grizha i zakrila v normativnite aktove)." *Istoriya*, no. 1 (2018): 31–45.

Pantov, Alexander V., and Daria A. Spichak. "New Light from the Russian Archives: Chinese Stalinists and Trotskyists at the International Lenin School in Moscow, 1926–1938." *Twentieth-Century China* 33, no. 2 (April 2008): 29–50. https://doi.org/10.1179/tcc.2008.33.2.29.

Paraskevov, Vasil. "Insecurity and Control: Bulgaria and Its Turkish Minority." In *Ethnicity, Nationalism and the European Cold War*, edited by Robert Knight, 123–46. London: Continuum, 2012.

Parla, Ayşe. *Precarious Hope: Migration and the Limits of Belonging in Turkey*. Stanford, CA: Stanford University Press, 2019. https://doi.org/10.1515/9781503609440.

Pavlović, Marko. "Problem izjednačenja zakona u Kraljevini Srba, Hrvata i Slovenaca / Jugoslaviji." *Zbornik Pravnog fakulteta u Zagrebu* 68, nos. 3–4 (2018): 493–523.

Pearson, Sevan Philippe. "Muslims' Nation-Building Process in Socialist Bosnia and Herzegovina in the 1960s: Muslims' Nation-Building Process." *Nations and Nationalism* 24, no. 2 (April 2018): 432–52. https://doi.org/10.1111/nana.12370.

Perović, Jeronim. "The Tito-Stalin Split: A Reassessment in Light of New Evidence." *Journal of Cold War Studies* 9, no. 2 (2007): 32–63. https://doi.org/10.1162/jcws.2007.9.2.32.

Petranović, Branko. *Istorija Jugoslavije 1918–1988*. 3 vols. Belgrade: Nolit, 1988.

Pezo, Edvin. "Emigration and Policy in Yugoslavia: Dynamics and Constraints within the Process of Muslim Emigration to Turkey during the 1950s." *European History Quarterly* 48, no. 2 (April 2018): 283–313. https://doi.org/10.1177/0265691418757391.

Pišev, Marko. "Između 'azijatskog' islama i 'pravoslavnog' slovenstva. Jugoslovenski muslimani u ranoj srpskoj etnologiji." *Antropologija* 19, no. 3 (2019): 171–208.

Polianski, Igor J. "*Pathologia religiosa*: Medicine and the Anti-religious Movement in the Early Soviet Union." *Journal of Contemporary History* 53, no. 3 (July 2018): 524–49. https://doi.org/10.1177/0022009416669421.

Poppetrov, Nikolay. *Fashizmat v Balgariya. Razvitie i Proyavi*. Znaem Li 41. Sofia: Kama, 2008.

Promitzer, Christian. "Interwar Bulgaria: Populism, Authoritarianism, and Ethnic Minorities." In Ramet, *Interwar East Central Europe*, 178–212.

Radeva, Mariya, ed. *Balgarski Darzhavnitsi 1944–1989. Epohata na sotsializma.* Sofia: Skorpio, 2005.

Radić, Radmila. "Islamska verska zajednica 1945–1970. godine." *Forum Bosnae,* no. 32 (2005): 99–134.

Rädle, Rena, and Milovan Pisarri, eds. *Mesta stradanja i antifašističke borbe u Beogradu 1941–44.* Belgrade: Rosa Luxemburg Stiftung SEE, 2016.

Rafailović, Jelena. "Agrarna reforma i industrijalizacija u Kraljevini SHS – studija slučaja poseda Đorđa Dunđerskog." *Tokovi istorije* 2 (2016): 93–120. https://doi.org/10.31212/tokovi.2016.2.raf.93-120.

Ragaru, Nadège. *Bulgaria, the Jews, and the Holocaust: On the Origins of a Heroic Narrative.* Rochester Studies in East and Central Europe 32. Rochester, NY: University of Rochester Press, 2023.

– "Symbolic Time(s) of Violence in Late Socialist Bulgaria." *Slavic Review* 82, no. 1 (2023): 48–68. https://doi.org/10.1017/slr.2023.103.

Ramet, Pedro. "Primordial Ethnicity or Modern Nationalism: The Case of Yugoslavia's Muslims." *Nationalities Papers* 13, no. 2 (1985): 165–87. https://doi.org/10.1080/00905998508408020.

Ramet, Sabrina P., ed. *Interwar East Central Europe, 1918–1941: The Failure of Democracy-Building, the Fate of Minorities.* Routledge Studies in Modern European History. New York: Routledge, 2020. https://doi.org/10.4324/9780429027222.

Randall, Amy E. "'Revolutionary Bolshevik Work': Stakhanovism in Retail Trade." *Russian Review* 59, no. 3 (July 2000): 425–41. https://doi.org/10.1111/0036-0341.00131.

Ro'i, Yaacov. *Islam in the Soviet Union: From the Second World War to Gorbachev.* London: Hurst, 2000.

Rowley, Alison. "Spreading the Bolshevik Message? Soviet Regional Periodicals for Women, 1917–1941." *Canadian Slavonic Papers* 47, nos. 1–2 (March 2005): 111–26. https://doi.org/10.1080/00085006.2005.11092380.

Savova-Mahon Borden, Milena. "The Politics of Nationalism under Communism in Bulgaria: Myths, Memories, and Minorities." PhD diss., University College London, 2001.

Scarboro, Cristofer A. "Living Socialism: The Bulgarian Socialist Humanist Experiment." PhD diss., University of Illinois at Urbana-Champaign, 2007.

Scheide, Carmen. "'Born in October': The Life and Thought of Aleksandra Vasil'evna Artyukhina, 1889–1969." In *Women in the Stalin Era,* edited by Melanie Ilič, 9–28. Studies in Russian and East European History and Society. Houndmills: Palgrave Macmillan, 2001. https://doi.org/10.1057/9780230523425_2.

Scott, Joan Wallach. *Sex and Secularism.* Princeton, NJ: Princeton University Press, 2018. https://doi.org/10.2307/j.ctvc7792k.

Siegelbaum, Lewis H. "'Dear Comrade, You Ask What We Need': Socialist Paternalism and Soviet Rural 'Notables' in the Mid-1930s." *Slavic Review* 57, no. 1 (April 1998): 107–32. https://doi.org/10.2307/2502055.

– *Stakhanovism and the Politics of Productivity in the USSR, 1935–1941*. Soviet and East European Studies. Cambridge: Cambridge University Press, 1988.

Silverman, Carol. "State, Market, and Gender Relationships among Bulgarian Roma, 1970–90." *Anthropology of East Europe Review* 14, no. 2 (1996): 3–22.

Simić, Ivan. "Building Socialism in the Countryside: The Impact of Collectivization on Yugoslav Gender Relations." *Journal of Social History* 51, no. 4 (Summer 2018): 1023–44. https://doi.org/10.1093/jsh/shx023.

– "Gender and Youth Work Actions in Post-war Yugoslavia." In *Gender in Twentieth-Century Eastern Europe and the Soviet Union*, edited by Catherine Baker, 143–56. New York: Palgrave Macmillan, 2016. https://doi.org /10.1057/978-1-137-52804-9_9.

– *Soviet Influences on Postwar Yugoslav Gender Policies*. New York: Palgrave Macmillan, 2018. https://doi.org/10.1007/978-3-319-94382-4.

– "Soviet Model for Yugoslav Post-war Legal Transformation: Divorce Panic and Specialist Debate." *Annual for Social History*, no. 2 (2015): 83–101.

Simić, Marina, and Ivan Simić. "'Who Should Care about Our Children?': Public Childcare Policy in Yugoslav Socialism and Its Serbian Aftermath." *Journal of Family History* 44, no. 2 (April 2018): 119–44. https://doi. org/10.1177/0363199019831402.

Slipičević-Bubić, Samija. "Žene Mostara u prvim godinama rata." In *Žene Bosne i Hercegovine u Narodnooslobodilačkoj borbi: 1941–1945 godine. Sjećanje učesnika*, edited by Rasim Hurem, 45–7. Sarajevo: Svjetlost, 1977.

Smith, Jeremy. *Bolsheviks and the National Question, 1917–23*. Houndmills: Palgrave Macmillan, 1999. https://doi.org/10.1057/9780230377370.

Smolkin, Victoria. *A Sacred Space Is Never Empty: A History of Soviet Atheism*. Princeton, NJ: Princeton University Press, 2018. https://doi.org/10.2307 /j.ctt1zgb089.

Staar, R.F. *Communist Regimes in Eastern Europe*. Stanford, CA: Hoover Institution Press, 1984.

Stanev, Vladimir. *SHumat ot debri i Balkani … Partizanite v Balgariya (1941–1944)*. Sofia: UI-"Sv.-Kliment-Ohridski," 2022.

Sternadori, Miglena. "Heroines under Control: Unexpected Portrayals of Women in the Organ of the Bulgarian Communist Party, 1944–1989." *Women's Studies in Communication* 36, no. 2 (June 2013): 142–66. https://doi. org/10.1080/07491409.2013.795510.

Stoyanov, Valeri. *Turskoto naselenie v Balgariya mezhdu polyusite na etnicheskata politika*. Sofia: Lik, 1997.

Stoyanova, Plamena Slavova. *TSiganite v godinite na sotsializma. Politikata na balgarskata darzhava kam tsiganskoto maltsinstvo (1944–1989)*. Sofia: Paradigmi, 2017.

Stoyanova, Zhanina. "Kam modernizatsiya i emantsipatsiya – mazhkite momicheta na sotsialisticheskiya svyata." *Epohi* 22, no. 2 (2014): 251–62.

– "Modernization and Emancipation: Masculine Women in the Communist World (Bulgarian Case 1944–1956)." *Venets* 6, no. 3 (2015): 339–53.

Studer, Brigitte. *The Transnational World of the Cominternians*. London: Palgrave Macmillan, 2015. https://doi.org/10.1057/9781137510297.

Sygkelos, Yannis. *Nationalism from the Left: The Bulgarian Communist Party during the Second World War and the Early Post-war Years*. Balkan Studies Library 2. Leiden: Brill, 2011. https://doi.org/10.1163/ej.9789004192089.i-291.

Tasar, Eren. *Soviet and Muslim: The Institutionalization of Islam in Central Asia*. New York: Oxford University Press, 2017. https://doi.org/10.1093/oso/9780190652104.001.0001.

Thelen, Tatjana. "Shortage, Fuzzy Property and Other Dead Ends in the Anthropological Analysis of (Post)Socialism." *Critique of Anthropology* 31, no. 1 (March 2011): 43–61. https://doi.org/10.1177/0308275X10393436.

Thibault, Hélène. "Labour Migration, Sex, and Polygyny: Negotiating Patriarchy in Tajikistan." *Ethnic and Racial Studies* 41, no. 15 (2018): 2809–26. https://doi.org/10.1080/01419870.2017.1400086.

Todorova, Maria. *Imagining the Balkans*. New York: Oxford University Press, 1997.

– *The Lost World of Socialists at Europe's Margins: Imagining Utopia, 1870s–1920s*. New York: Bloomsbury Academic, 2020.

Todorova, V. "Family Law in Bulgaria: Legal Norms and Social Norms." *International Journal of Law, Policy and the Family* 14, no. 2 (August 2000): 148–81. https://doi.org/10.1093/lawfam/14.2.148.

Tsoneva, Penka. "Zhenskite druzhestva i neformalnoto obrazovanie v Balgariya 1857–1990." *Balgarsko spisanie za obrazovanie*, no. 2 (2017): 6–32.

Tursunova, Zulfiya. "Women's Narratives: Resistance to Oppression and the Empowerment of Women in Uzbekistan." *Journal of Indigenous Social Development* 3, no. 2 (December 2014): 1–16.

Urdea, Alexandra. "Enacting Culture in a Romanian Village." *East European Politics and Societies* 34, no. 3 (August 2020): 663–84. https://doi.org/10.1177/0888325419874450.

Vachkov, Daniel. "Ikonomikata na Komunisticheska Bylgariya (1944–1962)." In Znepolski, *Istoriya na Narodna republika Balgariya*, 263–302.

Valiavicharska, Zhivka. *Restless History: Political Imaginaries and Their Discontents in Post-Stalinist Bulgaria*. Montreal: McGill-Queen's University Press, 2021. https://doi.org/10.2307/j.ctv1m0khrn.

Valkov, Martin. "Mezhdu natsionalno obedinenie i zavoevatelna voyna. Voennopoliticheskite tseli na Balgariya prez parvata svetovna voyna kato istoriografski problem." *Anamneza* 13, no. 1 (2018): 1–47.

Varsa, Eszter. *Protected Children, Regulated Mothers: Gender and the "Gypsy Question" in State Care in Postwar Hungary, 1949–1956.* Budapest: Central European University Press, 2021. https://doi.org/10.7829/j.ctv18b5c4c.

Vlašić, Anđelko. "Modern Women in a Modern State." *Aspasia* 12, no. 1 (2018): 68–90. https://doi.org/10.3167/asp.2018.120104.

Wiesner-Hanks, Merry E. "Crossing Borders in Transnational Gender History." *Journal of Global History* 6, no. 3 (November 2011): 357–79. https://doi.org/10.1017/S1740022811000374.

Wood, Elizabeth A. *The Baba and the Comrade: Gender and Politics in Revolutionary Russia.* Bloomington: Indiana University Press, 1997.

Yusufjonova-Abman, Zamira. "State Feminism in Soviet Central Asia: Anti-religious Campaigns and Muslim Women in Tajikistan, 1953–1982." In *The Palgrave Handbook of Women and Gender in Twentieth-Century Russia and the Soviet Union,* edited by Melanie Ilic, 299–314. New York: Palgrave Macmillan, 2018. https://doi.org/10.1057/978-1-137-54905-1_20.

Znepolski, Ivaylo, ed. *Istoriya na Narodna republika Balgariya.* Sofia: Ciela, 2009.

Znepolski, Ivaylo, Mihail Gruev, Momchil Metodiev, Martin Ivanov, Daniel Vatchkov, Ivan Elenkov, and Plamen Doynov. *Bulgaria under Communism.* Routledge Histories of Central and Eastern Europe 3. London: Routledge, 2019. https://doi.org/10.4324/9781351244916.

Index